COMPLEX SYSTEMS THEORY
AND DEVELOPMENT PRACTICE

ABOUT THE AUTHOR

Dr Samir Rihani is Senior Research Fellow, School of Politics and Communication Studies at the University of Liverpool. He is a member of the Institute of Civil Engineers and the Chartered Institute of Marketing, and holds a doctorate in development studies from the University of Liverpool. His long and varied career, both in Britain and elsewhere, has included lecturing, consultancy and public service. A former director of planning at the Merseyside Passenger Transport Executive and chief executive of the Merseyside Tourism Board, he is currently a non-executive director on the board of the South Liverpool NHS Primary Care Trust, having served as a non-executive director at the Liverpool Women's Hospital NHS Trust from 1994 to 2001. In June 2001 he launched a website, www.globalcomplexity.org, on which he publishes news and articles on complexity, development and international relations.

COMPLEX SYSTEMS THEORY AND DEVELOPMENT PRACTICE

UNDERSTANDING NON-LINEAR REALITIES

SAMIR RIHANI

with a Foreword by
Hernando de Soto

ZED BOOKS
London & New York

Complex Systems Theory and Development Practice
was first published in 2002 by
Zed Books Ltd, 7 Cynthia Street, London N1 9JF, UK,
and Room 400, 175 Fifth Avenue, New York, NY 10010, USA

Distributed in the USA exclusively by Palgrave, a division of
St Martin's Press, LLC, 175 Fifth Avenue, New York, NY 10010, USA

Designed and typeset in Monotype Ehrhardt by Illuminati, Grosmont
Cover designed by Andrew Corbett
Printed and bound in Great Britain by Bookcraft Ltd, Midsomer Norton.

A catalogue record for this book is available from the British Library

Library of Congress Cataloging-in-Publication Data applied for

ISBN 1 84277 046 2 (Hb)
ISBN 1 84277 047 0 (Pb)

CONTENTS

ACKNOWLEDGEMENTS

I have learnt a good deal from those who have taken issue with my radically different viewpoint on development, and it is only right that I should express my gratitude to them first of all. On the other hand, I was fortunate to have the willing support of others. They might not have agreed with everything I said, but they gave me the benefit of the doubt and then went on to aid and abet me in my efforts. Barry Cooper introduced me to Complex Systems theory and nonlinearity some years ago. What was at the time a casual conversation assumed greater significance when I began the work that finally led to the publication of this book. His contribution did not end there, as he continued to act as an ever-present sounding board.

I am also indebted to Duraid Yawer for his support and assistance. He kept me supplied with a flood of reference books in the Arabic language. One of my aims was to look at development in a broader geographical and historic context. I needed a well-read friend to point me in the right direction. His intimate knowledge of regional planning and Middle Eastern affairs was an added bonus.

I am pleased to record my gratitude to Barry Munslow and Robert Geyer from the University of Liverpool. At critical stages in the work, they put forward ideas and suggestions that greatly improved the arguments and the narrative. Barry Munslow is an authority on development and has published several books on the subject. His breadth of knowledge and experience was of considerable help to me. Robert Geyer, a social scientist with a particular interest in the European Union, is also the author of several textbooks. His American background was of special assistance in explaining some of the vagaries of American policies at home and abroad.

Finally, I wish to thank Robert Molteno of Zed Books. One is able to count on the unqualified support of family and close friends. However, I was pleasantly gratified to receive the enthusiastic backing of an experienced publisher who is also a scholar in his own right.

FOREWORD

HERNANDO DE SOTO

In the course of the extensive research that led to the publication of my book *The Mystery of Capital*, several key elements emerged that, in my opinion, determine how nations develop economically. First, development is primarily a home-grown product rather than a blessing bestowed by foreign benefactors. Second, effective action often takes place at the local level between ordinary people trying to better themselves in ways that they consider relevant in the face of existing opportunities and hindrances. Often they are forced to operate outside the official legal systems and bureaucracies that tend to be impossibly rigid and Byzantine, and far removed from how most people live and work. Third, communities in need of growth and development are not helpless, and they certainly do not lack many of the resources needed to improve their fortunes. In fact, they already have most of the tools for economic success – homes and small businesses, for example – but such assets are typically held outside the law, where they cannot be transformed into useful capital. The trick is to transform such 'dead assets' into active economic instruments for progress. Fourth, that transformation can only come about when the right conditions are made available, principally through democratic property rights and institutional reforms.

The empirical research that provided the basis for *The Mystery of Capital* was prompted by the frustrations I encountered when I came back to my native Peru in 1980 after many years of living and working in Europe. I quickly discovered that, in a developing country like Peru, a massive effort was needed to create and manage even the smallest business. To find out why, I put a group of researchers to work. We soon discovered that Peru had passed an astonishing 28,000 laws and regulations since 1947 regulating how citizens produced and distributed wealth. Yet those laws – and the institutions that spawned them – had little relevance to the real needs of ordinary people. In fact, existing laws made it virtually impossible for most Peruvians to title their businesses and homes.

My own experience along with that of my colleagues from the Institute of Liberty and Democracy (ILD), a non-profit think-and-act tank in Lima, convinced me that the only way governments could improve the economic life of most of their people was to reform their legal systems to integrate the ways that people manage to work and succeed in the 'underground economy'. A year ago, Samir Rihani realised that we were mining the same intellectual territory and brought his exciting work to my attention. At the time, Rihani was considering the possibility that communities as well as nations develop as complex adaptive systems driven by local interactions between people. That seemed to provide additional theoretical backing for the work that the ILD has been pursuing for years. My initial expectations were confirmed when I read the manuscript for *Complex Systems Theory and Development Practice*. Although Rihani deals with the wider field of development and the theoretical framework within which that critical activity should be approached, the groundbreaking concepts advanced in this book, I believe, complement and reinforce the findings and proposals for reform that are outlined in *The Mystery of Capital*.

Complex Systems Theory and Development Practice redefines our current notion of development. Samir Rihani gives us a new perspec- tive on the balance of power between the local, national and international actors involved in development. He argues convincingly for a vision of development as an open-ended cyclical process that has three inseparable components: survival, adaptation and learning. Most important, he puts the emphasis uncompromisingly where it belongs – on people as the interacting elements of the complex systems we recognise as communities or nations. Thus, Rihani crystallises the argument between supporters of economic development, such as the IMF and the World Bank, and advocates of human development, such as the United Nations Development Programme. Rihani reasonably concludes that this is a false dichotomy: there can be no effective economic development without progress on human development.

Illiterate, malnourished, diseased and oppressed people shackled by an impenetrable web of rules and regulations are in no position to sustain growth on the economic front.

Complex Systems Theory and Development Practice also challenges a number of long-held views on development. Rihani makes no bones about his ultimate aim, which is to take an active part in causing a paradigm shift in the study and practice of development. This is an enormous task, but Rihani welcomes the challenge – not to mention the controversy – that inevitably accompanies these kinds of intellectual revolution. For Rihani, the benefits far outweigh the difficulties. I agree: simply discussing these issues is bound to help development efforts around the world.

How would a framework for development that views the unfolding events in the lives of communities and nations as a tapestry of complex adaptive processes change things for the better? To start with, it would provide an objective yardstick for selecting effective policies and actions. More significantly, Rihani's revised framework provides theoretical explanations as to why initiatives such as sustainable development focused on poverty alleviation and institutional reforms offer better and more consistent results. The new paradigm also gives cogent reasons as to why other programmes have failed so spectacularly. Those failures, according to Rihani, are not due to lack of funding, individual or constitutional incompetence, powerful external conspiracies, or any of the other usual explanations cited by commentators. He argues convincingly that such programmes were doomed to fail because they mistakenly presumed that development is a linear, Newtonian process.

For Rihani, development is a Complex Adaptive process. The ILD's work certainly bears this out. Ordinary people manage to survive and even prosper in developing economies by finding – or inventing – Complex transactions that work. We theoreticians and reformers have to be equally adaptive and creative. As Rihani suggests, we too have to identify objective means of assessing policies and actions that stand a higher probability of success. This alone would be a huge step forward in a field that seems to have meandered aimlessly through a mishmash of ideologies and theories. The paradigm shift advocated in this book offers a sound theoretical structure for substantive progress in the field of development. Certainly, many scholars, development professionals, and reformers will find similar synergies between their work and the thought-provoking ideas advanced in this book.

A WORD OF EXPLANATION

Others might enjoy sudden revelations, more often than not it seems while on a trek through the Andes or the Himalayas, but for me the spur to put pen to paper was the end product of years of puzzlement tinged with exasperation. My concerns were simple: why do development efforts regularly fall short of their targets; and, just as intriguing, why do the powers that be persist in committing the same mistakes? That conundrum took a long time to unravel, and the answer came as something of a surprise: failure, it turns out, cannot be attributed to the usual culprits of incompetence, lack of funds, conspiracy by wicked powers, or even misfortune.

After four chaotic years in the Middle East, I came back to England in 1967 and started another equally baffling period in planning and development. In place of chaos there was apparent order and control. Analytical methods in vogue at the time relied heavily on the use of models understood by a few eggheads, supported by another set of high priests who fussed over the huge computers on which the models were run. We dreamt up ideas for the future and these were left at the door of the modellers for testing. They went into a mystifying huddle and then came back a few days later with a precise picture of what would happen twenty-five years later if our wish list were turned into action. An elaborate bureaucracy considered the results minutely, but at every turn the ubiquitous computer print-outs were much in evidence. It was unheard of, and practically impossible, to challenge the printouts as they wove their magic over all else, including common sense. The aura of order, predictability and control over long-term events was intoxicating. Development was seen as a finite and tidy process that obeyed known universal laws. Certain inputs produced predictable results, each and every time. It was as simple as that. And the implicit aim was *economic development* first and last.

As long as the experts did not think the unthinkable, they lived a charmed life in which work and play intermingled seamlessly. The unthinkable was whether their feverish activity had any tangible meaning as dreams and plans were replaced by the mundane realities of unfolding events. In the meantime, the rest of society took millions upon millions of decisions that had at least as much relevance and influence on events as all the agonising that went on at the presumed seats of power. And all the while there were others, from foreign states and central banks to faceless boards of multinational corporations, who it seemed were intent on imposing their will from afar.

A few decades and jobs later, any expectations I might have had of order and predictability lay in tatters. I have to confess to an obsession at this stage: I never throw documents away, and worse still I return to them every now and then. Audit of past performance is frowned on when it comes to political promises, economic forecasts and development plans. That is a pity, as comparing past pronouncements with present events could be a source of endless entertainment and, for those directly involved, painful embarrassment. Admittedly, it can also be a most unsettling experience, as I know to my cost. Black–and–white certainty was replaced at an early stage by murky uncertainty. I worked with the stargazers for many years, but by inclination – and possibly because of a childhood spent in the Middle East, where most things were left to the capricious will of God – I suspected that life was moulded just as much by chance as by science. I was not satisfied with the modernists' suggestion that experts could reliably forecast the future. Equally, I could not agree with the fatalists and postmodernists who questioned the wisdom and utility of getting out of bed.

I decided by the mid-1990s that the time had come to revisit the original question: why are development experts not more expert at what they do? There seemed to be more to their shortcomings than met the eye. Regular failure on that scale often points to major systemic problems, and that is the line I followed in the research on which this book is based. Possibly the most challenging concept in what follows concerns a shift in development's frame of reference from one suited to *linear*, highly predictable, systems to an approach based on *nonlinear*, less predictable, systems in which internal chaotic interactions between local actors produce self-organised global order. That shift would also redirect the spotlight onto *human*, as opposed to economic, development.

I argue in this book that nations behave as nonlinear Complex Adaptive Systems. Their human development is an endless, exploratory and uncertain trek through the rugged global landscape, with no shortcuts or promises. In effect, I am asking the reader to discard an inbuilt structure of beliefs and assumptions, based on Newtonian positivist certainties, in favour of another little-known setup founded on nonlinearity which sets strict limits on our ability to predict the future in detail. I will devote much space in the book to highlighting the need for, and implications of, that transition. I fully recognise, of course, that fundamental transitions of this nature are exceedingly contentious and long-winded. However, I also believe the case for a shift in viewpoint is overwhelming, and unavoidable in the long run.

I am asking a great deal more of the reader. Gleick (2000: 14) said, in describing Feynman's work in quantum mechanics, 'It was not knowledge of or knowledge about. It was knowledge how to.' Using that mode of expression, this book is not of or about development; certainly not what is commonly understood by that term at any rate, which is strictly economic development. It is, on the other hand, about how nations behave as systems with millions of interacting constituent parts and how that behaviour could be animated to achieve better, more sustainable, results in human development terms, or hampered to accomplish little or nothing.

Fundamentally, I do not find the word 'development' of much utility in describing what nations should strive for. Despite all assurances to the contrary, economic influences and targets are put at the top of the agenda. Worse, the expression suggests a common end-state achieved by some clever or fortunate nations that is, or should be, sought by others. To compound the problem, those lagging behind are now pressed to adopt a set of prescriptions that the leaders are presumed to have followed on their way up the ladder of success. In sum, there is one escalator to the promised land of development and that destination is the same for one and all. The West sent missionaries in the past to convert misguided foreigners to Christianity. Nowadays missions from the World Bank and the International Monetary Fund (IMF) pour out of Washington to sell their prepackaged ideas of development to all nations. And those at the receiving end stand in awe, and with open hands, always ready to accept handouts from abroad. There is one thought that hardly ever crosses their minds: beyond a shadow of a doubt meaningful development is what you do and not what others do for you.

The book's starting position is that current wisdom has let down billions of people. A radical and overdue change in direction is necessary and inevitable. Development, it is argued here, is essentially a local affair; a marathon dogged by unexpected twists and turns rather than a rush to a nearby summit. Evidence is presented in forthcoming chapters to show that sustainable economic development has to follow consistent progress on the human development front, and not the other way round. Will the book bring about an overnight revolution? Hardly, but we have to start somewhere.

ONE

THE WHOLE CASE
IN A NUTSHELL

I had a choice to make in structuring this book. Should I present the evidence over several chapters and then end with a dramatic denouement? Or should I reveal my hand at the start and then argue the case? For clarity, I went for the latter approach. This chapter, therefore, outlines the arguments for a paradigm shift in development, while Chapter 10 describes the consequences that flow from that suggestion. The chapters between provide the detailed supporting evidence.

TWO SIDES OF A PARADOX

Development was given star billing during the second half of the twentieth century. Commissions, institutions and world summits focused their attention on that worthy cause. The best talents were recruited for the task, and these experts, led by equally dedicated politicians and administrators, unleashed a flood of reports on how to help so-called Third World countries to develop.

Despite fifty years of intensive activity by movers and shakers of the day, and costs amounting to billions of dollars, too many deprived regions on Earth have stubbornly failed to develop. The developing countries received over $1 trillion (in 1995 dollars) in aid alone between 1950 and 1995 (Easterly, 2001: 33). That is an intriguing paradox. Millions live in abject misery, racked by disease, hunger and war. Too weak and illiterate to help themselves, they rely on help from abroad. The gap separating them from more prosperous nations continues to grow and it seems there is little anyone could do to change that pattern. In short, progress has been thoroughly disappointing, and that is now beyond dispute. Those working in development are well aware of that fact. Their reports on the subject ritually start with a litany of shortcomings associated with past efforts. This is a key point. The experts seem to be unwilling or unable to change course. Variations on the same failed prescriptions are repeatedly adopted in spite of their obvious inadequacy. Even when ardent and justified calls were made for sensible changes in direction, as has been done for instance by successive annual *Human Development Reports* produced by the UN Development Programme since 1990, the results have been disappointing. Why? That is the other side of the same paradox.

LOCKED INTO AN INAPPROPRIATE MINDSET

Explanations based on the presumed incompetence of development professionals are nonstarters. Well-paid positions at the World Bank, for instance, attract graduates from the most prestigious universities worldwide.[2] Their counterparts in the Third World are also highly qualified, and usually graduates of the same institutions. Could there be a long-running conspiracy against the Third World? That is improbable too, as it would have had to involve a large number of participants over lengthy periods of time. In any case, who would benefit from such a conspiracy? Increased consumption by the vast numbers of people who would gain access to the world market would more than offset any detrimental effects. Unrelenting efforts by leading economic powers, and the World Trade Organisation (WTO), to entice China and other countries to open their borders to international trade leave little doubt on the balance of benefits.

The scale and frequency of development failures, and the inability of the experts to change course, point to systemic problems associated with the framework within which development is conceived and pursued. For instance, is there just one escalator to success, along which time and little else separates nations? And is there just one common destination to that journey? Moreover, does development obey deterministic laws of universal applicability? That certainly seems to be the general impression given by most of the policies and actions adopted in the past. In scientific terms, such assumptions would accord with a *linear* view of the development process that assumes a high level of order and predictability. Conversely, is development an uncertain, lengthy and open-ended evolutionary process that is driven by chance as much as by science? The development process would then conform more closely to a *nonlinear*, less predictable, mode of behaviour. In that case, it would be more productive for nations to optimise their performance in their own different ways within prevailing circumstances without worrying unduly about where other nations are in the development league and how they got there. Such a stance would be more than a major departure from the norm. It would constitute a paradigm shift in the study and practice of development. I believe that is the radical nature of change needed to achieve more consistent and sustainable results.

DEVELOPMENT'S CURRENT PARADIGM

Thomas Kuhn (1996: 10) argued that a scientific discipline progresses through a series of revolutions, or 'paradigm shifts', separated by long periods of relative calm. The paradigm in force at any stage defines the boundaries for what is considered to be legitimate practices in that field. In the last three centuries the natural sciences have adhered to the dictates of a linear paradigm that originated from ideas advanced by scholars such as Hobbes, Descartes, Locke and Newton.

Linearity, as typified by an industrial assembly line for instance, is correlated with order, predictability and knowable universal laws. Desirable results can be obtained by application of the requisite inputs to a system. The same association between specific causes and effects applies at all times and places, and the mode of behaviour of the whole system can be determined simply by studying the constituent parts. Additionally, linear processes are deterministic and finite, with clear beginnings and ends. Consequently, they respond well to top–down management structures, and to reductionist, rather than integrative, methods of analysis: the system is divided into smaller units and these are then dealt with separately.

Linear thinking gradually spread beyond the original scientific discoveries to embrace other facets of life. The success of the Industrial Revolution, in particular, engendered a belief that most problems could be resolved by the positivist application of reason to empirical observations. In that way, Smith and Ricardo claimed to have captured the laws of economics, and Marx enunciated his 'immutable' laws of capitalist development. On the same basis, Bell (1965) predicted an end to ideology while Fukuyama (1992) claimed history has come to an end following the fall of communism. Belief in determinism and the single escalator to success is all too evident.

So far, the study of development has mainly proceeded within a linear paradigm. Rostow (1960), for instance, reduced economic development to five distinct stages, and Toye (1987: 11) reported that development was commonly envisioned as a move 'through a series of stages of development derived essentially from the history of Europe, North America, and Japan'. However, the International Monetary Fund (IMF) and the World Bank's highly specified structural stabilisation and adjustment programmes provide the most striking examples of a linear conception of development.

Despite changing perceptions in the 1980s and 1990s that recognised development as a 'multidimensional concept' (see Elliott 1996: 5), it continues to be seen as a reasonably predictable activity that responds to laws of general applicability; in short a linear process. Research seeks to distil from specific instances lessons useful to the so-called developing world as a whole. Fashions in development have come and gone but the objective of determining these laws has endured.

Reliance on top–down management styles is another telltale sign of linearity. When development became a global priority after World War II, it was implicitly viewed as a task that required direction from the top through the UN, the World Bank and IMF, world leaders, and specialist governmental agencies in developed and developing countries. The Brandt Commission is one example amongst many. Brandt, in his passionate introduction to the Commission's 1980 report, called for focus to be 'not on machines or institutions but on people'. He added, 'We must not surrender to the idea that the whole world should copy the models of highly industrialized countries' (Sampson 1980: 7). Nevertheless, these sentiments did not inhibit his Commission from putting forward a unified policy package for nations with diverse problems, potentialities, and constraints (Sampson 1980: 267). The package was clearly based on a bird's eye view of what should happen down below.

The Brundtland Commission is another example of the same standpoint. By accident or design, the title of the Commission's 1987 report, *Our Common Future* was identical to a phrase used by Brandt in the introduction to his report several years before (WCED 1987). The title itself hints at a linear view of life. It conjures a comforting vision of commonality that has more of a spiritual than a practical meaning.

The message is clear though: we are riding the same escalator and we share a common destiny. In essence, we sink or swim together; a creditable moral notion that is hard to recognise in concrete terms. The Commission advanced many sensible proposals, especially in relation to the need for sustainable practices. Nonetheless, it clearly was guided by a linear conception of development. In that spirit, it defined core problem topics – population, energy, industry, and so forth – and then described the political, economic, production, technological, international and administrative systems that should be put in place to deal with them. It was yet another bird's eye view of development.

I wish to underline a key point at this stage. The prevailing linear paradigm is not an explicit notion agreed between those working in development. In the main, a paradigm embodies an assemblage of implicit assumptions that exert their influence in subtle ways. Those operating within a paradigm are often unaware of its very presence, and they would be offended by suggestions that their opinions and actions might be guided by anything but the objective facts.

A PARADIGM SHIFT TO COMPLEXITY?

My initial research suggested that the assumptions underlying development actions merited closer scrutiny. By degrees, a key question came to the fore: could top-down management structures and reductionist methods of analysis, best suited to linear systems, work in a field that involves such a bewildering array of actors and influences, most of which are difficult if not impossible to model or predict? Scientific thinking in which the search for truth proceeds on the basis of objective observation was not at issue. On the other hand, the implicit assumption that parts of the development process could be tackled separately and then the results added up to predict and manage the overall system, was undoubtedly in question.

I was aware that nonlinear phenomena, more specifically for the present purpose a group known as *Complex Adaptive Systems*, are not amenable to that form of treatment. When their parts are assembled unexpected *emergent properties* appear that could not have been deduced by observing the system's components. If it were to be shown that development, and its underlying political, social, and economic processes, behaved as a Complex Adaptive System, then linear assumptions would have led naturally to unwarranted presumptions about order and predictability in that field. As explained in more detail in later chapters, the evidence I have gathered left no doubt that the non-linearity hypothesis was essentially correct. Small wonder, therefore, that development interventions and forecasts have proved so lamentably wide of the mark. Similarly, working within an inappropriate framework would have made it virtually impossible for the experts to learn from past mistakes and, hence, to change radically their traditional prescriptions. A paradigm shift to nonlinearity would resolve both aspects of the paradox.

Before proceeding further it is necessary to clarify a couple of key points. First, the paradigm shift described above is broader than the standard argument between system-based and unit-based theorists. Some scholars, notably Waltz (1979), have advocated an approach to theory that deals with international politics, for instance, on system-wide bases. That is accepted entirely in the vision of development advocated here. But Waltz, and others, assumed that causes and effects can be linked and future events can be predicted accurately as long as the system is taken as a whole. These assumptions would be invalid for nonlinear situations. Second, references to 'Complex' and 'Complexity' do not necessarily signify the same meanings understood in everyday usage. I have capitalised the first letter throughout the text to highlight this distinction. Complex and Complexity refer to certain systems that have large numbers of internal elements that interact locally to produce stable, but evolving, global patterns. There is nothing complicated or obscure about Complexity. Admittedly, however, it ushers in a few unfamiliar terms and concepts.

RECOGNITION OF NONLINEARITY WITHIN THE SCIENCES

The success of scientific discoveries allowed determinism, and its linear paradigm, to reign supreme over science well into the twentieth century. In 1926, however, Heisenberg advanced his uncertainty principle, and then he, Schrödinger and Dirac pioneered quantum mechanics and proved that some phenomena are probabilistic. That discovery at the heart of the 'hard' sciences marked in some respects the birth of the nonlinear paradigm that became in time an accepted part of mainstream science.

Researchers became progressively interested in nonlinear situations where a system exhibits extreme sensitivity to variations in initial conditions. Trivial events could be magnified, through positive feedback, into major upheavals. On the other hand, they might come and go without leaving a trace. A given cause might lead to more than one outcome, and if the process were repeated the results could be, and often are, different. Basically, emergent properties ensure that in this case the whole is more than the sum of the parts. Assimilation of nonlinearity is now well established within the natural and life sciences.[3] It has, furthermore, begun to spill slowly into the social sciences.[4]

Complex Adaptive Systems

Certain nonlinear systems attracted the attentions of scholars as a potentially useful avenue for analysing natural and social phenomena. They are commonly described as being *Complex*, because their behaviour is defined to a large extent by local interactions between their components. When such systems are capable of evolution they are also known as Complex Adaptive Systems. It is my contention that the development process behaves as a Complex Adaptive System, and from this point onwards, therefore, the discussion will be confined to this class of system.

To consider the significance of Complex Adaptive Systems to development it is necessary first to describe three regimes of behaviour: *order*, *chaos* and *self-organised Complexity*. Several metaphors have been used to describe these regimes, but water in a bathtub is the most straightforward illustration (Kauffman 1996: 21). When tap and plughole are closed, the water is in a state of unchanging order, but when the tap is fully open the movement of the water assumes a regime of chaos that is almost impossible to specify. However, with the water running at a controlled rate and the plug removed, the water *self-organises* itself into a Complex regime represented by the familiar vortex. A state of chaos might exist at the detailed level, with constant flow of new particles of water, but globally the system exhibits an orderly pattern. Chaos and order combine to produce a state of self-organised Complexity, and that will persist as long as there is a constant flow of water through the system.

Boolean networks, as well as other techniques, have been used to study the above three regimes. Each network has many internal elements with two possible states: active or inactive – for instance, light bulbs that can be turned on or off by some or all of the other bulbs depending on the *connectivity* of the network. By altering connectivity and the local rules that dictate how the elements interact order, chaos or organised Complexity can be created and observed (Kauffman 1993: 36).

As interactions between the elements proceed, a system scrolls through different *states*. In an orderly regime all regions of the system 'freeze in fixed states of activity', while an infinite number of different states are involved in a chaotic regime (Kauffman 1993: 174). In organised Complexity the system cycles through a large but finite number of similar, but not identical, states (Coveney and Highfield 1996: 166; Byrne 1998: 26). The near-identical states differ but they do so within specific limits. In Complexity parlance they are said to fall into one *basin of attraction* or *attractor*. As described more fully in Chapter 4, the attractor in force at any time gives a Complex system its global pattern, which remains stable while the states are in the grip of that attractor.

Minor variations between states cause some change but this is normally contained within the attractor. Despite the frenetic internal activity, outwardly the system seems to be unchanging. Occasionally, however, minor variations can trigger a major shift into an altogether different attractor that presents a new global pattern, but there is no way of knowing which initial perturbation will shunt the system into a new pattern. In evolutionary terms the sequence of large upheavals separated by long periods of global stability, but energetic local activity, is sometimes referred to as *punctuated equilibrium* (Coveney and Highfield 1996: 232).

To evolve successfully, a Complex Adaptive System must change in response to shifting conditions, but it must survive long enough for the next cycle of adaptation to begin. Both necessary activities are dependent on the flow of time. In essence, evolution is an open-ended process that involves small but effective adaptations by which the system tries to improve its chances of survival. In the first instance, however, the system must gather knowledge about its environment, including activities by other co-evolving systems. Intelligence helps, but is not necessary. Copious internal variety ensures that some elements will survive and prosper under the new conditions.

The significant links between survival and adaptation and between knowledge, Complexity and evolution will be discussed in Chapter 4, but it is important to highlight at this point a key feature that will be stressed repeatedly: evolution is not a rush to the nearest summit but a leisurely process of exploration of possibilities. Another critical point that should be underlined here relates to a regularly observed characteristic of Complex Adaptive Systems whereby 'the greatest complexity represented has a tendency to grow larger with time' (Gell-Mann 1994: 244).

In summary, therefore, for a system to exist in a state of self-organised Complexity its internal elements should be capable of interacting at an appropriate level of connectivity and in accordance with suitable local rules. Complex Adaptive Systems exhibit an ability to evolve over time through small but effective modifications, but their evolution is an uncertain and lengthy process that does not lead to an optimal end-state. Finally, average Complexity increases over time, and systems with the highest complexity stand to gain the most.

A VISION OF DEVELOPMENT BASED ON COMPLEXITY

Within a Complex regime, some global patterns are predictable, but in the main useful interventions are restricted to enabling interactions to proceed in a manner that produces self-organised stable patterns in preference to either order or chaos. Local freedom of action, learning, flexibility and variety are vitally important, as control is limited to observation of outputs and encouragement for the elements to interact in a way that moves the system towards desirable ends. Management of Complex Adaptive Systems is, therefore, a reiterative process that relies on slow, and uncertain, evolution. Command-and-control methods and detailed forecasts and plans, effective for linear systems, are inappropriate as it is not possible to select sensible actions to achieve desired objectives in situations driven by internal dynamics that involve vast numbers of interactions, and where results cannot be traced back to specific causes.

Hence, the key to resolving the dual paradox discussed earlier lies in the recognition that nations, political economies, and the process of development itself behave as Complex Adaptive Systems, with egoistic individuals as internal elements. Clearly, a frame of reference that utilises Complex Systems theory will change not only what is done but also how it is done.

Complexity in the developed countries

Detailed evidence to support the assertion that the process of human development accords with the mode of behaviour of Complex Adaptive Systems is presented in later chapters. However, a few examples drawn from today's developed countries will help in giving a preliminary illustration of the case for Complexity. First, these nations present a stable common pattern typified by a welfare state, liberal democracy and a market economy. Within the uniformity of that global pattern there is massive variation between and within these nations, which has given them stability that has overcome many, expected and unexpected, challenges for several centuries. That setup is reminiscent of the healthy variety provided by near-similar *states* within one *stable attractor.* Capitalism.

Second, the governments concerned value the social capital represented by the diverse interactions that take place locally between ordinary people. The government of the USA, for example, is 'the world's biggest enterprise' (Samuelson and Nordhaus 1995: 299). Its public spending patterns have changed little in recent decades under different administrations. In essence, high spending, on law enforcement, nutrition, health, education and income protection, is dictated by the wish to endow citizens with the freedom and ability to interact and pursue their varied interests. In essence, human development is given top priority over all else.

Third, today's developed countries followed an evolutionary path characterised by the steady accumulation of modest growth over *very* long periods. It would be most unusual for anyone to argue that they have reached the end of that process; their evolution is implicitly accepted as being gradual and open-ended. The process also exhibited signs of punctuated equilibrium and *gateway events*, such as the invention of the steam engine and computers. Parallels with Complexity are self-evident.

Fourth, development in these countries stemmed largely from uncoordinated efforts by individuals and groups concerned exclusively with their particular businesses, intellectual pursuits and hobbies. The unplanned emergence of the Industrial Revolution in Britain, driven by inventions such as Hargreaves's spinning jenny and Watt's steam engine, illustrates this feature to perfection. The same is true of the significance of the *zaibatsu*, a diversified business group owned by one family, in Japan's growth prior to World War I (Chandler 1977). Yet again, pointers to a Complexity view of development are unmistakable.

Finally, today's developed countries are becoming richer, and the gap between them and poorer nations is inexorably widening. That is precisely what one would expect if the development of nations behaved as a typical Complex Adaptive System: average Complexity increases and the highest Complexity stands to gain the most. Basically, developed countries selected, through trial and error, practices that optimised their performance. Recent discoveries in the field of Complexity simply provide explanations of why these particular practices proved to be better than others.

Complexity in the developing countries

It is possible to consider the analogy between development and Complexity from the developing countries' perspective as well. In this instance conditions are in general the exact opposite of those needed for the system to achieve a stable but evolving pattern of self-organised Complexity. Hence, it is only to be expected that the countries involved would find it difficult to develop successfully, which mirrors their current situation. The Complexity argument is straightforward: the stimulating layer of self-organised Complexity that lies between deathly order and wasteful chaos could only emerge if people were *free* to interact and *capable* of interacting, and if their interactions were facilitated by *appropriate rules* that command popular support.

Few of the developing countries meet the *freedom* criterion. State repression, against whole populations or sectors targeted by gender, religion, or ethnic background, is widespread. The pattern of control by a small and ruthless elite that sets out to stifle diversity of independent action is all too familiar and does not require elaboration. However, it is appropriate to underline the damaging association between repression and corruption. Directly or indirectly, all these features curb healthy interactions between individuals and, therefore, impede development.

The factors that affect individuals' *capability*, as opposed to freedom, to interact are equally clear. The main culprits are malnutrition, disease, illiteracy and war, or preparation for war. For a nation to evolve properly as a Complex Adaptive System, interacting individuals must be able to accumulate knowledge and interpret and respond to opportunities, threats and other events in their environment. Most people in the developing countries are hardly capable of fulfilling that requirement.

Furthermore, interactions between people have to be facilitated and protected by a framework of rules and regulations that command popular support from the population. Yet again, most developing countries do not fulfil this basic condition. There is either wasteful chaos, brought about by constantly shifting, unclear, and often conflicting rules; or stifling order, created by arbitrary and rigid rules that prevent healthy interactions. One example, identified by de Soto (2000: 15, 63) to explain the failure of certain nations to develop, will help to illustrate this point. He described in some detail the hundreds of bureaucratic steps, and the years, required in Peru, the Philippines, Egypt and Haiti to start a small business or build a modest dwelling. He approached the topic from a different perspective, but again the link to Complexity is plain to see.

As explained in later chapters, the significance of the above impediments to development is well understood by one and all. For instance, Summers, former chief economist at the World Bank, said, concerning the failure of some countries to develop, 'I am convinced that there is a common element of a lack of social connection – a lack of links between people because governments have pre-empted not just all the political and economic space, but also much of the social space.'[6] The language might be different but the meaning in Complexity terms is abundantly clear. A shift to a Complexity viewpoint merely provides a plausible scientific explanation of why and how the above hurdles to development exert their influence in practice.

IS A PARADIGM SHIFT TO COMPLEXITY FEASIBLE?

In this chapter, I have sought to give a concise picture of the main theme, and some of the supporting arguments, elaborated later. Doubts about the soundness of the primary proposition, namely that the development process behaves as a Complex Adaptive System, can be settled one way or the other by scrutiny of the facts and arguments presented. However, two questions require an early response at this stage.

One question can be framed as follows: everyone knows development is complex, so what is new? As already mentioned, Complexity as used here denotes a description of a system that has certain distinctive properties. It does not necessarily concern features related to how difficult or complicated development might be. Once grasped, the ideas associated with Complexity are quite simple to the point of being virtually self-evident. The development process itself is, has been, and will always be complicated and difficult. My aim is to define a radically different framework within which that process could be advanced more effectively.

The second question might run something like this: the Complexity paradigm seems a reasonable idea but is it all a pipedream? Would those involved in development accept such a radical departure? The answer is definitely Yes. Calls for paradigm shifts do not come with a rush of blood. On the contrary, there is always a lengthy lead period of dissatisfaction with the existing paradigm and experimentation with alternative ideas. The study and practice of development is already undergoing a major change. To a large extent, the new ideas being tried were arrived at through experience and intuition. However, not unexpectedly perhaps, they sit very comfortably within the paradigm shift proposed here, as I argue in more detail in Chapter 10.

WHAT WOULD A PARADIGM SHIFT MEAN IN PRACTICE?

Recent innovations in development strongly connote an unintended move towards a concept of development founded on Complexity. The new ideas were adopted as moral responses to the consequences of policy failures or as sensible improvements, but are not yet integrated within a unified theoretical framework. Complexity offers compelling possibilities in this respect. That line of approach, however, would imply acceptance of a number of challenging concepts that go well beyond the tentative ideas currently on trial. Consequently, it would be misleading, and counterproductive, to undersell the revolutionary nature of the fallout that would ensue from adoption of the proposed paradigm shift in development.

For a start, world powers, governments of developing countries, and international institutions would have to accept the unpalatable fact that development is largely a messy and uncertain affair, driven in the main by millions of local actors. Development cannot be imported from abroad. Second, those involved in development would have to concede that development is a lengthy and open-ended evolutionary process that can take many paths. Hence, a balance would have to be struck between the unifying forces of global capitalism and the critical need to maintain abundant local diversity and freedom of choice. Finally, and above all else, improving standards of health, nutrition, literacy, security, human and property rights, and good governance could not wait for development to take place. The horse must come before the cart. There is basically no choice in the matter.

It is not safe to assume that the above radical shifts would be welcomed necessarily by all, or any, domestic and foreign interest groups. One aspect relating to armed conflict would help to illustrate this point. Much has been said and written about the role of arms transfer to, and concentration of civil and interstate wars within, the developing countries. Significantly, and as discussed in Chapter 9, the five permanent members of the UN Security Council, with supposedly a keen interest in peacekeeping, are also the main suppliers of arms, accounting for more than four-fifths of weapons sold. Corruption, local interest groups, global business, and international power politics present additional formidable forces against change. The potential benefit in considering a paradigm shift to Complexity within the development field, however, lies in its ability to leave little doubt about what would and would not help to drive the development process forward. If the shift were to gain general acceptance, politicians and experts would be less able to blame laziness, incompetence, shortage of funds, conspiracies by evil powers, or whatever when their efforts end up in a cul-de-sac.

THE BOOK'S STRUCTURE

The book follows a natural structure that presents successive layers of evidence to support and elaborate the concepts outlined above. Ideologies and theories associated with the international political economy (IPE) are tackled first as they form, at least in part, the foundations for past and present policies and actions in development.

The primary aim in Chapter 2 (A False Sense of Order) is to demonstrate that the main IPE schools of thought currently abide by an implicit linear paradigm. Their relevance as scientific models capable of yielding stable prescriptions of universal applicability is, therefore, analysed in some detail. For that purpose, emphasis is placed on the concurrent variety of interpretations within and clear overlaps among the leading ideologies. Attention is also drawn to the incessant process of revision that has affected IPE theories as their advocates sought in vain to model – in effect to predict or explain – the continual twists and turns of political economic events.

Chapter 3 (Ancient Roots to Modern Ideologies) delves into the distant past to trace ancient origins to what are thought to be modern, and essentially Western, international political economic concepts. The object is to test the possibility that the key ideologies might be behavioural consequences of commonplace human interactions. Evidence in Chapter 3, therefore, helps to pave the way for the introduction, in Chapter 4, of Complex systems as potentially useful tools in the study and practice of development.

Chapter 4 (Dawn of the Probabilistic Age) describes nonlinearity and assesses its applicability to social, political and economic processes. Causes of unpredictability are outlined and evolutionary change – including fitness landscapes, gateway events, survival, adaptability and learning – is described to trace potential parallels with social, political and economic events. Game Theory is also discussed to explore co-operation and competition, and hierarchies and elites. The overall aim is to specify the features that set Complex Adaptive Systems apart from linear systems.

Chapter 5 (Linear Recipes for a Complex World) moves the discussion away from ideologies and theories and onto global and national institutions and activities. It continues the search for evidence of the telltale signs of linear thinking in present-day development efforts. Discussion focuses principally on the roles of the United Nations and the World Bank, and on the thorny topics of international debt, aid and trade.

Chapter 6 (The Wealth and Poverty of Nations) underscores the huge, and growing, gap separating the few exceptionally wealthy nations from the rest. It identifies steady long-term evolution as a key feature of the path followed by the leading nations in their climb up the ladder of human development. The purpose is to show that developed countries adopted, albeit without prior design, integrative methods suited to nonlinear situations. They sought progress on a wide front that went beyond economic growth. In conclusion, the chapter argues that progress on basic social needs could be achieved in the absence of wealth. Poverty and human development are not mutually exclusive.

The next three chapters explore the factors that help or hinder individuals' ability to interact in social, political and economic activities. Chapter 7 (Freedom to Interact) focuses on international and domestic forces that limit personal choice and the freedom of individuals to take an active part in the affairs of their communities. Chapter 8 (Capability to Interact) examines influences that curtail the capability of individuals to interact, principally malnutrition, disease and illiteracy. Chapter 9 (Conflict and Incapability) continues the theme started in Chapter 8 by analysing the high cost exacted by potential and actual war in all its formats in preventing interactions within the communities affected.

Chapter 10 (Agenda for a New Paradigm) is the business end of the book. It focuses attention on what individual nations could most usefully do to optimise their chances of success in an uncertain and highly competitive world. It underlines the point that success or failure is largely determined by what is, and is not, done locally. The chapter addresses the thorny subject of how fast and how far the development process could be driven, when that activity is viewed in its true colours as a Complex Adaptive System. In addition, the chapter defines what more prosperous nations and global agencies should, and should not, do to help, and not hinder, other nations in their efforts to make effective and sustainable progress. Chapter 10 has a tough but positive message: nations could make substantial progress by harnessing their local energies and resources, but local makers and shakers have to bite the bullet and accept that human development comes first and foremost.

NOTES

1. As described in Chapters 5, 6, and 7. The balance sheet of human development from 1990 to 1997 presented in *Human Development Report 1999* paints possibly the bleakest picture in this context, although it does highlight the successes as well (UNDP 1999). See also Rich (1994), Allen and Thomas (1995), and Caufield (1996).
2. For a detailed description of rates of pay and fringe benefits, see Caufield (1996: 46, 189).
3. Detailed supporting evidence for this point could be seen in Gleick (1988), Nicolis and Prigogine (1989), Waldrop (1994), Kauffman (1993,

1996), Gell-Mann (1994), and Lewin (1997).
4. As argued, for example, by Day (1994), Byrne (1998) and Ormerod (1994, 1998).
5. See Chapter 6 and Chandler et al. (1997).
6. Summers, then deputy secretary at the US Department of the Treasury, was speaking at the eleventh Annual World Bank Conference on Development Economics held in April 1999 (Summers 1999).

TWO

A FALSE SENSE OF ORDER

Development is a derivative science rooted mainly in political economic ideology and theory. Clearly, the search for the telltale signs of a linear paradigm in development must start at these origins. To that end, I seek to establish three key facts in this chapter. First, that political economic ideologies and theories are founded on assumptions of order, predictability, and stable cause-and-effect relationships. The ideologies originally evolved as articles of faith, and then their respective advocates, buoyed no doubt by the scientific age, tried to translate them into scientific theories of universal applicability. Second, I set out to show that the different ideologies share extensive common ground, and that their so-called scientific theories are essentially working hypotheses relevant only to given times and places. My third and final objective is to demonstrate that the leading political economic powers are well aware of the above facts. They take ideologies and their associated theories with a large pinch of salt. Their policies and actions are based on a pragmatic outlook that contrasts sharply with efforts, by the World Bank and the IMF, say, to impose dogmatic and highly specified political economic recipes on nations struggling to develop.

REGULATED GLOBALISATION?

The latest wisdom on development advocates what could be described as 'globalisation with knobs on'. The United Nations Development Programme (UNDP) recommends that faith should be put in the powers of globalisation to breathe new life into development efforts. However, the UNDP (1999: 2) makes one proviso: globalisation should be regulated to ensure that it 'works for people – and not just for profits.' The proposal to square that circle underlines the penchant of the development community to cling to the cherished hope of finding the one and only reliable escalator to success, and one that is driven in the main by economic forces.

Economic development above all else

It is fashionable for reports and commentators to stress the multi-dimensional nature of development as well as the need to put people right at the heart of that activity. Having done that, they quickly narrow their field of vision to mainly economic matters.[1] Politics comes a close second and everything else is given third place. Based on the premiss that the distinction between developed and developing countries concerns wealth and little else, development is seen principally as *economic development*. Economics was treated until recent decades as a linear science endowed with order, predictably and well-established theories.[2] That mature science, it was thought, offered the most controllable and assured chances of success in development. Get the economy right and all else will naturally fall into place. It was inevitable, therefore, for the linear paradigm to sneak unobserved into the development field.

That frame of reference produced differing concepts of the process of development. One, often ascribed to Rostow (1960), envisions distinct stages of development, from initial *takeoff* to sustained future economic growth. Another viewpoint suggests that poorer, 'more backward', countries could make faster progress by benefiting from economic and technological advances made by those at the top of the development league. A third idea asserts that nations develop in a gradual manner that does not materially affect the gap between haves and have-nots. But in all these approaches the inputs to development are seen as being mainly economic, with contributions from politics and other fields.

Consideration of the adequacy or otherwise of the present development paradigm must be based, therefore, on analysis of the above primary influences, and the ideologies and theories of international political economy (IPE) provide a rational medium for that task. My objective, I must stress, is not to give a fully fledged presentation of the topic; others have covered this field thoroughly.[3] Instead, I will delve into IPE ideologies and theories only to the extent required to meet the aims I outlined at the start.

INTERNATIONAL POLITICAL ECONOMY: IDEOLOGIES AND THEORIES

IPE ideologies are traditionally classified into mercantilist, liberal, and Marxist schools of thought (Gilpin 1992). According to that convention, each doctrinal approach is primarily a view of the relative supremacy of economic versus political factors internationally, and state versus social forces domestically. Schools also differ in their assumptions about the main driving forces behind change, and the vision of what that change would bring over time. Delineation between schools is not one of absolute values but depends on the weights to be given to each factor. This would explain in part the hazard of labelling a nation as being, say, liberal or mercantilist. To muddy the waters further, I will contend later that a nation could easily be both at the same time. I will take that contention a step further to show that, in the case of IPE ideologies, ambiguity is the normal state of affairs. However, the didactic convention of treating the three schools as identifiable separate entities will be adhered to for the present to allow a brief description to be given of each school.

Mercantilism

Recognised traditionally as the oldest of the three, the mercantilist school, also referred to as *nationalist* or *realist*, views international relations primarily as an endless struggle between states over political power. This ideology, therefore, does not envisage an end–state; nations simply jostle for position within the international hierarchy. It does not dispute the efficacy of the free market, but it maintains that while states continue to be the building blocks of the global system they would pursue their national interests in all events. Inevitably, the contest would result in a global hierarchy, with a few nations as an elite at the apex. Mercantilists traditionally saw other nations in the hierarchy as colonial rewards or, at best, occasional allies.

At the domestic level, mercantilism places the state at the top of the hierarchy. It is paramount, all other actors being subservient to its needs, designs and, quite often, whims. Mercantilism nonetheless takes it as a matter of course that the state is a rational institution that acts objectively to optimise the national interest in any situation. In this context, the doctrine has a sense of morality as it correlates the absolute power of the leader, or state, with the need to deter individuals from pursuing their egoistic interests at the expense of society as a whole.

Niccolò Machiavelli (1469–1527) is recognised as the archetypal mercantilist. He presented his book, *The Prince*, to the Duke of Urbino in 1513 as a manual for securing and holding on to power (Machiavelli 1981).[4] Most nations had their own mercantilist advocates though. Their views are of significance here as they mirror distinct parallels in modern times. For example, the German scholar Friedrich List (1789–1846) asserted that protection was desirable in some cases to enable nations, meaning Germany at that time, to catch up with the leaders. He had no quarrel with free trade 'in a union of states', as long as it was understood that the union would have massive advantages over others (List 1977).[5] In the USA, Alexander Hamilton (1755–1804) presented a *Report on Manufacture* to Congress in 1791 in which he discussed relations with Europe. His remarks are interesting as they foreshadow to a remarkable degree those advanced by developing countries vis-à-vis today's leading powers.

Convention decrees that mercantilism, having attained its zenith in England in the first half of the eighteenth century, went out of fashion in the first half of the twentieth century. Most advanced industrial states adopted policies that conformed to that philosophy during the Depression years of the 1930s, but that was the last flourish until it was revived in the 1970s as *neo-mercantilism* or *neorealism*. Nevertheless, I take a contrary stance, later in this chapter, to argue that all states retain unmistakable mercantilist traits to this day.

Liberalism

John Locke (1632–1704), one of the fathers of the Enlightenment, concerned himself mainly with political liberalism. He commented at length on the balance of power between governments and individuals. But liberalism has a more familiar economic dimension, now recognised as capitalism. In the international arena, liberalism un-waveringly believes in the supremacy of economic influences un-hindered by national boundaries and state power. Domestically, liberalism abhors big government. The state is there to protect indi-vidual freedoms and property rights, and to secure public goods that might not otherwise be provided by the private sector. Theory and practice diverge though. America is by all accounts the bastion of liberalism, but its government is also the biggest enterprise on earth. It exercises functions that go well beyond those advocated by this doctrine, including redistribution of incomes on a vast scale (Samuelson and Nordhaus 1995: 278, 299).

The principal actors are assumed by liberalism to be egoistic indi-viduals, as persons or corporations; rational actors driven by self-interest and guided by perfect knowledge of all the factors that affect the choices they make. In pursuing their selfish ends, however, they confer benefits on society as a whole. Adam Smith (1723–1790), the Scottish economist and the recognised architect of classical econom-ics, defined the market, and its *invisible hand*, as the medium for that hopeful scenario. It is useful to stress at this point that Smith was a near contemporary of Isaac Newton (1642–1727), who published his groundbreaking *Principia* in 1678. The fundamental laws of linear mechanics that the publication revealed to the world had a massive impact in later years on the way people viewed social as well as natural phenomena.

The market's invisible hand, liberalism asserts, steers economic activity towards a state of equilibrium blessed by efficient allocation of resources and just distribution of rewards. Later liberal theorists advanced the idea of *diminishing returns* to explain how the market exerted its virtuous power over the economy: through negative feed-back, large fluctuations are offset by the reactions they create.[6] Division of labour, Smith rightly predicted, would increase productivity and profits. Capital deepening – increasing the capital to labour ratio, through greater reliance on mechanical power – and division of labour paved the way for the appearance of massive factories and the assembly line.

David Ricardo (1772–1823) widened the concept of specialisation to include trade between nations. He advocated *comparative advantage* as the more appropriate basis for international trade in preference to absolute advantage. (Ricardo 1971). The idea was breathtaking at a time when Europe was staunchly mercantilist, and hence protectionist. Comparative advantage argued that it would be more beneficial if a country were to concentrate its resources on what it could produce most efficiently. Given free trade across boundaries, it could then import what others produce more cheaply.

Liberalism is founded on a firm belief that prosperity, borne on the tide of spreading capitalism, would radiate outwards from richer to poorer nations. When taken to the extreme, liberalism is sometimes described as *laissez-faire*, and such a state is said to have existed in Victorian England and the USA in the nineteenth century. However, the doctrine, as envisioned in modern times, involves an inevitable element of intervention by the state. In that format, it acquired in the 1990s almost religious status as the only escalator to success following the demise of the USSR and America's re-emergence as the undisputed hegemon.

Marxism

This is the last in the trilogy of core IPE ideologies. The founder, Karl Marx (1818–1883), was born and educated in Germany but had to flee to England when his revolutionary ideas became unacceptable to the authorities. Shortly before leaving, in 1848, he penned the *Communist Manifesto* with Friedrich Engels (1820–1895). Marx's move to England, and his friendship with the wealthy Engels, was a decisive factor in crystallising his thoughts along the lines presented in *Capital* (McLellan 1995). England at the time was past its mercantilist phase and in the grip of liberalism in its most unyielding form. Slums amid the opulence of London, Liverpool and Manchester were all too plain to see.

Marxist philosophy is based on a deterministic concept of history that charts the progress of humankind through precise and identical steps. The escalator ends at the door of communism. In effect, the doctrine treats the transition from a state of barbarism, through feudalism and capitalism, to communist civilisation as a predictable linear process. Centre stage is given to an apocalyptic vision of the end of the capitalist mode of production in the aftermath of a revolt by the working classes against the capitalists. That vision was given expression in the first line in the *Communist Manifesto* (Marx and Engels 1998: 34), which stated, 'The history of all hitherto existing society is the history of class struggles.'

Perhaps surprisingly, other key tenets of Marxism exhibit clear similarity to liberal beliefs. For instance, the Marxist doctrine is decidedly international in scope. In addition, it recognises economics as the leading factor that conditions political and social life. Moreover, Marx saw capitalism and the market as inevitable tools for progress, and he predicted that capitalism would in time envelop the whole world. It is only at that stage that Marx's vision departs radically from liberalism. The escalator continues beyond capitalism, through a concluding fight between capitalists and the proletariat, to communism as the final destination.

Marx blamed the 'Asiatic mode of production' for much of what he saw as being wrong with developing countries. Significantly, Soviet archaeologists researching ancient Eastern civilisations challenged his concept of an inferior mode of production indigenous to these nations (al-Tikriti 1986: 189). Beyond that, his attitude to nations at the lower end of the global hierarchy mirrored common European opinions of that era. He saw them as backward people in need of awakening. For that purpose, they had to mount the historic escalator, through capitalism. Writing in the *Communist Manifesto* (Marx and Engels 1998: 39), Marx and Engels proclaimed that the global capitalist mode of production 'by the rapid improvement of all instruments of production, by the immensely facilitated means of communication, draws all, even the most barbarian, nations into civilisation'.

Marxism, in summary, has a staged historic conception of economic development.[7] The key feature that distinguishes traditional Marxism from liberalism focuses primarily on the length of the escalator and the nature of the terminus at the end of the ride. Hence, even these supposedly divergent schools of thought share some common ground. It is perhaps worth mentioning at this point that the *Communist Manifesto* painted a picture of capitalism that is remarkably similar to that existing in today's global market. For example, the *Manifesto*, written in 1848 remember, referred to 'universal interdependence' as well as to the globalisation of 'intellectual production'.

SPURIOUS NEATNESS IN AN IDEOLOGICAL MAELSTROM

A simplistic version of the history of IPE ideologies enjoys surprising currency. It claims that mercantilism went into terminal decline after World War II, Marxism thrived and perished with the rise and fall of the Soviet Union, and liberalism has survived as the one and only viable ideology, and by implication the sole escalator to development. This neat historical perspective is as flawed as the assertion that the ideologies are discordant doctrines locked into a zero-sum battle for survival. Having described the core IPE ideologies earlier, it is now appropriate to dispense with this dogmatic myth before turning the spotlight on IPE's so-called theories.

Mercantilism lives on

Far from being an extinct ideology, mercantilism lives on. A glance at news headlines in any country leaves little doubt that mercantilist tendencies remain the norm, with variable inputs from the other ideologies. Given an opportunity to act freely, all states seek power and supremacy at home and abroad, and those with sufficient clout do so uninhibitedly. Liberal and Marxist regimes exhibit the self-same mercantilist preferences, as the following examples drawn from liberal, communist, and newly industrialising nations demonstrate:

- The USA is the bastion of liberalism, but closer scrutiny reveals that classic mercantilist undertones freely intermingle with the mainstream. Rivalry between the USA and the waning British hegemon at the end of World War II provides a prime illustration. Successive US governments, in true mercantilist fashion, master-minded a series of revolutions during the 1950s and 1960s to dislodge America's staunch ally from its areas of influence. The Free Officer's coup in Egypt in 1952 was one such event (Vatikiotis 1991: 374). Similarly, the USA, as befits a liberal state, has reduced barriers to trade over the years, but that mostly relates to tariffs, as opposed to nontariff barriers, which were maintained, and in some instances enhanced (Ray 1988).
- Russia in the days of the USSR provided convincing proof that mercantilism coexists with communism just as easily as with capitalism. Russia stuck to its nationalist traditions throughout the USSR era; power for mother Russia topped the priority list. Apart from relentless economic exploitation – as was the case in Uzbekistan, say – Russia's satellite states served much the same political and military purposes as city walls in ancient times, and Western Europe vis-à-vis the USA in modern times.

• South Korea presents another instance where the extremes of mercantilism and liberalism mixed quite comfortably, this time within a newly industrialising nation. Success was achieved because a repressive regime was prepared to adopt protectionist policies externally and a regulated but relatively liberal economy at home to attain its nationalist aims (Haggard and Moon 1983).

States and their fixation with the acquisition of power are, therefore, prominent and permanent features of the global system. On the other hand, the degree to which they succeed in that task is a function of many factors. The point I wish to emphasise here is the inclination for mercantilism to mix seamlessly with other political economic creeds. But then that statement is just as valid when applied to the other ideologies. Firebrands might cajole, but in the end compromises are always at hand.

Shades of Marxism

Similar to mercantilism, Marxism presents a concoction of beliefs chosen to suit circumstances. The Marxism found in textbooks is an idealised polar extreme of a range of options that range from rampant communism to mild socialism. Communism itself should not be confused with Russian communism, and that variant is not the same as the models practised in China, Vietnam or Cuba. To confuse matters further, each version has changed considerably over time.

European socialism, rooted in the Enlightenment, was initially an attempt by enlightened capitalists to introduce justice and equity into the capitalist mode of production.[8] Revolutionary overtones only came about when Marx appeared on the scene. Conversely, by the end of World War II some of the political and economic features of socialism, essentially nationalisation and the welfare state, were to be seen in all the leading nations regardless of ideological orientation.[9] As such, the average American would have been somewhat shocked, especially in the heat of the Cold War, to learn that socialists governed friendly Sweden from 1932 to 1976.

Ideology is not a primary concern in Europe; governments oscillate easily between socialism and liberalism while they maintain their mercantilist preferences. Although, socialism was in vogue after World War II, by the mid-1950s the pendulum had swung the other way until the end of the so-called golden age in the early 1970s. At that time socialist parties gained power in France, Greece, Portugal and Spain, a new departure for these nations. During the 1980s European nations took another turn to liberalism and that was underlined by the dramatic events that accompanied the collapse of the USSR. Then the late 1990s witnessed another revival in the fortunes of the left, as was the case in Britain, France and Germany for instance, but by that stage there was hardly a difference between parties of the left and right.[10] Later collapse of outright communism and the end of the Cold War allowed pragmatism to come out into the open. Ideologies had lost their utility as battle cries of the Cold War.

Pervasive variety and pragmatism are amply in evidence even at the communist end of the spectrum. Widespread public ownership, say, took hold only in certain locations with special needs, but even here diversity was commonplace. V.I. Lenin (1870–1924) himself was not antagonistic to a fair measure of private ownership and enterprise in revolutionary Russia, as seen clearly in his 1921 *New Economic Policy*. In essence, the Soviet Union was not strictly communist for long. Many socialist models were tried up to the early 1930s; the USSR then experienced brief periods of true communism up to Stalin's death in 1953; and that was followed by milder forms of communism that slowly led to the dramatic events of the late 1980s and early 1990s.

Mao Tse-tung (1893–1976) evolved a brand of communism in China that reflected his dislike of bureaucracy and his rural outlook. As a result, he singled out the peasants as the main revolutionary force, rather than the workers as preached by Marx. Local autonomy, as opposed to control from the centre, and communal ownership, in preference to public ownership, were adopted throughout China. After Mao's death a new generation of leaders evolved their own styles of communism. These culminated in the adoption of radical privatisation proposals at the Communist Party Congress held in September 1997, and further easing of controls has continued since. Significantly, however, those in power still believe that China is a communist state.

Vietnamese communism shows a similar level of diversity. Years of war against France and then America left their mark on the political economy of that country. Up to the end of hostilities in 1976, Vietnam was strictly communist. However, when the USA withdrew and the Republic of Vietnam came into being, a prompt metamorphosis took place that altered Vietnamese communism beyond recognition. The transition was formalised at the Sixth Party Congress in 1986 when the *doi moi* (renewal) reforms, comprising a mix of liberal and communist practices, were agreed. It is interesting to remember that the change in direction predated the collapse of the USSR.

Yugoslavia, during thirty-five years under Josip Tito (1892–1980), offered yet another version of communism. As usual, Yugoslav communism incorporated mercantilist tendencies, but it incorporated liberal pluralist convictions as well. Competition among public enterprises was actively encouraged, only 13 per cent of agricultural land was collectivised, and trade and other links with the West were firmer than those with the Eastern bloc. Annual growth in industrial production was about 10 per cent in the 1950s and 1960s. Significantly, policies to attain that level of growth were much the same in 'communist' Yugoslavia as those followed by 'capitalist' South Korea – basically a pragmatic mix of ideologies.

It was necessary to mull over the Marxist case at some length, as it often conjures up visions of doctrinal inflexibility. Nonetheless, as shown above, variety is as common here as it is in other ideologies. Fundamentally, for ideologies to survive they have to adapt in line with changing circumstances. That is the only viable strategy.

Ideological flags of convenience

To complete the picture, it is helpful to look briefly at the way communism and socialism fared in the developing countries. There are two key points to make in this context. On the one hand, ideologies display similar pragmatism when they are exported abroad. In practical terms, developing nations cannot afford the luxury of sticking to any particular ideological line. On the other hand, ideological tags are sometimes attached to this or that developing country for purposes commonly associated with local propaganda and the machinations of the leading powers.

India provides a good illustration. Jawaharlal Nehru (1889–1964), first prime minister after independence in 1947, adopted liberal policies laced with socialist expedients. He recognised that ideology hardly mattered in the tangled affairs of nations. A leading light in the non-aligned nations bloc, he was not drawn into the concocted antagonism between liberalism and Marxism. Mani Shankar Aiyar, past member of the Indian parliament and a supporter of liberalisation, is in no doubt that 'Indian socialism made Indian capitalism possible', an interesting reversal of Marxist philosophy (Ward 1997).

Leaders of weaker nations often proclaimed their allegiance or antagonism to socialism as a tool in negotiations with the Eastern and Western blocs, as seen in Egypt for instance. Gamal Abdel Nasser became president on the back of an American-inspired revolution. It was only the tussle over funding for the Aswan Dam that tipped him into the USSR camp. Up to that point, socialism in Egypt hardly ever strayed beyond rhetoric and actions that were necessary irrespective of doctrinal beliefs.[11] Egypt's flirtation with socialism continued for a while after Nasser's death in 1970, but his successor, Anwar Sadat, did not hesitate when it suited him to ask the Russians to leave in 1975.[12] At the time of writing, Hosni Mubarak has made certain that Egypt is firmly lodged in the liberal, meaning American, camp. But that is not the final word, if past events are any guide.

Abd al-Karim Qassem (1814–1963), leader of the revolution that overthrew the monarchy in Iraq in 1958, was a run-of-the-mill pragmatist. Only hours after the success of the coup he found time to send dispatches to Britain and the USA assuring them of his liberal intentions so far as oil was concerned. Later on he had to rely on communist support to shore up his regime against Nasser's Arab nationalist ambitions. Qassem's biographer (Fawzi 1988: 42) was in no doubt that 'Qassem was nothing more than a Qassemite.' Moscow was not fooled either, but Washington seemingly took Qassem's communist leanings more seriously: the CIA (Clark 1998: 3) 'formed a "health alterations committee" to plot the assassination of the new Iraqi leader'. In February 1963, the Ba'th party mounted a coup that cost Qassem his life and ultimately brought Saddam Hussein to power. A new socialist model was born.

Jacobo Arbenz, president of Guatemala from 1950 to 1954, was removed from power by an American-inspired coup, again on the basis of his alleged communist sympathies, a claim Secretary of State Dulles admitted was groundless. The operation was undertaken, it is reported, because Arbenz expropriated United Fruit's holdings without compensation (Ranelagh 1992: 81). The same pattern was repeated in the events during and after Muhammad Mossadegh nationalised the Anglo-Iranian Oil Company in May 1951. He was promptly, and wrongly, accused by the USA of being a supporter of Tudeh, the Iranian communist party. Mossadegh was removed from power with the help of the American CIA and spent the rest of his days under house arrest.

As the above examples reveal, polarisation was required in the Cold War years as a tool for intrigues by the superpowers and their secret services. Little has changed since the end of that era. Governments of developing countries find it useful, for local or external consumption, to declare allegiance to this or that ideology, and leading powers find it to their advantage to go along with that charade. Ideology is only a cover.

Dogma and eclecticism in the liberal camp

Undoubtedly, the ideology of choice at the moment is liberalism. It is hailed as the only escalator to development. That is a simple message for anyone to understand. Just to make sure, however, a number of global bodies, such as the IMF, the World Bank and the WTO, are charged with the task of exhorting all developing countries to come into line behind that doctrine. They devote massive effort to cajoling developing countries into reducing public spending and the size of their governments in line with stabilisation and structural adjustment programmes.

However, there is ample evidence that in the real world liberalism comes in all shapes and sizes. Basically, the doctrine in its pure form as *laissez-faire* – Thomas Carlyle's 'anarchy plus the constable' – is virtually unknown. Members of the select group of developed countries headed by America adhere instead to the *mixed-economy* model; a hybrid of capitalist and socialist components in various and varying proportions. A brief glance at the size and pattern of government spending, welfare, subsidies, and free trade is sufficient to put any doubts on that score to rest. Hence, while the US government, for instance, consumes around 35 per cent of national gross domestic product (GDP), state spending in Paraguay is limited to less than 10 per cent of GDP (Samuelson and Nordhaus 1995: 302, 278).

A similar pattern exists in respect to welfare. According to dogma, liberalism scorns welfare, a practice whereby the government re-distributes income and provides health and social services. Welfare, classical liberal economists sermonised, is a source of inefficiency in the economy, and the IMF and the World Bank forcefully underwrite that message in their dealings with developing countries. Again, this particular pillar of capitalist credo is a stipulation that is largely ignored by leading nations, as seen in the USA where 'virtually the entire growth in federal spending in recent years can be accounted for by entitlement programs, which grew from 28 per cent of the budget in 1960 to 59 per cent in 1994' (Samuelson and Nordhaus 1995: 302).

Liberal teachings disapprove of subsidies as well. Accordingly, the IMF and the World Bank managed to convince governments of some developing countries to reduce wages and price subsidies for most commodities including food. Mexico is a case in point. In 1983, a basket of basic goods for an average family of five cost 46 per cent of the minimum wage, but by 1992 the same basket absorbed 161 per cent (Brown et al. 1997: 123). Governments of developed countries, on the other hand, support their industries directly, as in the case of the European Union's notorious Common Agricultural Policy, which absorbs more than half its budget, or indirectly, through funding for research and development, say.

Furthermore, according to liberal economic theory, free trade is good without ifs or buts. Nonetheless, in practice it all depends on whether times are good or bad and on the winners and losers. In recent years, openness was in vogue until crises in Asia and Russia impacted on Europe and the USA. Predictably, following the mid-term elections in November 1998, President Clinton informed America's trading partners that he was not prepared to tolerate 'the flooding of our markets' with cheap imports. Protection is relatively common. For example, US steel imports from Russia are restricted, while Europe limits Japanese car imports to 11 per cent of the European market. Even the humble banana became for a while a major item of contention between Europe and the USA. Although tariffs have been substantially reduced, leading economic powers have instituted ingenious nontariff barriers designed to regulate trade to suit their purposes.

The examples quoted above underscore the fact that liberalism, in line with mercantilism and Marxism, does not offer natural laws written on tablets of stone. All ideologies evolve, sometimes in large mutations, to fit circumstances. The practice makes sense in terms of the survival of the overall system. Liberalism is not flexible because it is liberal and sensible. It has had to adapt constantly in order to survive – a clear sign of evolutionary change and nonlinearity. Regardless, the prescriptions handed down to developing countries seem to place obdurate reliance on order and rigidly.

THEORIES AT THE MERCY OF CAPRICIOUS EVENTS

It is necessary at this stage to draw a distinction between ideologies and theories. An ideology is a 'comprehensive and mutually consistent set of ideas by which a social group makes sense of the world' (McLean 1996: 233). A theory, on the other hand, denotes a 'deliberate effort to … separate out rules from special or accidental circumstances'. A successful theory should have two attributes, 'coherence and generality', and should apply to 'a whole class of situations' (Gell-Mann 1994: 77). At some point in the evolution of IPE ideologies attempts were made to fortify ideological debate with 'scientific' theories. That was the signal for matters to go seriously wrong. The theories failed to predict and explain events for 'a whole class of situations', and they did not converge but suffered incessant radical revision instead.

Theorists, it seems, failed to ask themselves a simple but fundamental question: is it feasible to formulate a theory to model political economic phenomena characterised by copious diversity and constantly fluctuating events that in the main followed no rhyme or reason? We are now entering the heart of the matter. Those working on the theories lived in a scientific era that believed implicitly in order, predictability, and stable cause-and-effect relationships. Though they did not realize it, they went in search of what we now recognise as linear scientific theories. However, nations and their political economies are not as straightforward as the motion of solids under gravity, say. They give every impression of being nonlinear phenomena. It is not surprising, therefore, that theorists of all ideological persuasions were left chasing their tails.

COURSE CORRECTIONS AND CROSSOVERS

Rival IPE theories were troubled over time by three problems. First, the market did not live up to classical liberal expectations. Second, contrary to Marxist predictions, capitalists and workers did not clash, and the final leap into communism never came. Third, in a highly interconnected world, mercantilists had to revise their ideas on trade protection and state autonomy. Radical course corrections became unavoidable and these led to crossover theories that merely succeeded in undermining the validity of all the core theories.

Frailty of the invisible hand

Classical economists, led by Adam Smith and David Ricardo, asserted that rational and informed sellers and buyers, guided by the *invisible hand* of the market, could settle without involvement by third parties the three elementary questions of what goods and services to offer, how to produce them, and for whom. Their confidence reflected the rational spirit of the scientific age launched by Isaac Newton and his colleagues.

Some economists have kept faith with that view, as in the case of followers of the Chicago School of Economics, but others disagreed and for good reasons. First, booms and busts, the evident inability of the market in some cases to correct business cycles, were constant reminders that reliance on the market mechanism might not be enough. The Great Depression in the late 1920s and early 1930s, in which the invisible hand was unable to come to the rescue, put that weakness under the microscope. Second, imperfect competition – the proliferation of monopolies and colossal multinational corporations, and powerful speculators – and imperfect information by buyers and sellers were additional features that did not obey the cardinal conditions defined by classical theories. And finally, positive and negative externalities complicated the picture even further. Externalities are activities that affect others without a price being charged from or paid to those affected. A firm might pollute the environment, say, at a considerable cost to the community, without any effects on its costs. In theory, a price must be allocated to all items within the market, but in practice externalities escape that net.

These and other market failures cast serious doubt on the ability of classical theories to model real-life situations adequately. In consequence, the theories had to be amended to permit external regulation, by the state, say, in an attempt to rectify failures in the economy, to reduce inequality, or to dampen booms and busts.

Revolution in liberal ranks

Adam Smith was concerned for the most part with what we recognise today as microeconomics: the behaviour of single elements in the economy. There is little doubt that these individual parts are tolerably orderly, predictable and linear. Microeconomic theories have been expanded or modified but in general they withstood the test of time. By contrast, macroeconomic theories that addressed the behaviour of the economy as a whole proved less durable. In particular, excessive bouts of unemployment and inflation imposed several rethinks. Doubts about the efficacy of classical economics came to a head during the Great Depression, preceded in the USA by the Wall Street crash of October 1929, which was caused by a number of factors that gathered force after World War I.[13]

Liberal recipes had not delivered on their promises and rising trade unionism and expanding welfare programmes were stamping their imprint on domestic political economies. In addition, international trade had entered a new phase of closure that was to prove harmful to all nations. In addition, there was also a power vacuum: the British Empire was a thing of the past and the new hegemon, the USA, was not yet ready to take the lead. Governments of the leading industrial nations had to abandon their inherited liberal policies, and the search was on for better theories.

In time, the USA, Britain and other major economies were forced to undergo a peaceful revolution, led by activists from within the liberal fraternity. That revolution proved to be the undoing of Marx's concept of the violent overthrow of capitalism by the proletariat. But it also dealt a heavy blow to classical liberal theory. John Maynard Keynes (1883–1946) played a major role in that transformation. He uttered the unthinkable: from time to time the state has to step in to resuscitate the economy when it stagnates or to dampen it down when it overheats. Keynes's prescription of how this was to be achieved defined the fundamental principles of macroeconomics. The boldness of his conception was impressive. For over two centuries classical economists treated the independence of the market as an article of faith. Keynes's format turned that viewpoint on its head and ushered in modern economics. The market shapes microeconomics through the supply-and-demand mechanism. The government, on the other hand, influences macroeconomic affairs by means of fiscal measures, taxes and government spending, for instance, and monetary levers, such as interest rates and actions to meter money supply.

Keynes was an influential member of the British delegation at the Bretton Woods Conference, which led to the setting up of the IMF, the World Bank and GATT (General Agreement on Tariffs and Trade). These organisations, backed by considerable economic and political resources, were deemed to be essential for the proper regulation of the global political economy in accordance with the new definition of liberalism. In many ways, these international regimes assumed the powers of a 'global government' charged with the task of managing the world system to the satisfaction of the leading powers.

Cracks in Keynes's neoliberalism

Macroeconomic policies are, by definition, at variance with the cherished vision of a free global economy unencumbered by state rules and national borders. If capital, as money or people, could roam unhindered here and there, then a state's room for manoeuvre is drastically curtailed. Keynes was not unaware of this potential difficulty. That was one reason for his proposal to set up an international currency union that would issue its own universal currency and would eventually lead to the formation of an economic world government, but the Americans quickly disabused him of such notions (Caufield 1996: 41).

Not unexpectedly, Keynes's *General Theory*, the fundamental base of neoliberalism, did not go unchallenged; it was considered unnecessary when matters were going well, and it was blamed when events turned sour. There were good reasons for both viewpoints. On the one hand, Keynesian ideas, so effective in the early years, faltered under new conditions characterised by currency speculation on a vast scale, easier movement of capital across borders, and the sheer volume of international trade. On the other hand, dissatisfaction emerged when neoliberalism failed to combat high inflation that was triggered in part by the oil price shocks delivered by the Organisation of Petroleum Exporting Countries (OPEC) in the 1970s.

Intense debate ensued and a number of competing theories appeared on the scene. These ranged from *monetarism* with emphasis on money supply, to *supply-side economics* concerned with incentives and lower taxes, and, of course, a return to classical economics, in the style of the Chicago School. The most interesting aspect of the debate, for the present purpose, was the role played by politics in radically changing economic theory. Events in the USA illustrate this feature well. Reagan and Bush Sr, elected presidents in 1980 and 1988 respectively, followed to a large extent an economic policy based on supply-side economics, which favoured efficiency and productivity over virtually all else. Clinton promised a U-turn and won the presidency in 1992, and then his successor, George W. Bush, took over the presidency in 2001 on the promise of another radical shift in economic policy. Clearly, trial and error continues to reign supreme on the liberal political economic landscape.

While theorists try in vain to discover universal scientific formulations and ideologues nit-pick their way through claims and counterclaims; those taking actual decisions select suitable actions from a wide range of options. Essentially, there was nothing wrong with Keynesian macroeconomics or any of the earlier or later ideas as time- and place-specific working propositions. They were picked up, revised and discarded pragmatically by the leading powers. Matters went off the rails only when ideologies were repackaged as so-called scientific theories and then imposed willy-nilly on nations and governments in the developing world.

Marxism's feeble record

Liberal theories might be flawed but any failures here are put in the shade by the lame performance of Marxist ideology and theory. In their competition against capitalism they have exhibited a conspicuous lack of staying power. Furthermore, events have not conformed to Marx's vision of history; so far, advanced industrialised economies have not experienced the predicted violent confrontations between capitalists and workers. The capitalist mode of production was expected to spread to all developing countries, to be followed shortly thereafter by a move to socialism and communism. Facts again refused to fall in line with Marxist expectations. Entrepreneurs from richer and more powerful countries came, invested, and then exported the profits without materially transforming the societies concerned. Classical Marxist theory was, therefore, as flawed as its liberal counterpart, and something had to be done to retrieve the situation.

Discord in the Marxist cadres

A radical course correction, the social-democratic model, was the response. It had a profound effect on political economic thought, especially in northern Europe. Again change came from within the fraternity. Karl Kautsky (1854–1938) and Eduard Bernstein (1850–1932), the German Social Democratic Party leader, disagreed with

Marx's view that the final sprint to communism would come about after a violent revolution brought about by capitalist excesses. They clearly set communism as the ultimate aim, but they went on to define reforms that could be implemented within capitalism. These included universal suffrage, equal rights for women, and pensions and health services for all; features now accepted as axiomatic in all the advanced liberal states.

Social democracy, as was the case with Keynes's reforms of liberalism, allowed socialism to survive, especially after the fall of the USSR. The aim again was to search for a stable strategy through a move to the centre of the political economic spectrum. Social democracy came from the left and Keynes's ideas from the right. Mercantilism was not immune from the drift to the centre either, as outlined in the next section. In effect, differences between ideologies have been obliterated by the eclecticism of the mixed-economy model that is now *de rigueur* for developed countries.

Realism confronted by reality

Mercantilism, also known as realism, did not escape the reassessment that engulfed other ideologies and theories, but here the affair was less dramatic. In its classical form, the creed envisioned extensive state regulation of economic activity as part of the effort to enhance national power against other states. That description could apply in principle to all states, past and present. Inevitably, the extent to which a state succeeds in its quest for power is conditioned by obvious limiting factors, including its political, military and economic relative strength. In recent decades, however, the ability of states to pursue that line had to be reconciled with a shrinking world of linked interests in which capital, expertise and people move freely across political borders. Mercantilists, with avowed belief in the supremacy of the state, had to find a theoretical path through that maze.

Traditionally, classical mercantilists such as List asserted that political precepts shape economic outcomes, but that view was not always as clear-cut. For instance, Max Weber (1864–1920) envisioned a two-way relationship that bound economics and politics into a state of constant flux. Faced by irrefutable evidence, mercantilists veered towards Weber's way of thinking, as argued nowadays by Waltz, Gilpin, Katzenstein and other *neorealists*. They envisage the interplay between politics and economics as a process of push and pull. The state tries as far as possible to have its way at home and abroad, but all the while it is buffeted by international political economic forces and domestic social pressures. Interestingly, Waltz, recognised as the founder of neorealism, advocated 'systemic theory' in his analysis of international relations and highlighted the anarchic nature of these relations, which he envisaged as being complex and chaotic (Waltz 1979). He was, of course, writing at a time when Complex Systems theory was in its infancy.

In short, mercantilist theory had to be substantially altered to accept that politics is not an independent variable in the overall equation. Moreover, present-day neorealists do not subscribe to naked protectionism and other actions based on outdated beggar-thy-neighbour attitudes, mainly because prescriptions of that nature have been shown to be counterproductive. Once again, real life did not tally with so-called realist theory. Mercantilist theory was replaced, therefore, by an amalgam of ideas that suggest states would always do their utmost to acquire power and wealth, but they would be restrained by economic interdependence abroad and by social forces at home. In effect, the mixed economy is overlaid by mercantilist aspirations, and vice versa. Inevitably, perhaps, the interplay between state autonomy and an open global system was tackled later by yet another set of hybrids, *interdependence theories*.

The many faces of interdependence

Interdependence theories provide a further illustration of the turmoil that gripped all IPE theories as they attempted to explain and predict fast-changing events within linear formulations that took order, predictability and cause-and-effect relationships for granted. The uneasy tension between the state and its innate wish to promote national interests and a global economy operating substantially beyond the reach of politicians posed difficult questions to the three core ideologies and their associated theories, and a crop of interdependence theories was the inevitable outcome.

Theorists differed in their view of the nature and virtue of interdependence. Those originating from the liberal camp argued that interdependence, regulated in part by international regimes, such as the IMF, confers net joint benefits to all. Others, with a mercantilist spin on life, defined interdependence as *mutual dependence*, in which nations derived markedly different relative gains and losses. Certain scholars described the system as 'complex interdependence' to underline the variety of relationships that might exist at any time. Ultimately, they asserted, the balance point is determined, as ever, by an amalgam of factors, such as relative economic and military power between states, their relative vulnerabilities, and the issue areas involved (Keohane and Nye 1977).

Taking the debate a step further, *dependency theorists* of a Marxist persuasion contended that underdevelopment was a natural consequence of the global spread of capitalism. Santos (1970), for instance, defined dependence as 'a situation in which the economy of certain countries is conditioned by the development and expansion of another economy'. Advocates of dependency suggested the existence of a global division of labour: a *core* of rich and powerful nations and a *periphery* of other nations.

Interdependence theorists, from liberal and mercantilist backgrounds, concur with dependency theorists, of Marxist convictions, that interdependence might in some cases be akin to dependency. The two disagree, however, on what those disadvantaged by interdependence should do to improve their position. Far from shunning the global system, as proposed by dependency theorists, those in the liberal camp advocate that all nations should link themselves to a free market system that is regulated only by global institutions and international regimes set up for that purpose. The continuing debate underlines yet again the state of turmoil that has affected IPE theories, on the one hand, and the diminishing significance of demarcation between them, on the other.

CROSSOVER THEORIES COMPLETE THE CIRCLE

The centre ground is now replete with theories. Powerful restraints imposed by dependence and interdependence between nations and by international regimes, such as the WTO, designed with the express purpose of conformity in mind, generated an irresistible centrifugal force. Equally, shifting circumstances and the unpredictability of events made it almost impossible for theorists to set common rules that would apply to more than a few specific cases. And even here applicability was transient; unexpected developments quickly rendered models that worked well in the past more or less obsolete. Accretion of qualifications and compromises had two effects on theories: they became less specific and, in the course of increasing generalisation, they became progressively more similar to each other. IPE theories, therefore, merged into vague generalised models composed of largely similar tenets.

Drastic revisions led in the end to the emergence of *crossover theories* with links to more than one ideological root. Keynes's General Theory as a reform to liberalism, social democracy's attempt to revise Marxism, and interdependence and dependence theories – all exhibit elements borrowed from more than one ideology. However, the latest attempts to fuse roots into unified theories entailed a thoroughly comprehensive rethink. An outline is given below of the main crossover theories that have been added to IPE thought recently. The aim, of course, is not to give an exhaustive review of the topic, but to venture only as far as necessary to illustrate the principal theme of tactical variety within an amorphous central core.

Regime analysis

International regimes, such as the IMF and the WTO and global agreements concerned with telecommunications and postal services, are a prominent feature on the world stage. Crane and Amawi presented two complementary approaches to Regime Analysis: one from a liberal tradition and the other from a realist perspective (Crane and Amawi 1991: 266). Puchala and Hopkins, representing the former strand, argued that regimes stand for specific views of life that they are reluctant to jettison without a fight. Advocacy by the IMF and the World Bank of a single, mainly economic, escalator to development based on an idealised concept of the free market system is an illustration of this institutional obstinacy. Moreover, Puchala and Hopkins suggested that regimes have their own internal hierarchies, but they also fit into a global hierarchy in which they protect and promote the interests of the leading powers.

Neorealists, as in the case of Krasner (1981), on the other hand, view regimes as an essential part of the international distribution of power. Hegemons create and fund regimes to promote their interests, but soon the regimes themselves acquire their own preferences. States, therefore, have every incentive to infiltrate regimes to derive more benefits or to alter them to better suit their purposes. Far from engendering order and control over states, the regimes are seen in this case as the battleground for the exercise of power politics between states. The neorealist interpretation provides interesting food for thought for developing countries; there might be costs to pay, but on balance it might be beneficial in some cases to work with the regimes on the inside.

Hegemonic stability theory

At base, this model could be seen as a crossover between Marxism and mercantilism. A hegemon is defined (in Wallerstein 1983) as a power that is able to 'impose its rules and its wishes ... in the economic, political, military, diplomatic and even cultural arenas'. *Hegemonic stability theory* postulates that a hegemonic power at the zenith of its power favours openness in international affairs. The hegemon expends effort and financial resources to set up and maintain the system, including international regimes, because it stands to benefit most from such a structure.

Advocates of this theory have argued with convincing historical evidence that openness of world trade is determined by the international distribution of potential state power (Krasner 1976). In a multipolar setup involving a few large states of roughly equal power, world trade would range from *autarky*, a completely closed system, to low openness. However, when the distribution of potential economic power is very skewed, as in the presence of a single hegemonic power, then world trade would gravitate to a high degree of openness. That line of argument naturally leads to the conclusion that world trade is in slow flux, its structure drifting between relative openness and closure.

Hegemonic stability theorists suggest that as a hegemon goes into decline the system begins to break down. World affairs, including trade, enter a period of turmoil and the system edges towards closure. In that phase the hegemon, challenged by aspiring rivals, adopts more aggressive policies designed primarily to preserve, or prolong, its supremacy. Scholars have speculated that the USA began the long descent from the summit in the 1960s. Undoubtedly, the rise of the 'United States of Europe' and East and Southeast Asia, led by China or Japan, presents a new phenomenon. The international distribution of power is drifting to a multipolar structure, and the global system might slowly move to relative closure. Irrespective of the eventual outcome, the merging of theories from Marxist and mercantilist backgrounds underlines once more the pattern of variegated sameness.

Public choice analysis

This crossover theory is not new on the field; Schumpeter pioneered the concept over fifty years ago (Schumpeter 1950). A short while later, Downs cast the initial ideas into a theory. His conclusion that all political parties gravitate to the centre of the political spectrum is particularly interesting in the context of the above discussion. Anthony Downs also expressed the view that politicians, as egoistic individuals, select policies in a way that maximises their chances of being re-elected (Downs 1957). James Buchanan added further dimensions to the theory and subsequently received the Nobel Prize in 1986 for his contributions in that field (Buchanan and Tullock 1962).

Public choice theory, sometimes referred to as the *economic theory of politics* or the *new political economy*, is grounded in liberalism. It models interaction between politics and economics by using the tools of modern (neoclassical) analysis (Frey 1984). Theorists of that viewpoint have applied it, for instance, to explain how political intervention might impede optimal economic outcomes as prescribed by liberal theory. However, analysts from realist and Marxist backgrounds have deployed the same theory to put their own spin on international relations.

The link to Marxist and neorealist theory is highly significant. Public choice theory, a variant of a wider rational choice theory, focuses on a key liberal tenet: individual rationality. Egoistic individuals, not social classes or the state, are paramount in this model. Decisions in the political economic field are seen as the result of a bargaining process that is driven by the aspirations of many actors, as persons, interest groups, firms and government departments. Each actor separately considers the costs and benefits as they affect him or her and then behaves accordingly in supporting or resisting change. That is quite a radical U-turn for Marxists and mercantilists alike.

An important point that deserves emphasis here relates to the significance of internal dynamics, driven by a web of local interactions between many players, in determining overall global patterns; an unmistakable pointer to Complexity (see Chapter 4). However, public choice theory is also of interest because of its close affinity to *Game Theory*. Rational choice theory conceives the IPE field as an intricate medium of complementary and competing interests that are actively involved in a hectic process of bargaining. The rational individual is the basic unit of analysis. The concepts of nation and state are themselves seen for what they are, a collection of actors pushing their particular causes to the fore against other equally egoistic individuals and interest groups. Rules of Game Theory, consciously or otherwise, are used to minimise penalties and maximise rewards. I will return to this point in Chapter 4 and, later, in Chapter 10.

IN CONCLUSION

This chapter established that the core IPE ideologies are flexible ideas that ebb and flow. It also showed that as theories emerging from these ideologies were challenged by events, they were comprehensively revised in a bid to rectify the perceived defects. The revisions entailed substantial compromises on previous ideological tenets. Demarcation lines between the theories were blurred through a process of generalisation rather than convergence. Revision proceeded next on a path that led to crossover theories that had links to several ideological and theoretical roots, and they eventually merged into a common pool. Contradictions were resolved through further compromises, leading to an inevitable conclusion that none could be accepted without reservation as a scientific theory that 'separate[s] out rules from special or accidental circumstances'. They did not apply to 'a whole class of situations' either.

Signs of dissatisfaction with the linear paradigm that dominates the study and practice of political economic issues are now quite clear, although they are not recognised as such. For example, Chase-Dunn argued for a holistic IPE theory that views political and economic processes as integrative forces (Chase-Dunn 1981). In similar vein, Frey, in looking into public choice theories, considered it an advantage that the analysis should be based on 'an explicit and unified *theory of human behaviour*' as that 'makes it possible to isolate and analyse relatively simple relationships' (Frey 1984). Debate between reductionist and integrative approaches, or linearity and nonlinearity, is gathering momentum, as the remarks made by Chase-Dunn and Frey exemplify.

In the meantime, however, and as I explain in Chapter 5, the developing countries are under pressure to accept prescriptions that treat the liberal ideology, and its associated models and theories, as fixed articles of faith. Divergence from strict compliance with their tenets is seen as a punishable challenge to the 'world order'. There lies the dilemma for nations in search of development. As I argue in Chapter 10, they are being led down the garden path by, on the whole, well-intentioned leaders and international organisations eager to help. However, before moving on to the topic of nonlinearity and Complex Adaptive Systems, in Chapter 4, I would like to take a backward look at the core IPE ideologies to argue that they have deeper and broader historical roots.

NOTES

1. The Human Development Index (HDI), pioneered by the late Mahbub ul Haq when he was at the United Nations Development Programme, brings three components together: life expectancy, education and income. The HDI was adopted to supplement gross national product and other economic indicators. It has had some impact, but the effort to reduce reliance on economic factors is still a struggle.

2. Several scholars have advocated a shift to a nonlinear framework for economics. Brian Arthur (Stanford University and the Santa Fe Institute of Complexity) is one of the leading proponents for a transformation of this kind (Arthur 1990, 1994).

3. Crane and Amawi (1991) and Frieden and Lake (1995) offer excellent introductory readings in the topic.

4. I will show in Chapter 3 that Machiavelli did not pioneer the format or, for that matter, the creed itself. Ibn Khaldun (n.d.: 143–8) expounded similar ideas several centuries earlier. However, over the years hordes of politicians have seized, often highly selectively, on Machiavelli's injunctions to condemn him or to justify all manner of deeds and misdeeds. Interestingly, Mussolini (1883–1945) chose Machiavelli as the topic for his doctoral thesis.

5. The role of regional alliances is considered in Chapter 10.

6. Some scholars have challenged diminishing returns. They maintain that increasing returns describe actual economic events more accurately. In that nonlinear view of economics, positive feedback is seen as the mechanism that could magnify minor fluctuations into major upheavals (Arthur 1990).

7. See discussion of the idea of a Universal History in Fukuyama (1992: 55).

8. As seen, for instance, in the works of Robert Owen (1771–1858), the Welsh capitalist cotton mill owner, and William Hesketh Lever (1851–1925), the philanthropist soap maker from the north of England.

9. In France, for example, the Monnet plans, after Jean Monnet (1888–1979) involved extensive nationalisation. Monnet himself was not a socialist. In Britain, on the other hand, a socialist Labour government nationalised coal, railways, electricity, health services and gas in 1947, 1948 and 1949.

10. The drift to the middle ground is not a new phenomenon. The German Social Democrats, for example, changed most of their beliefs at the Bad Godesberg Conference in 1959. See also Crosland (1956).

11. For detailed analysis of relations between Egypt, Russia and the USA, see Heikal (1975).

12. He went further by handing Washington a complete battery of Russian SAM 6 missiles. Later Egypt gave Russian weapons to Afghan mujahedeen for use against Soviet troops (Heikal 1992: 87).

13. Detailed analysis of the circumstances that led to these events can be found in Cohen (1977) and Kindleberger (1973).

THREE

ANCIENT ROOTS
TO MODERN IDEOLOGIES

The evidence I presented in the previous chapter showed that ideologies, from Marxism to *laissez-faire* liberalism and all those in between, are not fixed canons. However, the matter does not rest there. The instances outlined in the present chapter leave little room for doubt that the motley collection of notions we recognise as IPE ideologies are neither European in origin nor recent in vintage, and they are certainly not freestanding world-views. Those who argued, and in some cases fought and spilled blood, over the contending creeds will be dismayed by my assertion, but the historic evidence is compelling. Longevity and variability are germane to the concepts considered in future chapters as they corroborate the hypothesis that social, political and economic processes, and human development itself, are in a permanent state of evolutionary change that follows a nonlinear mode of behaviour.

WHOSE DARK AGES?

Knowledge is accumulated piece by piece from here and there over a long period of time, but the Chinese, Greeks, Romans, Arabs and, in recent history, Europeans and Americans all claimed a unique contribution to advancing knowledge while underplaying efforts by others. Europeans, for instance, assume unquestioningly that the Dark Ages, roughly from the fifth to the fifteenth century, were 'dark' everywhere. In fact that period witnessed the flowering of Islamic culture and science, which itself borrowed heavily from previous civilisations.[1] There is, in addition, an absurd conviction that everything else pales into insignificance in comparison with the discoveries and inventions of the last few centuries. Naturally, all discoveries seem miraculous in their time. The use of symbols to record facts and events must have been a truly magical innovation when the Sumerian cuneiform and Egyptian hieratic systems were developed 5,000 years ago. The magnetic needle, invented in China at the time of the Chou dynasty about 1000 BC, is another instance that would have appeared to people of that era as a peerless step forward in human knowledge.

Technical inventions tell only part of the story though. It is routinely assumed that individualism and humanism came to the fore only during the Renaissance in Europe. But that assertion ignores individualists of the calibre of Akhenaten (d. 1362 BC), the heretic pharaoh who is credited with influencing Moses' thoughts on monotheism a century later.[2] That contention also does less than justice to giants of individualism such as Moses, Confucius, the Buddha, Plato, Christ and Muhammad.

Similarly, philosophical speculations about life, the rights of people, and the distribution of power and wealth led to conflicting beliefs, revolts and wars, thousands of years before the age of popular revolutions and the Enlightenment in Europe and America. The increasing sophistication of human affairs generated an unavoidable need for rules and regulations that even in ancient times extended well beyond purely domestic matters to address political and economic issues. The Code of Hammurabi in Babylon (c. 1751 BC), Draco's Laws in Greece (621 BC) and Solon's later reforms (594 BC) provide a clear picture of the modernity of these ancient civilisations. Following that train of thought, I will present in the next few sections anecdotal proof to show that Adam Smith did not invent liberalism, Marx was hardly the first devotee of socialism, and Machiavelli was not the founding father of mercantilism. These ideas might have modern names but their traits have been in evidence for thousands of years.

ELITES AND HIERARCHIES: AN ENDURING MODEL

The above remarks underline the need for a measure of historic reorientation when considering human development. The essential task in looking for evolutionarily stable development strategies is to search for underlying patterns that endure, though they might evolve and assume different guises in line with prevailing beliefs. The French philosopher Auguste Comte (1798–1857) identified three paradigms to trace the course of human history: theological, metaphysical and scientific (Saad 1990: 285). That categorisation is helpful as it explains why practices at times far removed from the present appear so different although the basic patterns are essentially the same.

The most enduring feature in human societies is a hierarchical structure based on monopoly of power and wealth by an elite at the top and a concomitant quest by the rest of the community for equity and justice. Over the centuries, ideologies were invented to justify the privileged position of the elite, and to offer a glimmer of hope for the rest of society. During the theological era priests and kings accumulated wealth and wielded power in the name of the gods, while their slaves sought rewards as well as protection from punishment through prayers and sacrifices. Later, elites of princes and noblemen acquired riches on the basis of metaphysical ideas of virtue, wisdom and valour. In the present era, the mainstream is represented by theories advocating a variety of so-called scientific explanations for the lopsided distribution of power and wealth. Some elites claim they are there to provide jobs and income for the rest of the community, while others assert their right to be at the top because they are the sole guardians of the revolution, religion, or whatever.

Justifications might vary but the end result is the same. Basically, when people come together order is needed even at the lowest levels of social organisation, and that requires the exercise of authority by a group of people irrespective of how that particular clique reached the top. And individuals who enjoy power over others simply cannot avoid becoming wealthier. The concentration of power and wealth into a few hands, or a few nations, has technical significance related to the way Complexity increases over time, as I will explain in Chapter 4. Equally inevitably, dissatisfaction with the elite and their uses and abuses of power eventually comes to the surface. There is, therefore, a constant tussle between the two factions. This applies to the hierarchy within the global interstate system just as much as to the *sarpanch* and his friends and relations in a village in West Bengal.

An iron grip on power and wealth

History chronicles the ebb and flow of elites, their relations with the communities they ruled, and their shifting alliances and conflicts with other elites abroad. States, or the elites that lie behind them, have always tried to hoard power and wealth. That inclination was known well before mercantilism arrived on the scene. In recent times, wider networks of elites of individuals, interest groups and political parties replaced for the most part the priests and noblemen of old. It is claimed, with some justification, that this latest hierarchical model is flatter than previous models, but that is only a matter of degree; the elites in Britain or the USA, for instance, continue to be limited to at most a few thousand people (Herman and Chomsky 1994: 8).

The attitude of elites on the best way to preserve their exclusive grip on wealth and power evolved in response to changing conditions, particularly increasing assertiveness by the community at large. Nonetheless, dictators still rule by terror and brute force, while some continue to assert their right to govern on the basis of mandates from heaven.[3] But other, more enlightened, elites developed more subtle and effective strategies for keeping the majority quiescent. They concluded that it was generally more efficient to give the populace freedom to do what they liked, including a modest measure of income generation and retention, as long as they accepted the status quo and helped the elite to amass more wealth. That was the stance taken by slave owners in Mesopotamia when they found that better returns could be made with less effort and risk if slaves were allowed to run their own businesses; slave owners simply levied a tax on profits (al-Tikriti 1986: 94). The same concept lay behind the Taoists' advice to rulers in China to keep people's 'bellies full'. In that way, it was argued, they would not hold unsocial thoughts.

Pragmatic elites, therefore, realised early in history that a format that allowed people to lead reasonably free lives and to engage in trade for their own profit was an efficient model, as long as it benefited the elite and did not challenge their position. That scenario endured; it proved itself to be an evolutionarily stable strategy. Basically, liberalism won the contest thousands of years ago, but a degree of socialism was needed for the system to work efficiently. A fair measure of mercantilism was equally unavoidable as elites felt obliged to pursue, protect and promote their interests against other elites. That amalgam of ideologies is nowadays recognised as the mixed-economy model.

Today's developed countries have for several centuries kept an open-minded attitude to ideologies and beliefs. Adherence to one ideology might be proclaimed from time to time, but that is not allowed to cramp unduly their room for manoeuvre. In the main, the ideologies were taken for what they are: varying and variable sets of simplifications to be handled with a degree of caution and flexibility. Events took a turn for the worse only when that fundamental philosophy was abandoned, as happened in Nazi Germany. Sadly, the developing world is not allowed the same degree of freedom and pragmatism that the developed countries exercise as of right. I will return to that in future chapters, but for the moment examples drawn for the histories of Mesopotamia, Greece, Islam and China are presented below to show that all the IPE ideologies were in evidence, and coexisted side by side with each other, at all these locations and times.

MODERN IDEOLOGIES IN ANCIENT MESOPOTAMIA[4]

Archaeological studies of the Sumerian (c. 3000 BC) and Babylonian (c. 1800 BC) eras confirm the longevity of social, political and economic practices and reveal striking parallels with current norms. These civilisations were not insignificant city-states. They covered large regions; the Sumerian Empire in the reign of Lugalanemundu (c. 2525–2500 BC), for example, extended from the Zagros to the Taurus Mountains, in modern-day Iran and Turkey, and from the Persian Gulf to the Mediterranean.

Soon after the appearance of the earliest settled communities, temple priests appropriated land and property in the name of their chosen gods. They assumed responsibility for administration, irrigation, and distribution of work and rewards. Gradually, private ownership of slaves and land spread from the priests to noble families. Even at that early period, high volumes of international trade based on exchange of raw materials and finished products were meticulously recorded, and exchange relied on merchants who occupied increasingly important positions in society.

Eventually, the growth of domestic and international trade and 'the increasing importance of division of labour and the general increase in production capabilities' led to the disintegration of rural societies controlled by noblemen and the appearance of ruling elites of rich individuals who were not necessarily linked to land and agriculture (al-Tikriti 1986: 26). It is evident from reliable archaeological studies, therefore, that the drift from feudalism to mercantilism and capitalism and the associated dismantling of outdated social structures are more ancient phenomena than generally presumed.

Records give graphic accounts of the steady spread of capitalism and the emergence of wealthy individuals who proceeded to monopolise lands, slaves and other means of production. It was natural that the same process should involve growing control over strategic resources, mainly rivers and wells. The workers, mostly *muskenu*, free persons of low or no estate, were deprived of all means of earning their living apart from selling their services or themselves as slaves to the *awilu*, the elite. The tension paved the way for the inevitable emergence of 'socialist' revolutionaries. Uruinimgina (*c.* 2355 BC) led one such popular revolt against Lugalanda, the despotic ruler of Lagash.

A Sumerian socialist revolution

That revolution had a remarkably modern ring to it. Payments to the army were increased to forestall further uprisings; at the start of Uruinimgina's reign soldiers' monthly allocation of corn, for example, was doubled. Welfare payments from community funds to free persons were also restored after their suspension by the previous regime. In the year after, however, economic difficulties forced the government to cancel most of the reforms. The number of persons receiving welfare payments had increased substantially, while the new elite upheld the common practice of monopolising power and wealth. The economy was soon in ruins and, again in line with more recent events, the reforms disturbed neighbouring rulers, who feared similar revolts by their own subjects. On cue, Lugalzagesi (*c.* 2350 BC) from nearby Umma attacked and defeated Uruinimgina, the 'socialist' reforms were rescinded and 'liberalism' was once again the dominant policy (al-Tikriti 1986: 55).

Sumerian capitalist hegemony in full swing

Advanced administrative systems commonly in use at the time relied on division of labour, teamwork and analysis of productivity by measures such as 'the work one man could do in one day'. In Lagash, for instance, workers in factories were divided into eight basic tasks and brought together as a unit of production under one supervisor. Competition between units was encouraged and supervisors were moved often to maintain discipline and productivity (al-Tikriti 1986: 122). Rudimentary forms of the assembly line and specialisation were known, therefore, well before Adam Smith and the Industrial Revolution. The fact that production in Europe was organised differently, in craft guilds for instance, does not mean that it was thus everywhere.

Expansion of production and trade touched other facets of life. Metals – copper then silver and gold – were accepted as measures of value from an early date, and banks were established to provide many of the services known today. Enhanced dependence on and reliability of money changed the pattern of land ownership. Small landowners sold their properties and the pattern of large tracts of land under single ownership of one person or family emerged as a familiar feature. In consequence, massive regional irrigation regimes became feasible, which in turn relied on the security that only a strong state backed by a standing army could provide.

Lugalzagesi of Uruk made his city the centre of a large monarchy at about 2375 BC. Twenty-five years later he was defeated by Sargon I, who then proceeded to unite the whole of Mesopotamia and parts of Turkey, Syria and Iran into one of the oldest hegemonic powers in history. A thriving capitalist economy was manifestly in place at that time. The empire, which lasted from 2350 to 2260 BC, was a coalition of states, each of which retained its own king (Schneider 1963: 43). While hegemony persisted, domestic and international trade expanded rapidly, as demonstrated by the preserved records of local and foreign contracts. International trade entered another period of openness when the Assyrian Empire consolidated itself as the hegemonic power of the day during the first millennium before Christ; unexpected support for the hegemonic stability theory from distant lands and times. Affinity between hegemony and openness, it seems, is yet another feature that has longer ancestry than modern IPE scholars would have us believe.

Ancient mercantilism completes the set

Requirements of law, trade and religion prompted the Sumerians to invent writing. Hammurabi's famous Code (c. 1760 BC), and the lesser-known legal code of Ur-Nammu, predating Hammurabi's by three centuries, were preserved for humankind in that way. The Code dealt with property rights, minimum wages, loans, debts and deposits, in addition to marital and social matters. It reflected his socialist leanings as well as his mercantilist belief in the utility of power. In these respects he was even more determined than Uruinimgina, who preceded him by about six centuries. To implement his socialist programme successfully, Hammurabi decided to insulate the Babylonian Empire from the system of international exchange existing at the time (al-Tikriti 1986: 87). He failed miserably. His empire lacked the raw materials to maintain its productive capacity in all sectors apart from agriculture. Hammurabi, like his modern-day equivalents, had to learn the hard way that mercantilists and Marxists have to be sufficiently flexible to exercise, whenever necessary, a degree of liberalism.

Mercantilist traits were still in evidence in later centuries. Shalmaneser III, ruler of Assyria from 859 to 824 BC, mounted numerous campaigns against other states in the thirty-five years of his reign and his Assyrian Empire, stretching from Egypt in the south to Turkey in the north and Iran in the east, brought a new twist to warfare. Destruction was replaced as the main purpose of war by the desire to add assets and dominions in true mercantilist fashion. Trade in, and accumulation of, silver and gold were also high on the agenda; then, as in more recent times, reserves of these precious metals equated with power as well as wealth (al-Tikriti 1986: 388).

Continuing the mercantilist theme, but with liberal overtones, technology transfer was discouraged but trade, when profitable, was not hindered. Wool was produced where sheep were plentiful, in Syria say, transported elsewhere to be turned into cloth, and moved again to be coloured in Phoenicia and Caucasia before final dispatch to the marketplace. The Phoenicians deserve special mention in this context. Out of Tyre they founded colonies, at about 1400 BC, throughout the Mediterranean, and in England, Spain and North Africa and became the leading raw materials dealers of antiquity. They enabled Nebuchadnezzar II, who reigned in Babylon from 605 to 562 BC, to make use of English tin imported on Carthaginian ships (Schneider 1963: 127).

The examples selected from Mesopotamian history underline the longevity of political economic patterns that are often presumed to be of recent vintage. The existence of hierarchies with an exclusive elite at the top that monopolised power and wealth, and disgruntled people below seeking fairness and justice, was well established as a permanent facet of life. Most importantly, the cases presented confirm that liberalism, socialism, and mercantilism were, as they are today, attributes of everyday life that coexisted in a constant state of mutual contention and agitation.

THE GREEKS CHANGE TACK[5]

The Greeks opened a new chapter in human knowledge by moving the debate from a theological to a metaphysical paradigm. Philosophical abstractions and logical observations replaced outmoded mystical beliefs. The basic pattern remained the same as before though; some hoarded wealth and power while the majority sought fair play and protection. Similar to present-day custom and practice, Greek thinkers came in two varieties: those supporting the elite and those who championed the cause of the masses.

Greek laissez-faire yields to socialist reforms

Attica was progressively unified under the leadership of Athens between the eighth and the sixth centuries BC. The nobles, the Eupatridae, abolished hereditary monarchy in 683 BC and then went on to wield power in a vicious manner that caused severe discontent. Their reign epitomised the height of *laissez-faire* in pre-classical Greece. They were above the law, enjoying total freedom to accumulate wealth without interference from the state. In reality they were the state. Disparity between the rich elite and the rest of the population generated unrest, and the relentless swing of the pendulum was only a matter of time. On cue, Draco appeared on the scene and enacted his famous law in 621 BC, partly to limit the powers of the nobles but mainly to impose severe penalties on lawbreakers, especially those who fell into debt. In that way, many landowners lost their property to the rich elite when they failed to repay loans.

The stage was set for change, and civil disruption culminated in Solon's (638–558 BC) reforms. He was a poet and a lawmaker and his code, known as the Laws of Attica, was an early form of socialist revolution. After the rampant liberalism of the Eupatridae, it was natural for the political economy to take a left turn. Solon wrote off debts, implemented democratic reforms and limited private ownership of land. He also instituted a programme of agrarian reforms, encouraged progress in the crafts, growth in the industrial sector, and the importation of technology from abroad. One of Greece's Seven Sages,

Solon pioneered an innovation that has survived to this day. He acknowledged the right of 'groups that share a commonality of worship'
to set their own rules and regulations and to promote their interests
within the overall framework of the law (Saad 1990: 214). We recognise that pattern today as political parties, unions, interest groups and
companies. Rational choice analysis had to appear in time.

Greek mercantilists

The Sophists, roaming philosophers who acquired an enviable reputation in classical Greece during the fifth century BC, expressed views on
the relationship between individuals and society that covered very
much the same range as that encompassed by modern-day ideologies
(McLean 1996: 463). Some, such as Antiphon, one of the Ten Attica
Orators who led an attempted coup in Athens in 411 BC, believed that
man-made laws cut across the rights of individuals under natural law
to pursue their own advantage and pleasure. He argued that truth and
morality were matters of opinion, and that might and right were one
and the same. Anticipating Machiavelli by over two thousand years,
Antiphon advocated realism in facing conditions as they are and not
as they ought to be. That early form of mercantilist thinking is seen
even more unambiguously in the writings of another Greek historian,
Thucydides (c. 460–400 BC), who is identified by modern scholars as
one of the earliest political realists.

The concept of the virtuous city cropped up regularly in the
musings of Greek thinkers. Plato (427–347 BC) painted a vivid picture
of such an entity in his *Republic*. It would be modelled on the principle that 'virtue is knowledge'; an interesting starting point when
viewed in the light of today's near-obsessive stress on information. A
knowledgeable elite who would guarantee justice to all would rule
Plato's ideal state, but the rulers would not be allowed to own private
property and their salaries would be strictly controlled. Evidently,
there was no place for popular democracy in 'Plato's communism'
(Saad 1990: 221).

Advent of the scientific era

Aristotle (384–322 BC), who attended Plato's Academy in Athens, came
from a wealthy family. It was only to be expected, therefore, that he

should rebel by advocating democratic and socialist reforms. He took the first tentative steps to shift the emphasis away from metaphysical speculation to scientific analysis. In line with Plato's thinking, and in marked contrast to Antiphon's mercantilist views, Aristotle, while teaching at the Lyceum, insisted that politics and economics could not be divorced from issues of morality. Moreover, he underlined the need to treat knowledge as an indivisible whole. He is also credited with elevating politics to the status of science to merge it with economics as one unified field of research. As mentioned in the previous chapter, neorealists belatedly came to the same conclusion. Aristotle innovated another concept that seems to have endured. He defined three key elements in government: the deliberative, the executive and the judicial (McLean 1996: 21), a structure that was faithfully observed when the US Constitution was drafted in 1787.

This brief glimpse into early Greek history supports the propositions that the core ideologies are coexisting features of human behaviour that share common ancient roots. The Greeks moved Mesopotamian theological beliefs into a metaphysical phase, but Aristotle then initiated the jump to positivist methods based on scientific experimentation and objective observation that was later to influence Islamic thought.[6]

AN ISLAMIC BRIDGE TO THE RENAISSANCE

Muhammad (570–632 AD) was born in Mecca, in western Arabia, into the wealthy tribe of Quraysh, whose power rested on its religious position in Mecca and its extensive trading links with the outside world. At the beginning, Muhammad's mission was purely religious and beamed principally at pagan Mecca and Arabia beyond. Gradually, the message acquired social, political and economic dimensions concerned with the rights and wrongs of wealth, privilege and inequality. Yet again the familiar pattern repeated itself: reform came from within the ranks of the elite.

Clash of Arabian capitalism and socialism

When his activities attracted too much hostility from senior members of his influential tribe, Muhammad left Mecca for Medina in 622 AD and promptly started to hit Quraysh where it mattered; he attacked its trade caravans. After several military defeats, Quraysh sued for peace and invited him back to Mecca in 630 AD. Soon thereafter all members of the tribe converted to Islam; an act of pragmatic realism worthy of special note by some of today's weaker nations. Commercial and trading considerations played a part in that sudden conversion.[7] Although the interests of Quraysh, elitist and capitalist by tradition, and those of Islam, egalitarian and socialist by definition, differed materially, it was futile to meet the challenge head on. The classic tension between egoistic interests, on the one hand, and public welfare, on the other, marked Islam for centuries to come.

The death of Muhammad in 632 AD was a signal for that contest to come to the surface. One faction, and, it is claimed, the Prophet himself, wanted his cousin and son-in-law, Ali, to be his successor. Ali was disliked and distrusted by Quraysh, and for good reason. He did not belong to the elite branch of the tribe, and worse still he was a fanatical socialist with definite views about the piety of sharing wealth and the impiety of earning interest from loans; practices dear to the tribe's coffers. In the event Abu Bakr was chosen instead. He ruled for only two years and was followed by Umar, who reigned from 634 until his assassination in 644. Finally Quraysh had the opportunity to place their man, Uthman, in the caliphate. His years were distinctly liberal; free trade and the accumulation of private wealth and power were given full rein.

Matters had to come to a head and the power brokers of Quraysh foresaw the drift of events and took steps to protect their interests. Their base was progressively transferred to Syria. When Uthman was in turn assassinated, therefore, life continued with little disruption despite the fact that Ali was at last installed as caliph in Arabia. He ruled from 656 to 661, when he also was assassinated. The Syrian contingent of Quraysh was heavily implicated in the murder. The followers of Ali (*Shiat Ali* in Arabic) who believed in succession to the caliphate on the basis of lineage from Muhammad gave the world *Shiism*, a distinctive Islamic sect now comprising about 10 per cent of Muslims worldwide. The schism from the Sunnis, representing the dominant sect of Islam, undoubtedly stems from specific religious differences. In the early days, however, the split was caused by political and economic disagreements as well, reflecting mercantilist disputes over power and wealth, and socialist versus liberal interpretations of what an Islamic society should stand for (Musawi 1978).

Six centuries of Islamic hegemony

The caliphate moved to Damascus and Muawiya ruled from 661 to 680. In that time he managed to create a vast empire that stretched from North Africa and Spain in the west to the Oxus valley in India in the east. The Umayyad dynasty lasted until 750 when the Abbasids succeeded in moving the power base to Iraq, and that empire lasted until 1258 AD, when it was devastated by the Mongol hordes. Muawiya is of special interest in the present context. He had a genius for politics and power that compared favourably with that envisioned by Machiavelli in *The Prince* many centuries later. Analysis of Muawiya's political attitudes and methods shows unmistakable mercantilist traits. He had few if any moral scruples when it came to the exercise of statecraft and his security system and terror methods were unsurpassed. His philosophy left its mark on succeeding dynasties, and some would say on the style of government in present-day Syria (al-Wardi 1995: 55).

Islamic hegemony, up to 1258 AD when the Mongols sacked Baghdad, comprised several independent states held together by ties of culture and religion. The centre moved from Arabia to Syria and then to Iraq but the extensive empire remained substantially intact. Hegemony gave a boost to far-flung international trade; the fragmentation of political power did not imply weakness, as other social and economic ties linked people over long distances (Hourani 1991: 144). Basically, international traders worked outside the confines of the prevailing political system in true capitalist fashion. Inevitably, 'an internationally recognised monetary system grew up', but the state did not interfere in day-to-day economic matters (Hourani 1991: 46).

The private sector reigned supreme in a fashion that would have received enthusiastic approval from the IMF. There were no significant barriers to trade. Records written at the time indicate beyond question that being a trader was almost as sought after as being a religious leader, a doctor or scientist, or a dignitary at court. The key point to note here is, therefore, the comfortable association between socialist religious beliefs, an obvious mercantilist outlook by the elite and the state, and liberal economic practices by one and all.

Islam's Machiavelli

To complete the picture, it is important to discuss the special contribution made by an eminent Islamic scholar, Ibn Khaldun (1332–1406), for a time a professor at the world famous Al-Azhar Islamic University in Cairo. He took a sabbatical of four years in a castle in the Algerian countryside to write an exhaustive history of the Islamic dynasties in North Africa. The publication was prefaced by a prologue (*Muqaddima* in Arabic), recognised by universal acclaim as a milestone of immense social, political and economic significance. The *Muqaddima* covered a vast range of topics including expositions on the rise and fall of dynasties, the development of societies, and the acquisition and retention of power by elites (Ibn Khaldun: n.d.). His theories on these and other subjects trigger in the mind of the modern reader distinct parallels with mercantilist writings of a much later age.

Ibn Khaldun penned his monumental work to educate rulers of his time in the art of statecraft in a similar format to that followed by Machiavelli when he dedicated *The Prince* to the Duke of Urbino. Others adopted the same style, as in the case of Al-Ghazali (1058– 1111), who dedicated his *Advice to Kings* to Sultan Muhammad Ibn Malikshah. The genre is often referred to in Islamic literature as *Mirrors for Princes* (Saad 1990: 233). One particular statement by Al-Ghazali helps to illustrate his political stance. He wrote: 'the tyranny of a sultan for a hundred years causes less damage than one year's tyranny exercised by the subjects against each other' (Saad 1990: 43). Centuries later mercantilists gave the self-same reason for their advocacy of the monopolistic exercise of benevolent power by the state for the public good.

The above selected instances from Islamic history support the contention that today's ideologies are not of recent vintage. Muslim thinkers added their own innovations to science, politics and economics, as well as the obvious topic of religion, but their role in translating ancient textbooks was crucial in preserving that legacy for later generations. Occupation of Spain by the Arabs gave the process a physical dimension. Ancient knowledge, translated into Arabic, was converted into Latin and then transmitted through Andalusia to the rest of Europe.

FORGOTTEN CIVILISATIONS OF CHINA[8]

The Chinese contribution to political economic thought is underrepresented. Language is an obvious barrier, but there might be a deeper reason for this oversight. The Chinese have always put more emphasis on social harmony and less on abstract discussions of rights and wrongs. In consequence, McLean (1996: 63) argued, 'China produced a political culture rather than a political philosophy.' Nevertheless, the signature of all the major schools of political economic thought were evident in China's long history, but they congregated in a pattern that was unfamiliar to Western minds. There was the usual trinity of approaches: those who envisioned human beings as hopelessly selfish and in need of rigid control by the state; those who believed in the innate goodness of people open to corruption by big and interfering governments; and those who took the middle way.

State power over all else

The *Legalists* epitomised the first line of thought. In today's terms this school, which enjoyed popularity up to the third century BC, was strictly mercantilist. People had to be protected from their base selfish instincts and a powerful state was the means to achieve that laudable aim.[9] Han Fei (*c.* 230 BC), one of the leading lights behind legalism, was the Machiavelli of his age. He was concerned with the study and practice of totalitarian statecraft. Legalism defined laws, for strict enforcement by rulers, founded on the purportedly modern assumption that the state was the primary element in the life of a nation. Its purpose was to acquire power and, in that quest, to wage wars on others. This creed was the product of its times; it emerged during the turmoil that characterised the dying days of the Chou dynasty (*c.* 1027–256 BC). Clearly, neither Ibn Khaldun nor Machiavelli invented mercantilism.

Supremacy of the individual

In contrast, Taoism elevated the individual above everything else and abhorred restrictions imposed by social dictates. Again, this school of thought appeared during the fourth century BC when the Chou dynasty was in the process of disintegration. The practical, as opposed to religious, strand of Taoism was intended to give guidance to rulers on how to govern at a time of uncertain but sustained change. It would seem that modern thinkers did not invent the lament about 'our changing times'. Some scholars view Taoism as a forerunner of modern–day ideas such as anti-rationalism and postmodernism in that it advocates minimal action by the individual. Conversely, as a philosophy of government it also praises the virtues of minimal action by the state.

Individuals, according to Taoist teachings, are concerned first and foremost with their own interests. Hence, as long as their basic needs are met they will live in social harmony and will not trouble the ruler and his entourage. Certain Taoist scholars, as in the case of Chuang-tzu (*c.* 300 BC), saw the ideal state as a dictatorship ruled by a philosopher-king; a concept much loved by Greek philosophers and latter-day dictators. Admittedly, the terms used to describe the tenets of the credo are different, but the likeness to present-day ideological lines of thought is discernable nonetheless.

The Chinese Third Way?

Confucius (*c.* 551–478 BC), representing another school of thought, advocated the attractions of the middle way. The role of good government, he suggested, should be to allow communities to be self-sufficient, to distribute wealth equitably, to restore unity to nations, and to extend learning to all people. Confucianism combined features of liberalism, Marxism and mercantilism. In accord with the first ideology, it defined the individual as a pivotal element in the system. In line with Marxism, the avowed object was to seek social justice. But Confucianism placed the state – in effect, the ruler and his elite – at the top of the hierarchy in true mercantilist fashion.

It is difficult to resist the temptation to compare Confucius's middle way with the Third Way, one of the most recent political economic fashions to hit the headlines (Giddens 1994, 1998). It influenced Tony Blair in his transformation of the British Labour Party into New Labour, and was also a source of inspiration to Bill Clinton during his years in the White House. Essentially, the Third Way is a development of the social-democratic model, but with several added ingredients stemming from a liberal ancestry. Now, as in ancient China, the natural state of political economic affairs appears to be a middle ground offering a fluid amalgam of concepts borrowed from several ideological roots.

The ancient tradition of trade across borders

Chinese views on international trade were essentially the same as those held by the other civilisations discussed earlier. At base, it was seen as a self-evident activity that benefited importers and exporters alike. Commercial links were sufficiently advanced by about 100 BC for Emperor Wudi of the Han dynasty to order the building and operation of the 4,000 mile Silk Route. Goods changed hands several times on the way to their final destination. The administrative and financial management of the enterprise, therefore, imposed considerable demands, but by then the Chinese Grand College for civil servants, complete with civil service examinations, had been in existence for about a quarter of a century. In short, both international trade and global bureaucracy are not new; again, circumstances simply imposed their own solutions.

THE STORY SO FAR

It is useful to highlight here the main points that emerged from this and the previous chapter. Earlier discussion established that the core IPE ideologies are coexisting sets of generalised beliefs that have much in common with each other. In short, there is nothing sacrosanct about liberalism, Marxism or mercantilism; they should be used cautiously for support rather than for guidance. Moreover, additional evidence presented in this chapter demonstrated that the core ideologies are neither modern nor European.

It is now possible, therefore, to state that the different ideologies are flexible global patterns that emerge as outcomes from local interactions between people, as individuals and groups. This critical point leads naturally into the next conclusion: the efforts to transform the ideologies into scientific theories of universal applicability were doomed to failure. They were built on unsustainable assumptions that took certainty and stable cause-and-effect relationships for granted. Development was dragged unresisting, and in fact unknowing, into this conceptual quagmire, with not unexpected results.

The last point I would wish to underline here concerns international trade. Adam Smith remarked with his usual acumen that the 'propensity to truck, barter and exchange one thing for another' is an innate part of human nature. Marco Polo (c. 1256–1323) and Ibn Battuta (c. 1304–1377), in recording their observations during their extensive travels, provided ample evidence to back Adam Smith's comment (Ibn Battuta 1984). Today's leading powers and their global organisations would no doubt be amazed to learn that al-Muqaddasi (*c.* 1000) and al-Yaqut (*c.* 1200) advanced robust academic evidence, in their studies of the political and economic geography of their period, to explain and support the disposition of people to trade across borders (Hourani 1991: 201). The World Trade Organisation need not fret.

It is fitting to end a chapter that sought to highlight longevity and diversity by referring to early signs of growing doubts about the adequacy of the liberal global economic system to bring prosperity for all. George Soros (1998), a legend in the world of capitalism, argued that assertions by 'market fundamentalists' that markets should be regulated by nothing more than profit and competition distort global capitalism into 'a greater threat to open society than any totalitarian ideology'. Advocates of liberalism should not panic if that criticism gains popularity. Judging by the evidence presented here, that course correction is likely to be only the latest in a long history of twists and turns. Unfortunately, the leading powers and the international regimes they support do panic at the least sign of a threat to the hallowed ideals of globalisation and free trade. That sensitivity spells disaster to the developing countries, as I argue in Chapter 10.

NOTES

1. Ya'qub ibn Ishaq al-Kindi (c.801–866), one of Islam's foremost thinkers, said, 'We should not be ashamed to acknowledge truth from whatever source it comes to us, even if it is brought to us by former generations and foreign people ... there is nothing of higher value than truth itself' (Hourani 1991: 76).
2. See also informed speculation in Qasha (1998) on the influence of Babylonian writings on the Torah.
3. Despite plentiful evidence to the contrary, modern dictators have persisted in misinterpreting Machiavelli's opinions to justify their view of power. In *The Prince,* Machiavelli advocated the use of force and cunning to gain power, when necessary, but he unequivocally highlighted the futility of adopting such methods as a permanent feature of statecraft (Bull 1981).
4. Some of the information presented in the next few sections is derived from al-Tikriti (1986) and Schneider (1963). Pollock (1999) and Bottero (2000) offer more detailed commentary on Mesopotamian history and its relevance to the present. Bottero (2000) also provides an interesting link between Greek and Near Eastern civilisations.
5. Sources for information on this topic are plentiful, including Ehrenberg (1973), Green (1979) and Pomeroy et al. (1998).
6. For the link between the two eras, see Fakhri (1958) and Farrukh (1970).

7. See al-Wardi (1995).
8. Buckley et al. (1999) gives a comprehensive exposition of China's history from ancient times to the present.
9. See Watson (1967) and Zhengyuan Fu (1996).

FOUR

DAWN OF THE PROBABILISTIC AGE

Ideologies and theories are set aside at this point in order to put the spotlight on paradigms and their pervasive, but subtle, role in determining how we perceive and respond to most of what life has to offer. Discussion will concentrate on the growing utility of nonlinear Complex Adaptive Systems in the study of social, political and economic phenomena. Of necessity, in the context of development, much of the chapter is devoted to the key topic of how these systems evolve and the factors that play a significant part in that process of change and survival.

COCOONED IN PARADIGMS

Kuhn described the way scientific disciplines trudge through lengthy periods of relative stability punctuated by intense 'paradigm shifts' (Kuhn 1996: 10). A paradigm defines what is and is not considered, by implicit general acclaim, to be sensible and legitimate at that juncture. Those working within a discipline are wholly convinced they are guided by unassailable scientific and objective facts and nothing else. But that, as the histories of astronomy, light, nuclear physics, and other subjects convincingly demonstrate, is simply not the case. A few scholars eventually encounter problems that could not be handled within the prevailing paradigm and a new paradigm is adopted after a long period of hesitation. The course of action is of course not clearcut; there is no formal agreement on the tenets of the old or the new paradigm and there is certainly no distinct procedure by which the transformation is accomplished.

Galileo Galilei (1564–1642), for instance, ventured outside the established paradigm when he declared his preference for the theory, propounded by Nicolaus Copernicus (1473–1543), that the earth revolved round the sun. He was promptly put under house arrest. Curiously, the Roman Catholic Church finally rehabilitated his name as late as 1992. The paradigm shift initiated by Copernicus prevailed and it is now inconceivable for anyone to suggest that the earth is the centre of the universe. But that was exactly what scientists believed up to that point on the basis of the state of knowledge available to them. With the benefit of hindsight that belief sounds improbable, even simple-minded, but that judgement would be highly unjust. Some of our most hallowed scientific convictions might prove to be equally off the mark in future.

Paradigm of certainties

The Enlightenment had a substantial impact on the way life is viewed at all levels from the mundane to the profound. Science was liberated from centuries of control by religious stipulations and blind trust in ancient philosophies. René Descartes (1596–1650) and, slightly later, Isaac Newton (1642–1727) set the scene. The former advocated rationalism while the latter unearthed a wondrous collection of fundamental laws. A flood of other discoveries in diverse fields such as magnetism, electricity, astronomy and chemistry soon followed, injecting a heightened sense of confidence in the power of reason to tackle any situation. By and large, that vision of life survived well into the twentieth century, and the linear paradigm it reflects is founded on four golden rules:

- Order: given causes lead to known effects at all times and places.
- Reductionism: the behaviour of a system can be understood, clockwork fashion, by observing the behaviour of its parts. There are no hidden surprises; the whole is the sum of the parts, no more and no less.
- Predictability: once global behaviour is defined, the future course of events can be predicted by application of the appropriate inputs to the model.
- Determinism: processes flow along orderly and predictable paths that have clear beginnings and rational ends.

The linear paradigm worked remarkably well, yielding guaranteed results each and every time, up to and including space travel. Success in the technological arena had a profound effect on attitudes in all sectors of human activity, spreading well beyond the disciplines covered by the original discoveries. Economics, international relations and development were no exception, as it was natural for scholars working in these fields to adopt methods that were so effective and reliable elsewhere.[1] Linear precepts are attractive for obvious reasons; events are not left to chance and humankind can enjoy life in the knowledge that someone, customarily held up as an expert, is at the controls.

Vast corporations committed themselves to long-term business strategies and nations pinned their hopes on elaborate five-year plans. Advocates of liberalism deified the market, with occasional micro- and macroeconomic diversions. Marxists countered with the ultimate in linear thinking: a command economy based on rigid central planning and ceaseless class conflicts, leading inevitably to the promised land of communism. In both cases, there was an assumption that the process moves inexorably towards a natural end-state of perfection along an orderly path predetermined by universal laws that are accessible to humankind. The future is predictable and inevitable, and history it-self, some brave souls were moved to assert, will eventually come to a natural end (Fukuyama 1992).

Spreading ripples of doubt

Certainty and predictability for all, the hallmarks of a linear frame of mind, were too good to last. Fissures came to the surface soon after World War I, although there were earlier indications that a shift was in the offing. Jules Henri Poincaré (1854–1912), the supreme physicist of his age, was one of the first to voice disquiet about some contemporary scientific beliefs. He advanced ideas that predated chaos theory by some seventy years (Coveney and Highfield 1996: 169). Later, Albert Einstein (1879–1955), Niels Bohr (1885–1962), Erwin Schrödinger (1887–1961), Werner Karl Heisenberg (1901–1976) and Paul Dirac (1902–1984) played a decisive role in pushing conventional wisdom beyond the Newtonian limits that enclosed it centuries before. These scientists, all Nobel laureates, set in motion a process that eventually transformed attitudes in many other disciplines.[2]

The new discoveries did not prove Newton to have been in error. Essentially, they revealed circumstances where linear methods yielded excellent results, and others where they did not. More fundamentally, they established beyond dispute that some phenomena, now referred to as nonlinear systems, are essentially *probabilistic*. They do not conform to the four golden rules associated with linearity: order, reductionism, predictability and determinism. Causes and effects are not linked; the whole is not simply the sum of the parts; *emergent properties* often appear seemingly out of the blue; taking the system apart does not reveal much about its global behaviour; and the related processes do not steer the systems to inevitable and distinct ends.

The shift in scientific analysis from utter certainty to considerations of probability was not accepted lightly. The sea change radiated slowly outwards from the more esoteric disciplines, particularly quantum mechanics' domain of sub-atomic particles. Naturally, there was a wide schism between the exclusive niches occupied by leading particle physicists and mathematicians, on the one hand, and the rest of the scientific community, on the other. A high degree of specialisation meant that even scholars involved in the same discipline were not immediately aware of discoveries being made by their colleagues. Moreover, the language of science itself became almost unintelligible beyond a select circle of specialists. In any case, their intriguing speculations were not thought at first to be of everyday concern. Traditional metaphors and reductionist methods built on certainty and order lingered for a while, therefore, but ultimately the ripples of doubt about the inadequacy of the linear paradigm became all too evident to scholars from a broad spectrum of backgrounds, including mathematicians, physicists, meteorologists, chemists and geneticists. They administered the final *coup de grâce* to the prevailing linear paradigm in the second half of the twentieth century.

NONLINEARITY ARRIVES ON THE SCENE

Science crossed the Rubicon; uncertainty was recognised as an inevitable feature of some situations.[3] It had to be accepted, confronted and then scientifically dealt with somehow. In effect, the envelope of formal science was expanded to add *nonlinear* phenomena to those already in place. Over time, a group of nonlinear entities attracted particular interest. These systems are variously described as being *complex*, because they have numerous internal elements; *dynamic*, because their global behaviour is governed by local interactions between the elements; and *dissipative*,[4] because they have to consume energy to maintain stable global patterns. In addition, when the stable patterns are capable of evolution the systems are also depicted as being *adaptive*. In the context of development, I will focus on Complex Adaptive Systems in what follows.

Extending the confines of science to embrace nonlinear phenomena was a lengthy process that moved in fits and starts. The bitter reaction of the scientific community to the early pioneers was only to be expected. Linear systems comprised the bulk of past analytical work in the applied sciences, and the new tools based on integrative (as opposed to reductionist) methods were unfamiliar. A ball falling to the ground under the force of gravity is a linear system. It is close to equilibrium and simple rules are readily available to calculate how long it will take to hit the ground. And the same result will be obtained repeatedly. These systems are safe and seductively computable through the conventional reductionist methods, and, most importantly, the process fitted well into the institutional structure of academic life. By contrast, analysing nonlinear systems 'is like walking through a maze whose walls rearrange themselves with each step you take' (Gleick 1988: 24).

Stable patterns far from equilibrium

Complex Adaptive Systems are able to assume stable global patterns although they exist in conditions that are far from equilibrium. This is a key feature and it merits a few initial words at this stage. The second law of thermodynamics, the most fundamental law of nature, states that when a system is left alone it drifts steadily into disorder. The effects of the second law are plain to see. A deserted building, for instance, eventually turns into a pile of rubble. After a few centuries even the rubble disappears without a trace. Dust to dust, ashes to ashes is a biblical assertion that is backed by the full force of science. Ultimately, a system cut off from the outside world will fall into a deathly state of equilibrium in which little or nothing of interest ever happens.

Linear systems are found at or near equilibrium. A ball bearing inside a bowl is a classic example; it quickly settles at the bottom and that is that. Nonlinearity, by contrast, is exhibited by systems that are far from equilibrium.[5] In this instance, the system has to exchange (dissipate) energy, or matter, with other systems in order to acquire and maintain self-organised stable patterns. That is the only option open to it to avoid falling into the destructive clutches of the second law of thermodynamics. The most dramatic illustration of that process is planet Earth. Without the nourishing rays of energy from the Sun, Earth would perish into complete equilibrium, and therefore nothingness. A continuous supply of energy from the Sun keeps the planet in a highly active state far from equilibrium. The energy is absorbed, dissipated and used to drive numerous local interactions that in total produce the stable pattern that we perceive as life on Earth. One final word in this introductory outline of nonlinearity: local chaotic agitation is necessary to produce an overall stable pattern, as seen in the case of Earth. Complexity emerges from a mix of chaos and order.

Nonlinearity in the natural and life sciences

Schrödinger estimated that it takes more than fifty years for major breakthroughs to gain general acceptance. That is particularly true when discoveries pose a challenge to an entrenched paradigm. Concepts inherited from the sensational scientific strides made after the Enlightenment assumed over time the status of a paradigm. In consequence, the traditional methods based on linear assumptions were implicitly accepted as the standard means by which most problems could be tackled. Those that defied analysis in that way – we now know they fall within a separate scientific category of nonlinear phenomena – were classed as being *intractable* and were then left alone (Coveney and Highfield 1996: 34). The insistence by some scholars that so-called intractable problems affected significant sectors of everyday life, and that they should be dealt with as legitimate scientific topics, was ignored for a long time, but the advancing tide was irreversible.

Abstract mathematical ideas and esoteric experiments in physics and chemistry were followed by research in other topics. In time, biologists, geneticists and physiologists also began to consider their respective disciplines within the context of nonlinearity. Analysts in these fields set out to investigate the properties of systems, including human beings, composed of a large number of internal parts that interacted locally in what looked like a state of anarchy that somehow managed to engender self-organised, stable and sustainable global order. Gradually, these Complex Adaptive Systems revealed their secrets and the validity of the new methods designed to study them began to command general acceptance as legitimate analytical tools.

Nascent shift in the social sciences

The treatment of certain phenomena as nonlinear Complex Adaptive Systems is now well established within the natural and life sciences, but change is not at an end. Nonlinear thinking is spilling slowly into the social sciences.[6] An early development took place in the late 1950s when Benôit Mandelbrot, one of the pioneers of Complex Systems theory, explored the distribution of incomes over long periods of time. At the same time, Houthakker, Professor of Economics at Harvard, was involved in similar studies into historic fluctuations in the price of cotton (Gleick 1988: 83). Research in stock exchange movements was another early recruit for the nonlinear treatment.

Gleick's description of the consequences of 'organised complexity' in everyday events is important here. There is an understandable expectation that stock exchange movements, say, are random in the short term but that they are deterministic in the long term. Gleick argued convincingly that such an assumption might not be valid. He demonstrated that economics and, by implication, other similar phenomena do not present the Gaussian bell-shaped distribution associated with linear systems, where measurements cluster tidily round an average (Gleick 1988: 84). On the contrary, Mandelbrot and Gleick, among others, discovered that in some cases change is random and unpredictable, and it involves discontinuities, rapid changes as opposed to smooth ones, and *persistence*; low for instance does not necessarily follow high.

Economics was not left untouched

These early ventures into nonlinearity were followed by further studies in the social sciences. The debate among the economics community is of particular interest in the context of development. Several scholars, notably Brian Arthur from Stanford University, advocated a shift to a nonlinear framework during the 1980s and 1990s (Arthur 1994). The hallowed principle of diminishing returns was at issue. Conventional theory is founded on a fundamental stipulation that economic events create their own negative feedback, which stabilises the economy at or near equilibrium. In short, the economic system is assumed to be linear. Basically, the economists who led the field in the 1940s and 1950s were 'the Young Turks of their day, a pack of brash upstarts determined to clean out the stables and make economics into a science as rigorous and precise as physics' (Waldrop 1994: 24).

Their main aim was to use science, perceived within a strictly linear framework, to run society rationally. Arthur felt that 'most people in development economics have this kind of attitude' (Waldrop 1994: 26). He, supported by a few other economists, maintained that *increasing returns* described actual economic events more accurately than diminishing returns (Arthur 1990). In that nonlinear view of economics, positive feedback is seen as the mechanism that can magnify minor fluctuations into major upheavals. Arthur was particularly scathing in his criticism of the fashionable economic models in use at all levels of government.

These initial concerns spread to a wider circle of social science disciplines. Byrne supported Reed and Harvey in arguing that 'societies and institutions can be treated as if they were dissipative entities' and envisioned a strong link between realism and Complexity (Byrne 1998: 39; Reed and Harvey 1992: 354). He went on to suggest that this combination was fatal to positivism, which assumes total mastery over nature is possible, and to postmodernism, which rejects grand narratives and advocates, in essence, social inaction. Complexity, in taking a middle course, accepts that human beings may adopt some measures to improve their condition, but it concedes that there are limits to that action. Accordingly, it is helpful in conceptualising the relationship between Complexity and realism to see 'the linear and reductionist as a thesis, postmodernism as an antithesis and complexity as a synthesis' (Byrne 1998: 45).[7]

Nonlinearity is here to stay

Social scientists now regularly speak of interactions, interconnectedness, emergent properties and evolutionary change. That is also par for the course; learning the new language is an essential element in understanding and then accepting a radically different viewpoint. As far as development is concerned the shift in economics has been augmented more recently by a similar move in international politics (Jervis 1999). The main disciplines allied with development, therefore, are already being progressively treated within a nonlinear framework, and it is only natural that development should be tackled in a similar way. However, before discussing Complex Adaptive Systems in detail, I have to answer a niggling and, for the present purpose, fundamental, question: In embracing Complexity are we moving away from science?

THE HIERARCHICAL STRUCTURE OF SCIENCE

What makes the market an efficient economic medium? Should we simply take Adam Smith's word for it? Is Marxism dead forever, and why? Is there any future for socialism? Are the recommendations in *Our Common Future*, published by the World Commission on the Environment and Development (WCED) in 1987, more effective in promoting development than previous reports and in what way? Is emphasis on sustainable development and basic needs justified, and why? Is it better, or worse, to put faith in the structural adjustment programmes favoured by the World Bank and IMF? Present models and theories do not offer convincing answers to these questions, and gut feelings and demagoguery are no substitute. Chapter 2 revealed the core IPE theories as, at best, empirical efforts applicable to specific events at given times and places. Such theories are sometimes referred to as being *phenomenological*. They are resorted to when 'we see what is going on but do not yet understand it' (Gell-Mann 1994: 93). They are often little more than subjective assertions.

Rational explanations must be found in the study and practice of development for how the process behaves, and why? These explanations, furthermore, must prove their validity over most geographical and time horizons. I firmly believe that looking at development from a nonlinear perspective, as a Complex Adaptive System, will meet these demanding criteria. The potency of a move to a nonlinear viewpoint stems from the fact that scientific disciplines are not all the same; some are more fundamental than others. It is patently obvious that development is linked to economic, political and social factors, but such links may be envisioned as being horizontal; they do not tell us anything new or fundamental about the process of development. We must dig deeper.

Roots and branches

Sciences, and their theories, range themselves in a hierarchical structure best understood as a tree. So-called less fundamental sciences
occupy the upper branches. They require specification of additional
conditions to modify the more fundamental laws that apply at the
lower levels in order to cater for their less simple, more specialised,
requirements. Complexity, and nonlinear traits in general, become more
and more pronounced as we move away from the domain of the fundamental sciences at the roots of the tree. Biology, for example, is
more Complex, and hence less fundamental, than chemistry, while
particle physics is simpler, and therefore more fundamental, than
chemistry.[8]

In crude terms, one can think of the social sciences as being less
fundamental than the life sciences and these in turn as less fundamental than the natural sciences. That would be a rough-and-ready
but useful way of looking at the general hierarchy of the sciences in
order to underline the fact that many, possibly too many, caveats
would have to be understood and explicitly stated before basic, linear,
laws could be applied to activities in the social science arena, including the science of development. I should point out here that top and
bottom is a purely schematic reference and does not of necessity
imply other connotations such as better or worse, or more or less
important.

The search for pertinent roots is normal in the evolution of
scientific knowledge. Biology, for instance, was found in time to have
links to the more fundamental disciplines of physics and chemistry,
and that realisation brought about a revolution in our understanding
of the functioning and behaviour of living entities, including human
beings. That behaviour, it was discovered, is determined by biochem-
istry and genetics just as much as by conscious thought and external
conditions. The collective actions and desires of people, driven by
nurture and nature, determine outcomes in politics, economics and
development. That is only part of the picture. Control, as exercised
by people, institutions, or states is also a prominent factor, and that
suggests a link to cybernetics, the science of 'steering and governing',
and to Game Theory, the discipline that addresses the role of elites
as well as cooperation and competition between people and among
states.

Development's place in the hierarchy

Where does one begin the search for the hidden forces that energise the development process? Determining the approximate position of the social sciences, and then development, in relation to the other sciences, would be a rational point to start. Development is some distance away from the bottom of the tree of science. Scholars generally agree that elementary particles exploded from a *singularity* at a big bang that happened about fifteen billion years ago. Seconds after that event the fundamental laws of nature took charge and the whole setup was for quite a while reasonably simple, and essentially linear. Earth formed about ten billion years later, and some two billion years after that early self-replicating entities appeared spontaneously from the mixture of molecules existing at the time.

Things became steadily less straightforward from that point onwards. The primitive 'DNA' turned into bacteria-like organisms, which progressed slowly to more elaborate structures. Many momentous events unfolded long before the ancestors of modern humans, with the ability to exercise conscious thought and willpower, made their debut only a short 250,000 years ago. If the first self-replicating entities were assumed to have appeared thirty-five years ago, then the ancestor of mankind would have come on the scene only yesterday. Families evolved into tribes and these led to more elaborate social gatherings, which grew ultimately into warring empires. And it is only moments ago in the context of the world's long history that we finally arrived at the global village.

Beyond politics and economics

In effect, politics, economics and development are very recent phenomena that have, in the parlance of Complexity, a vast quantum of *depth* behind them. Depth could be taken as a measure of effective Complexity (Gell-Mann 1994: 59, 104). It is quite clear that by the time development became an issue many layers of innovation and evolution, natural as well as social, were already in place. In the intervening time, the fundamental laws of nature were amended by elaborations brought about by numerous *frozen accidents* that eventually acquired the status of specialised law for application to less fundamental phenomena.

These features will be discussed shortly, but the point I would like to emphasise here is that many so-called scientific laws are not wholly deterministic. To some degree they are probabilistic, and that indeterminacy mounts as one climbs the tree of science. At heart, there is much that is not knowable in advance and uncertainty increases at the less fundamental levels of science nearer the top of the tree (Gell-Mann 1994: 132). More to the point, to learn more about a certain science one has to move down to the lower branches to unravel the mysteries that surround that particular discipline. Staying at the same level, by contrast, is less rewarding. In effect, we must take development beyond its kinship to politics and economics to understand its intrinsic mode of behaviour.

RICHES AMID ORDER AND CHAOS

As described in Chapter 1, water in a bathtub can be made to illustrate three primary regimes of behaviour: order, chaos and self-organised Complexity. When tap and plughole are closed, the water is in a state of unchanging order. If the tap were to be fully opened, the water in the bathtub shifts into chaos. However, with the tap turned off and the plug removed, the water self-organises itself, as if by magic, into a vortex. Individual molecules of water come, interact with other molecules and in that way contribute to the global pattern, and then go. They are unimportant details. But the significant vortex is left behind.

The above simple illustration reveals three key features of major significance in understanding Complexity. First, a Complex regime is a mix of global order and local chaos. Later discussion will show that development, and politics and economics, share that pattern of behaviour. Second, speaking of a beginning or an end to a Complex process is largely meaningless. As long as the water flows at a steady rate the system will remain in a self-organised state of global order. In other words, it will avoid chaos, in defiance of the second law of thermodynamics. Finally, there is a strong link between information and Complexity. It is easy to describe the orderly regime in a few words. It would take practically an infinite amount of information to specify the chaotic regime, as each particle of water has to be described separately. Complexity lies somewhere between; it requires a moderate level of information to define it adequately.

Complexity in the laboratory

Order, chaos and Complexity have been studied by the use of Boolean networks, named after the logician George Boole (1815–1864). A typical network has a large number of internal components, light bulbs that could turn each other on or off, say, each of which has two possible states: active or inactive. The binary system is familiar in computer science, but it has similarities in more familiar life situations; a nation, for example, might decide either to join or to abstain from taking part in world trade. The letter 'N' denotes the total number of elements in the network, while 'K' describes connectivity, the number of other elements controlled by each element. Simple local rules are specified to dictate how the 'K' elements would be switched on and off by each element, and global patterns are then observed through successive cycles of engagement. By altering connectivity, K, and the local rules, uneventful order, rampant chaos or organised Complexity can be created and studied (Kauffman 1993: 36).

Regulated local interactions are the key

Repeated experiments demonstrated that local capability to interact is essential for a network to acquire the stable global patterns associated with a state of Complexity. Significantly, however, the tests revealed that simple rules that regulate the interactions were also of critical importance in preventing the network from drifting into chaos. Moreover, connectivity was shown to be of critical importance. Clearly, some of the elements must be able to interact with each other for anything to happen. In the case of a sparsely connected network, say K = 1 with each element linked only to one other element, the system rapidly settles into an orderly global state and that is the end of the matter. Turning next to a network in which each element is able to switch several other elements on and off, say K = 5 or more, the resulting patterns observed are typical of a chaotic regime. The system does not settle into an overall pattern worth observing as it hunts through an almost infinite number of *states* hither and thither. When connectivity is reasonably small, K = 3 say, the network enters a regime of organised Complexity. It cycles through a large but finite number of similar, but not identical, states (Coveney and Highfield 1996: 166; Byrne 1998: 26).

It is worth stressing here that we are talking about vast numbers of system-wide states. Potentially, a system comprising N elements, each of which has two local states, off and on, would have two to the power N possible states in all. Even for a small network of only ten elements this results in 1,024 states. Put another element in the network and the total adds up to 2,048; insert another and the total jumps to 4,096. In the normal course of events a network would have hundreds of interacting elements, and in real-life situations, as in the case of an economy, components might be counted in the thousands or millions. Consequently, in a chaotic regime, in which each element is able to control several other elements, there are an almost infinite number of states; therefore the system does not show any *regularities* and it takes just as long to study and describe the system as it does for the system to cycle through its numerous states. This last observation is of vital importance to some political, economic and social situations. As discussed later, in order to discover all the regularities in a given activity, for instance, an observer might have to watch the whole episode from start to finish.

Basins of attraction

It is necessary at this point to introduce the concept of *attractors* or *basins of attraction* as a feature of dynamic (linear and nonlinear) systems.[9] Basically, an attractor describes 'the long-term behaviour of a system' (Coveney and Highfield 1996: 424). In its simplest form it could be a *point* attractor, as seen in a pendulum swinging under gravity that invariably comes to rest pointing vertically downwards. Its different *states* while it is in motion ultimately converge on that attractor; they are said to drain into that basin of attraction. The next level is the *limit-cycle* attractor, described for instance by a frictionless pendulum swinging in a vacuum (Byrne 1998: 168). The attractor in this case is an envelop of space or time that includes every single state assumed by the system. A few simple facts, such as the initial position from which the pendulum is released, allow us to predict accurately the state of the system at any point in the future. Point and limit-cycle attractors occur in linear systems that are at or near equilibrium.

Life becomes more complicated as we move away from these simple instances. The next stage involves a system that draws a doughnut, or *torus*, shape as it scrolls through its many states. An engine controlled by a governor is one example of such an attractor. The governor is preset to keep the speed of the engine within a certain range. Negative feedback is used to slow the engine down when it reaches the upper limit and to speed it up when it approaches the lower limit. An acceptable level of uncertainty is designed into the system because it is not necessary to know the exact speed at any point as long as it remains within the specified limits. If the speed were to be plotted over a long period it would reveal the typical torus shape associated with this basin of attraction.

However, if the governor were to fail suddenly the engine would then race along driven by a multiplicity of internal and external factors. We have now moved into the domain of nonlinear phenomena, including Complex Systems, where basins of attraction are often referred to as *strange* attractors. As before, and what really matters to us for the present purpose, the attractor describes the space of all possible states traced by the system, but here it defines a domain of uncertainty. The strange attractor presents more than just one set of limits, as seen in the butterfly shape of the Lorenz attractor for example. Positive feedback in this instance means that insignificant perturbations could push the system from one wing of the butterfly to the other, resulting in radically different limits and hence new global patterns. Other strange attractors might have several sets of limits. These remarks underline the significance of Arthur's arguments for adopting positive feedback as the more likely mechanism in his vision of nonlinear economics (Arthur 1990). Minor events can, and often do, shift the economy in new and unexpected directions. And the same can be said of politics and development. They lead an eventful life at the outer branches of the tree of science.

LOCAL CHAOS BUT GLOBAL STABILITY

While it is in a regime of Complexity, a system scrolls through many states that differ only within specific limits defined by the particular basin of attraction in command at that time.[10] The system is pulled in that way into a repeating cycle, which gives the system its observable global pattern. All the while the internal elements interact feverishly and the system scrolls through the family of states that belong to the attractor in force.[11] That mode of behaviour is highly suggestive of Adam Smith's invisible hand that keeps the market in order overall while people chaotically 'truck, barter and exchange one thing for another' locally.

Minor variations between states cause some change but this is normally contained within the attractor. Sometimes, small mutations bounce the system into a very similar, neighbouring, attractor. Despite the frenetic internal activity, outwardly the system still seems to be essentially unchanging. Occasionally, however, positive feedback can turn minor variations into powerful avalanches capable of shunting the system into an altogether different attractor that displays a new global pattern. Hence, a system that appears stable for long might suddenly, and for no clear reason, undergo a radical transformation. But there is no way of knowing in advance which initial perturbation would precipitate such a revolution. In evolutionary terms the pattern of large upheavals separated by long periods of global stability, but energetic local activity, is sometimes referred to as *punctuated equilibrium* (Gell-Mann 1994: 238; Coveney and Highfield 1996: 232). The seeming durability of the communist system in Eastern Europe that lasted many decades and then its rapid collapse within a few years is a good illustration of that concept of change.

There is a delicate balance to be struck between variety of local states and global stability. Too few states produce unvarying order and too many create chaos: both are dead ends. Poised between the two regimes, Complexity is the zone where self-organisation allows new stable patterns to emerge and evolve without compromising the survival of the entire system. In all cases the system must have some variety to give it flexibility to withstand unexpected shocks, but limits on variety are also necessary to avoid chaos. Parallels with national economies or international relations are easily detectable. People, the internal elements of the system, interact with each other in ways that can produce organised Complexity when their interactions follow sensible rules. Conversely, a repressive regime can reduce a whole nation to a state of stultifying order, while prolonged loss of control, due to civil war, say, can result in total chaos.

In summary, Complex Adaptive System share the following traits:

- They have active internal elements that furnish sufficient local variety to enable the system to survive as it adapts to unforeseen circumstances.
- The systems' elements are lightly but not sparsely connected.
- The elements interact locally according to simple rules to provide

the energy needed to maintain stable global patterns, as opposed to rigid order or chaos.

- Variations in prevailing conditions result in many minor changes and a few large mutations, but it is not possible to predict the outcome in advance.

ONGOING CYCLES OF SURVIVAL AND ADAPTATION

Boolean networks have also been used to study evolution, the cyclical process of adaptation and survival in a changing environment. To adapt successfully a system has to survive long enough to evolve into its next stable pattern, otherwise the next cycle cannot begin. Essentially, survival of the fittest is really survival of the most stable (Dawkins 1989: 12). Living organisms are Complex Adaptive Systems, but in this case change into new patterns involves reproduction. Observing adaptation in the living world, however, presents a number of logistical problems, the most obvious being the elapsed time between cycles of reproduction.[12] Computers are utilised nowadays to explore more speedily metaphors for evolution, with benefits to genetics, computer science and the study of Complexity.

Thomas Ray designed a classic computer simulation of Darwinian evolution, TIERRA, in which replicating digital 'organisms' competed over limited computer memory space.[13] TIERRA combined the Complexity of Boolean networks with replication and mutation to mimic the behaviour of Complex Adaptive Systems. A most illuminating outcome was the realisation that inside the computer as in nature, and in accordance with Darwin's views, selection pressures for adaptation came from activities by other coevolving entities. The physical environment, in this case the central processor, was the junior partner in that struggle. Similarity with interdependence and competition between states in the world system is fairly obvious.

Computer simulations mirrored activities in real-life situations, from aggression and parasitic behaviour to cooperation and competition. In every case variety emerged as an essential asset for survival. However, a curiously underremarked phenomenon of critical importance to development was laid bare through these studies: evolution does not lead to an optimal end state. 'Good enough' seems to be the sum total of what nature hopes to achieve, successful evolution being an ongoing open-ended process of, often small, effective improvements by which the entity manages to improve its performance in a changing environment (Dawkins 1991; Kauffman 1993: 173; Coveney and Highfield 1996: 118). The quick skip to Nirvana at the end of a rainbow, promised by ideologues and politicians, does not feature on nature's agenda.

Treks in fitness landscapes

The environment for a given system is determined to a large extent by other coevolving systems sharing the same space, and better performance is achieved when the structure becomes more suited to that habitat. Topographical representations are utilised as metaphors for this continuous process of adjustment, as was the case with the basins of attraction discussed earlier. If locations on a tabletop were assumed to represent differing sets of conditions, then at each place the height above, or below, the table would indicate the level of fitness to that set of conditions. The *fitness landscape*, therefore, has flat lands of neutral significance, mountains representing degrees of fitness and valleys indicating lack of fitness. Variety provided by the large number of elements within a Complex system ensures that some elements would suit a given set of circumstances better than others. The former would flourish in the 'mountains' while the latter might perish in the 'valleys'. In that way the system manages to survive under a wide range of circumstances. That is the only evolutionarily stable strategy (ESS) in an unpredictable and continually shifting environment.

When coevolving systems exist together, the fitness landscape assumes a fluid nature. Its features alter over time to reflect the activities of all entities sharing the same space. What might be a peak at one point in time, indicating good fitness, can easily turn into a trough, suggesting lack of fitness due to the actions of others. Comparison with social, economic and political events is unavoidable. For instance, what nations choose to do or are forced to do affects the fortunes and responses of other nations, sometimes quite disastrously. Those with sufficient variety and freedom and those that are able and willing to adapt pragmatically survive, while inflexible regimes, as in the case of dictatorships, experience debilitating bouts of instability.

Rigid ideas are inappropriate

Sustainable evolution is not a rush to the nearest peak. A more efficient policy would involve leisurely exploration of the whole spectrum of opportunities. As fitness landscapes are in continual flux, optimal and inflexible solutions are not the answer; today's successful creature could be tomorrow's dodo. A pragmatic and resilient policy that makes allowance for chance events is the only evolutionarily stable strategy for survival. Here again the parallels with real-life situations are compelling. As discussed in the next chapter, the contrast with futile attempts by the World Bank and the IMF to impose a few preconceived ideas on all their client nations in the hope of speeding them through the development process is compelling.

A further point should be highlighted here: degree of connectivity between coevolving systems or, in the present context, nations is a key factor that can substantially alter the chances of survival and adaptation. As connectivity increases – the mad rush to globalisation springs to mind here – interdependence begins to impose conflicting requirements that can only be resolved through frequent compromises by all the systems. They shed variety and become fit or unfit to just one set of conditions; the fitness landscape becomes flatter and systems, and nations, lose their ability to adapt to unforeseen changes that could, and in all probability would, affect their particular environment. Studies have repeatedly shown that excessive connectivity often leads to *Complexity catastrophe*, at which point progress grinds to a halt due to repeated local failures. This point is significant in connection with the efforts being made by leading powers and international regimes to impose a single political economic model on all nations, come what may. Basically, forcing interdependence and sameness on nations is not likely to be an evolutionarily stable strategy in the long run.

Evolution: an uphill struggle

Nonlinear science revealed evolution for what it really is, an arduous task undertaken against considerable odds. A system has to be able to adapt, by having at all times some elements that are fit for the prevailing circumstances; and then it has to remain stable for long enough to adapt repeatedly. That cyclic process, survival and adaptation, entails a battle against nature. This sounds somewhat odd on first inspection. What could be more natural than evolution? Living organisms, from the humblest to the most complex, have been doing it for millennia apparently without thought or effort. That cosy picture is misleading and is the source of considerable misunderstanding when one moves away from evolution of living entities to tackle social, political and economic systems.

A glance at what is involved is sufficient to illustrate the difficulties. An evolving system, be it an animal in pursuit of life, a company struggling to grow, or a whole nation seeking development, has to traverse cycles of adaptation and survival, and time is the medium over which that precarious process unfolds. Progress is precarious because the system has to combat the destabilising punches thrown at it all the while by thermodynamics' second law. That law, which also requires time to achieve its devastating ends, dictates that things, when left to their own devices, must move towards disorder and decay. Put simply, but very accurately, the second law is based on an unshakable principle that chaos is a more probable state than stability. That is only natural; for example, a pile of rubble never assembles itself into a building, but the reverse, by contrast, is a self-evident occurrence. In short, continual action is required to maintain a system in a stable, less probable, state of survival and, hopefully, evolution.

Stability, technically self-organised Complexity, is achieved through a system's ability to exchange energy with the outside world through its internal dynamics. As discussed before, a system with many interacting elements has a potentially vast number of states. In chaos, a more probable condition, the system wanders through all its *state space* to visit an infinite number of possible states; it does not settle down to a recognisable pattern. However, in organised Complexity the system is locked in small, less probable, regions of its state space with a fewer number of states to scroll through. To keep it there is no mean task: too little effort and the second law triumphs by pushing the system into chaos; too much effort and it is 'killed' as unvarying order prevails everywhere; all regions 'freeze in fixed states of activity' (Kauffman 1993: 174). Living systems mastered the trick of remaining within the narrow layer of Complexity, between order and chaos, after millions of years of trial and error.

The accumulation of knowledge

A fundamental notion, that of learning, presents itself here. A living entity achieves homeostasis, a state of self-organised Complexity, and then lives long enough to pass on its past experiences through its genes. Essentially, the system records *regularities* and ignores random occurrences. A dog learns through that mechanism to distinguish between food and poison and also learns to bury unused food for later without being told by other dogs or by human beings. These features are regularities. Next generations receive the message, amend it by adding other regularities, and then in turn pass it on. There is, therefore, a recurrent process that includes the accumulation of knowledge in addition to adaptation and survival.

The trilogy of survival, adaptation and learning exists in all situations involving Complex Adaptive Systems, irrespective of whether one is dealing with phenomena in the natural or the social sciences. If the tools of knowledge building are impaired, the process of adaptation and survival is affected, slightly or catastrophically. Later, in Chapter 8, the significance of this feature will be highlighted in relation to illiteracy and disregard for indigenous knowledge as components of the capability divide that inhibits some nations from developing successfully.

Punctuated equilibrium

Discussion of how Complex Adaptive Systems evolve would be incomplete without consideration of *punctuated equilibrium*, *frozen accidents* and *gateway events*.[14] As mentioned earlier, evolving systems stay more or less as they are for relatively long periods of time and then undergo fast radical change. The interval of apparent inactivity is deceptive, however; at the local level change takes place continuously and the system scrolls through many states within one attractor. Ripples of change come and go without leaving a discernible trace, but occasionally relatively minor events succeed in shunting the system into another attractor. Only then does the observer recognise that a definite change had taken place, but in a stable system life quickly settles down to the new pattern. Variety, and hence flexibility, allows the system to bend with the wind, the only other alternative being extinction, the opposite of evolution.

Punctuated equilibrium is also observed in the affairs of humankind, as the rise and fall of ancient empires and hegemonic powers clearly shows. Immanuel Wallerstein, for instance, cited three lengthy periods of stable hegemony: the United Provinces, mid-seventeenth century; the United Kingdom, mid-nineteenth century; and the United States of America, mid-twentieth century. They all attained ascendancy after a relatively brief world war (Wallerstein 1983). More recently, and on a smaller scale, when Nicolae Ceausescu (1918–1989) stood on a balcony to address the people of Romania on 22 December 1989, it took only a few minutes for everyone to realise that things would never be the same again after decades during which his rule appeared solid as a rock. By Christmas Day he and his wife Elena were dead and Romania was in the domain of a new attractor. The abrupt fragmentation of the USSR after three-quarters of a century of stability is, of course, the ultimate illustration of punctuated equilibrium in action.

Frozen accidents

In natural evolution, chance events from the past sometimes become an integral part of life from that point on. For obvious reasons they are referred to as frozen accidents. They exert a decisive influence on the future course of evolution. The carbon-based form of life on Earth is a good example. Once that frozen accident was built into the system, the future of all creatures on earth was set on a distinctive path. Complex Adaptive Systems are affected in a similar manner by the incorporation of successive frozen accidents as *regularities*. Attitudes to women, multiparty politics, international trade, concepts of beauty, censure of incest, and the family group, for example, were all found appropriate at some stage and were then included in the overall framework.

Such haphazard inherited influences indelibly shape the course of history. At the same time, relentless daily adaptation fuelled by ever-changing circumstances imposes a counterbalancing force for constant transformation within the general direction imposed by past frozen accidents. The unending contest between the conservatory influences of frozen accidents, on the one hand, and adaptation, on the other, typifies Complex Adaptive Systems. I will return to this feature in Chapter 10 in the context of the need for a nation to exercise a degree of pragmatism in relation to its treasured historic, social and political ideas to survive and develop within an interdependent global environment.

As I argued in the previous chapter, people regularly traded across national borders and over long distances for thousands of years. At some point in human history, trade, and of course the market itself, became a frozen accident. People found that it paid to trade, and politics and geography were of little consequence, as asserted by Adam Smith centuries later. Advice and pressure from the USA, the WTO and the IMF are hardly necessary in this issue area. International trade is here to stay as a predictable global feature, but openness and closure are shifting matters of detail. In a similar manner, the particular reigning hegemonic power at any time is only a detail. The relevant frozen accident is the high probability that there would be at least one major power, or elite, somewhere in the global hierarchy.[15]

Gateway events

In contrast to the day-to-day sedate influences that drive evolution onwards, gateway events go through the system like a whirlwind. They are a major factor in creating the pattern of punctuated equilibrium. Unplanned gateway events crop up from time to time to open up niches that promise new and unexpected opportunities for some, and disaster for others. That happened at the end of the Permian period, 245 million years ago, when more than half of all species on earth disappeared, and during the Cretaceous extinction, about 185 million years later, when dinosaurs became extinct along with one-third of the world's animal and plant life. The rest of creation, organisms able to tolerate or benefit from the new conditions, flourished in abundance.

Gateway events in natural evolution have their social, economic and political counterparts. The Industrial Revolution and, later, the invention of the internal combustion engine and the computer are perfect specimens of gateway events, comprising the emergence of new developments and the subsequent steady filling of the niches they bring forth. But a system, or nation, must have sufficient variety and flexibility to survive the shock of the latest gateway event in the first instance before it can proceed to profit from the new opportunities on offer.

INFORMATION AS A MEASURE OF COMPLEXITY

The process by which Complex Adaptive Systems evolve, survive and gather information is a slow activity that involves the gradual assembly of successive layers of elaboration. Moving on from that premiss, it is now possible to advance a quantitative definition of Complexity, but it is appropriate at this point to underline the fact that Complexity does not mean more difficult or more important. Gell–Mann describes Einstein's relativity theory as being 'wonderfully simple', although he accepts of course that few people understand it. A mouse, by contrast, is a Complex Adaptive System.

Essentially, the length of message needed to describe a system determines whether it is orderly, chaotic, or Complex (Gell–Mann 1994: 16–17). Regularities play a decisive role in that system. An orderly system is highly regular; a short description of the few recurring regularities is all one needs to give a full account of that system, hence the ease of modelling linear phenomena. A chaotic regime, on the other hand, has few or no regularities; therefore every individual part has to be observed and then specified separately to give an adequate picture of the system. The message could be infinitely long in this case. A statement that defines a Complex Adaptive System would have regularities that can be summarised, in computer jargon *compressed*, and other items that are random and, therefore, incompressible; a mix of order and chaos.[16]

The above definition and the accumulation of regularities provide a robust explanation for the difficulties frequently encountered by scholars seeking to produce theories to model socioeconomic phenomena. Using traditional methods, founded in a linear paradigm, they select a few examples from here and there to turn their hypotheses into theories. That will not do for a nonlinear Complex Adaptive System, as all the regularities might not be captured by the basket of instances chosen. At bottom, procedures suited for orderly linear systems, with a handful of recurring regularities to be accounted for, are ineffective in the case of systems that include a large number of regularities. The turmoil in IPE theories, as described in Chapter 2, was inevitable.

RISE AND FALL OF COMPLEXITY

As time goes on new regularities are added to the system and the statement needed to specify it becomes progressively longer, indicating an inherent tendency for Complexity to increase (Kauffman 1993: 232). To put it more precisely, in each specific instance 'complexity can either increase or decrease', but 'the greatest complexity represented has a tendency to grow larger with time' (Gell–Mann 1994: 244). Moreover, while the lengthy process of evolution unfolds there is a high probability that the average Complexity of all systems will also increase. These are significant features in Complex Systems theory, which is now used to study 'living systems, organisations, communities and coevolving ecosystems' (Kauffman 1993: 173). The emergence of hegemonic powers among nations and the inclination for the rich to get richer hint at social, political and economic similarities.[17] At a broader level, the above features help to reveal the real nature of the development process: nations develop differentially along a wide variety of evolutionary paths. Those at the head of the procession might move faster, but others should not be diverted by what is happening ahead; their main concern should be to achieve optimal performance within their own circumstances.

CERTAIN UNPREDICTABILITY

The above features are certainties in a field that is characterised by a large measure of uncertainty. Coevolution, constant adaptation and accumulating regularities identify the causes of the chronic state of unpredictable flux that marks all Complex Adaptive Systems.[18] Present beliefs and methods, derived from a linear paradigm, are firmly based on implicit assumptions of dependable predictability. In almost all situations, the feasibility of forecasting future events is taken as an article of faith. Nowhere is this, and the ubiquitous expert, more valued than in business, economics and politics. Despite every indication to the contrary, this expectation is adhered to fastidiously; it forms a substantial part of the design principles round which society is structured.

There are two major factors that conspire to make unpredictability a standard component of Complex Adaptive Systems. First, and possibly most importantly, even infinitesimal local disturbances in initial conditions can be magnified by positive feedback to induce large global changes. This is often illustrated by a ball bearing precariously balanced on an upturned hemispherical bowl. An infinitesimally small disturbance can send the ball rolling down the incline, but to predict the exact direction taken by the ball one would have to be able to measure the initial disturbance with great accuracy. This is a critical point: nonlinear phenomena are not necessarily unpredictable in theory, but in practice infinite precision and computing power is required to forecast the future.

Moving from the simple example of the ball bearing to a Complex Adaptive System with a large number of interacting elements helps to clarify the second factor that limits our ability to predict the future in detail. To trace causes and effects through the millions of local inter-actions creates massive computing problems. Just think of a 'simple' game of chess and then multiply the difficulty of prediction in that instance many times over to gain a rough idea of what is involved in forecasting events in the political, social and economic arena. In order to know what a system is doing, why and how, it is often necessary to watch while it does it; ecosystems and socioeconomic systems might 'behave in ways that are their shortest descriptions' (Kauffman 1996: 22). Regularities must be identified and compressed to formulate a creditable theory; explaining once again why IPE theorists experi-enced insurmountable problems.

Life's unpredictable events

When asked what his biggest concern was during his term as British prime minster from 1957 to 1963, Harold Macmillan is said to have replied 'events, dear boy, events'. The above computing difficulty could have helped Macmillan to come to terms with his inability to antici-pate developments. His experts and his own considerable expertise were not, and could not have been, a match for the vagaries of life at the top of the political ladder. *Emergent properties*, a constant com-panion of all Complex Adaptive Systems and a bottomless source of surprises, make sure that real life is never dull despite the best efforts of theorists to model it accurately. Inescapably, theories and methods formulated within a linear paradigm give only an illusory feeling of knowledge and control. Ultimately, the only possible defence is to make certain the system is sufficiently robust and pragmatic to survive the knocks.

Attempts to derive lessons from South Korea's economic perform-ance are a case in point. It was studied from the liberalising reforms initiated between 1963 and 1965 and through the miracle decades (Haggard and Moon 1983: 131). A few regularities were unearthed but these applied to South Korea during that specific period. If the time scale had been extended other regularities might have become apparent. Additionally, if the search area had been enlarged to cover other geographical locations, then further regularities might have been revealed. To formulate a universal theory, the process would have to be studied for all time periods and in all locations, hardly a practical proposition.

In business to predict the unpredictable

The meanderings of the international economy demonstrate beyond doubt the difficulties experienced by even the best-informed commentators in predicting and explaining events. I shall take the period from 1997 to the present to underline the fact that whilst hindsight is always perfect, looking forward is by contrast a hit or miss affair even in the short-term. At the start of 1997, most observers were agreed that Asia presented the ultimate in growth and stability. The Japanese 'miracle' was looking slightly tarnished but it was still sufficiently impressive to merit admiration. Observers agreed at the time that American and European economies were languishing under the burden of supposedly well-understood problems. Then came one of those events that clearly mark a nonlinear system in full swing: Asian economies went into an unanticipated nosedive, while American and European economies performed well.[19]

Speculators, who were roundly blamed at the time for the collapse, were themselves not better able to predict the event; the international financier George Soros was said to have lost $2 billion in a matter of days. The experts did not linger long over their inability to forecast the shifts in fortunes. They were too busy debating whether the anticipated Japanese recovery would be V-shaped, meaning sharp and speedy, or U-shaped, meaning gradual and more prolonged. The sum total of their analyses was that no one knew when the recovery would happen and what form it would take.

As usual, the period of turbulence in 1997 and 1998 coincided with a flurry of crisis meetings between leading politicians, such as the world economic forum held in Davos in the first week of February 1998. That itself is a telling indication that events frequently catch politicians and their advisers by surprise, sometimes verging on panic. There was, of course, the all-purpose announcement that the meetings were necessary 'to make sure this sort of thing never happens again'. In the context of unpredictability, Larry Summers, America's deputy Treasury secretary, made a pertinent observation on the Davos meeting. He remarked that if an international group of top analysts had been asked in the late 1980s whether America, Europe or Japan would have the fastest growing economy they would have nominated Japan by a large majority, followed by Europe, and then America in poor third position (*Sunday Times*, 8 February 1998).

In the event, America led the field by a mile against all earlier expectations. That miracle is usually attributed to the acumen of Alan Greenspan, chairman of the US Federal Reserve Board since 1987. Interestingly, Greenspan himself is candid enough to consider the conjunction of circumstances that propelled the USA to the top of the class a mystery. He is said to be a believer in logical positivism, which accepts a measure of uncertainty in all things (Woodward 2000). Needless to say, the pendulum has already started to move the other way. At the time of writing, America, and therefore the entire world economy, is heading for a recession and that has rekindled the usual outbreak of speculation. It is not clear whether the recession, if it were to materialise, would entail a 'hard' or 'soft' landing. For instance, the cataclysmic events in New York of 11 September 2001 undoubtedly added to the economic gloom. On the other hand, on past record of wars, the ensuing 'war against terror' waged against the Taliban and Bin Laden in Afghanistan would have been expected to lift the air of depression somewhat. In truth, no-one knows.

Politics is an even chancier business

Politicians have learnt to take unpredictability in their stride; they unapologetically make things up as they go along. The disintegration of the USSR, and more fundamentally the retreat of communism, in the late 1980s were momentous events. Billions of dollars were spent over the decades to pore over every scrap of information emerging from the USSR openly or clandestinely, but the experts failed to predict the change, its rapidity, or the route it followed.

However, prediction of less dramatic political affairs is just as problematic. At the end of the Gulf War in January 1991, for instance, the odds on Saddam Hussein's reign surviving into the twenty-first century were exceedingly remote. He had just been soundly defeated by a massive coalition of powers, and apparently had few friends left. Against all expectations his government survived and was sufficiently strong to cause the USA much irritation throughout the 1990s and beyond. Recent indications suggest that the sanctions against Iraq are eroding and diplomatic relations with other countries are returning to normal. Conversely, the USA and Britain, and quite possibly Saddam Hussein himself, seem content to retain the status quo.

The point to note is not that Saddam is still here large as life, but that it is impossible to forecast how the whole saga will eventually end. Basically, notwithstanding assertions by all politicians, and their experts and spin doctors, no one is in charge of events. So-called great powers, such as the USA, are reluctant to accept this fact, and the inevitable frustration when events refuse to fall in line with their wishes often leads to tragic consequences. The traditional democratic processes in these countries make matters worse, as governments swing into action at every turn of events to refute claims of lack of foresight and ineptitude coming from the opposition parties.

Do we give up then?

The above inherent indeterminacy sets strict limits on what is possible to predict when dealing with Complex Adaptive Systems. Undoubtedly, this constraint is most uncomfortable when viewed in today's frame of reference. However, it is also unavoidable. The certainty associated with reductionist scientific methods is largely spurious when applied to nonlinear situations. The danger lies in trading real but admittedly limited predictability for chimerical certainty. Explanation and prediction in the case of such systems centres on their stable global properties rather than the details of what is going on inside. That gives an important clue as to the appropriate actions that could be taken to achieve positive results. Command-and-control methods are useless. They might succeed temporarily when applied with sufficient force but they are not sustainable as long-term policies. Complex Adaptive Systems respond better to light-touch styles of management based on constant monitoring of overall patterns of performance coupled with judicious small-scale incremental adjustments.

The larger Complex Adaptive Systems are themselves made up of internal elements that might be Complex Adaptive Systems in their own right. However, here and there some of the systems include perfectly predictable linear parts. For example, the linear supply-and-demand models pioneered early in the twentieth century by Cambridge University economist Alfred Marshall led to reasonably predictable equilibrium in the short and long term (Samuelson and Nordhaus

1995: 134). Detailed actions can be taken with confidence in these specific areas. The trick, however, is to determine in advance the nature of the system under consideration before actions are contemplated.

The downside of expertise

Does it matter that the 'experts' persist in their efforts to predict the unpredictable? Sadly, yes it does. At best, their efforts might have a neutral effect on events. To an extent, their pronouncements serve a purpose of sorts as they supply the reassurance sought by people. In previous eras priests and soothsayers performed that task, but nowadays people demand rational answers, and more importantly quick fixes, based on some sort of science no matter how imperfect. Regrettably, when words are translated into actions the results can prove harmful. The misguided efforts of local and international development experts over the last decades have left some countries worse off than they would have been had they been left to paddle their own canoes.

In other instances the question of expertise is relatively unimportant. Certain political economic systems will survive and prosper because they have learnt from past experience that the future is uncertain, regardless of whether that fact is explicitly recognised or otherwise. Pragmatism, variety and readiness to adapt are incorporated into their fabric to allow for this precondition. The USA, for instance, will do reasonably well come Democrat or Republican. Much to the amazement of foreign dictators devoted to 'strong' government, the local chaos that characterises America's social, political and economic affairs is also the means by which overall stability is achieved. Most nations in the so-called developing world are not so fortunate. They take the experts at their word and follow their recommendations all too literally and with disastrous results. But that anticipates the discussion in Chapter 10.

MORE THAN POLITICS OR ECONOMICS

It is essential when dealing with processes that operate as Complex Adaptive Systems, including the process of development, to gain a full understanding of their inherent mode of behaviour. At base, we need to know the nature of the primary factors that make them what they are. As highlighted before, my contention is that it is too crude in the study and practice of development simply to look at social, political and economic influences. Certainly these are important derived elements but they are not the cardinal forces that drive development this way or that. The next sections outline the principal parameters that have particular relevance in this context.

The irreversible arrow of time

The irreversible arrow of time was launched when the universe exploded from a singularity, some fifteen billion years ago, and the trinity of past, present and future was thus established as an integral part of existence. Passage of time is the medium over which internal elements of a Complex Adaptive System interact furiously to take the system through successive cycles of learning, adaptation and survival. That mode of progression imposes certain constraints. To begin with, the pattern of a system at any time is clearly a function of everything that happened in its past up to that moment, but what happens next depends on too many factors, which makes prediction hazardous, to say the least. In addition, time is needed for the system to evolve proactively with an environment that is substantially affected by what other coevolving systems are doing.

In effect, systems have to expend energy to stay within stable, but evolving, self-organised patterns that accumulate in Complexity over time. I will provide evidence in Chapter 6 to underline the very long time taken by prosperous nations to amass wealth through small but steady increments. That span of time itself is merely a brief moment in a lengthy project of Complexity acquisition that has gone on for thousands of years, a sequence of occurrences that does not have a beginning or an end. In that context, it is quite wrong to imagine that the sum total of conventions and beliefs that describe what we know as Europe, say, started at the Renaissance or the Enlightenment. There was something there before these, admittedly important, episodes made their presence felt, and that past was instrumental in what happened later. The history of that continent evolved along a punctuated equilibrium path; the Enlightenment is one spike on that journey.

Culture, society, economics and politics evolve towards increasing Complexity and it takes time for that build-up to occur. That imposes yet another constraint: many layers of interconnections and adaptations have to come into being at a pace that could not be accelerated appreciably. Money, imported expertise, and grim determination to succeed are no substitutes for the time needed to generate 'depth'. In sum, the past affects the future, the future itself is unpredictable in detail, change follows a pattern of punctuated equilibrium, and above all else there are no shortcuts to sustainable evolution. As I argue in Chapter 10, these features have a decisive impact on how development is perceived and promoted.

Predictable inequalities

Average Complexity, in a group of Complex Adaptive Systems, increases and entities with the highest Complexity experience the largest growth. This is a key feature of Complex Systems theory, as explained earlier. Communities of people, and nations, are therefore stratified in wealth, as in most other respects, and the gap between those at the top and others has a propensity to grow larger. It would be unnatural for the system to work differently; hence the failure of good intentions to eliminate or reduce inequality at personal, national and international levels. Massive effort has to be expended in a determined and constant manner, well beyond what appears reasonable, to effect even a modest realignment. Sustainable evolution is a long-term process aimed at producing best results under prevailing conditions. It does not promise equality.

The impact of the above deceptively simple statement on our vision of development is nothing less than dramatic, as I argue later. Suffice it to say for the moment that international comparisons lose much of their significance. Developing countries would be better occupied in pursuing consistent, albeit modest, results over long periods without being concerned as to their position in the global or regional hierarchy. That after all is what developed countries had to do on their long march forward. But that is easier said than done, as discussed in Chapter 10.

Elites and hierarchies

Inequality, elites and hierarchies are facets of the same phenomenon. Study of social, political and economic elites that exercise disproportionate power over others is a vast subject. Remarks made here are only intended to present a few aspects of direct relevance to the present subject.[20] As described in the next section, it is natural for egoistic individuals to compete in the search for survival and dominance. The hierarchical model is an inevitable consequence of that process, and it is now firmly fixed as a frozen accident in most instances where people are involved, including the international political economy.

The rigidity and shape of the hierarchy in the context of a political economy is determined by a number of factors, including history, tradition and form of government. The hierarchy is steep under a dictator or a despotic royal family; those who monopolise political and economic interactions might amount to no more than a handful of people. In a democratic country, by contrast, the hierarchy is somewhat flatter; the elite embraces more individuals, and people are free to interact locally in many secondary hierarchies where they have 'bosses' above and 'underlings' below. The elite in this case is a flexible group with slowly changing membership. This distinction is a critical feature that will recur in later discussion.

The global hierarchy, comprising leading powers, international regimes, and less developed countries, is a typical manifestation of the above feature of Complexity. Interactions, within bounds, are crucial for self-organised Complexity. They energise the system and thereby confer positive benefits. However, too many interactions could shunt the system into chaos: Complexity catastrophe is an ever-present risk. Conversely, too few interactions might push it into a deathly state of order. Ultimately, a balance has to be struck somewhere between the two polar positions. It will be argued in later chapters that dictatorships as well as the regulating activities of regimes such as the IMF and the World Bank often go too far towards stultifying order. Hierarchies are inevitable, and their shape and mode of behaviour, steep or shallow and rigid or flexible, are major factors in improving or inhibiting performance. Fundamentally, understanding of this aspect of the way Complex Adaptive Systems behave is a positive step towards achieving better results in human and economic development.

THE FUNDAMENTAL UNIT

The driving force in natural selection is not the good of the species, or group, but the good, meaning survival, of the individual gene. The most significant action in natural evolution takes place, therefore, at the level of the basic unit, the selfish gene (Dawkins 1989: 19). Selfishness in this instance describes self-interest rather than ill will to others. Similar traits in the affairs of humankind could be observed in the behaviour of egoistic individuals, as appreciated by Adam Smith centuries ago. Furthermore, Dawkins suggested that if there were a general principle that is true of life it would be that it 'evolves by the differential survival of replicating entities'.

Genes develop for themselves increasingly more elaborate 'survival machines', including of course human beings. In consequence, Dawkins pointed out that although the main aim in evolution is strictly gene survival, 'for many purposes individual survival is a reasonable approximation' (Dawkins 1989: 55). Humans, therefore, are essentially 'selfish'; they basically want to prevail and then survive long enough to pass their genes to their offspring. In consequence, individuals focus almost exclusively on their own concerns. However, that does not mean that they could not, or would not, cooperate to achieve societal aims. Even here the welfare of the species as a whole has no real meaning in practice. At heart, decisions to compete or cooperate are meaningful in the main only at the level of the individual. The phenotypes of the conscious world – groups, committees, businesses, sectors of an economy, communities, whole nations, and ultimately the entire international political economy – are shaped substantially by the interactions pursued egoistically at the local level of conscious individuals.[21]

Survival machines for individuals

To continue Dawkins's theme, families, tribes and nations can be thought of in turn as survival machines for individuals. The terminology might be modern but the idea is ancient and does not require elaboration. Nevertheless, it is important to present that simple concept to see the picture in its true colours. Looking at events through ideological, moral, religious or nationalistic glasses obscures the most salient feature; one would be observing the vehicle rather than the purposeful driver within. Buddhism, Judaism, Christianity and Islam, to name only four instances, were all triggered by a single idea that germinated in the supreme intellect of one individual.

In a similar vein, if the history of the British Empire were analysed, there would be little argument about the identities of the handful of individuals who took part in that grand design through its long history.

One fundamental fact must be kept clearly in mind though: they did not set out to create an Empire. They simply wished to promote or safeguard their interests and to impose their opinions on others.[22] The history of other nations shows similar traits. One needs only mention George Washington, Atatürk, de Gaulle, Gandhi, Mao Tse-tung, Stalin, Hitler, Franco, Castro and Mandela, to illustrate the point.

A long tradition of egoism

The basic concept is essentially the same whether we consider ancient or modern events. Ibn Khaldun (1332–1406) and then Machiavelli (1469–1527) described in vivid detail the process through which certain individuals attain power, but it is not necessary to go that far back in history to illustrate the point. For example, Ramsay MacDonald (1866–1937) and a few other trade-union leaders formed the British Labour Party in 1906. It is only to be expected that the party should have evolved over the decades. However, a glance at its recent history exposes the extent to which the party is stamped by the will of its leader and his close associates. The contrast could not be greater between the party under Kinnock, Smith and Blair. When Blair became leader in 1994, the party ceased, for the moment at least, to be recognisable as a socialist party. The Conservative Party followed an identical path. The difference between what the party stood for under Heath, Thatcher and Major is manifest. Ultimately, any party, institution or corporation could become the means for a few individuals to gain control and power and all that goes with them. Naturally, that has to include a certain 'spin' of political, social, religious or economic ideology.

The same comparisons can be made in the case of Russia between Stalin, Khrushchev, Gorbachev, Yeltsin and now Putin. A differentiation must be drawn between what had to be done under force of circumstances and what was actually done. Gorbachev and Yeltsin confronted an almost identical situation, but their responses were materially dissimilar. The tussle between the two during 1990 and 1991 was not over politics or economics. It is of interest to recall, as an illustration, that when the Central Committee of the Communist Party voted in February 1990 to abolish the leadership role of the Party, Yeltsin opposed the motion. To that extent, his popular image as the defender of liberal reforms was not completely beyond question.

In business as in politics

The interests of a few individuals, often those of a single person, shape businesses as well as empires. Weinstock, to cite one instance, dominated Britain's electrical and electronics industry through his grip on the General Electric Company. He battled for over two decades against the Clark brothers, who ran Plessey, GEC's main competitor at the time. At base the battle was between individuals not businesses. Far from being an exception, such sagas of dominance and rivalry are common. For example, plans to merge Glaxo and SmithKline, a £100 billion deal that would have created a company second in size only to General Motors, seem to have failed in early 1998 because of disagreement over who would take the top jobs (*Sunday Times*, 15 February and 1 March 1998). Again, it should be stressed that a degree of belief is involved. Individuals convince themselves and others that they are working for the public good. That, indirectly, often turns out to be the case eventually.

Cascading rewards and penalties keep the hierarchical system in being, structured around the needs of a few egoistic individuals at the top. For instance, chairmen of companies ostensibly recruit non-executive directors to their boards to foster good governance. But non-executive directors also set salaries for chairmen and executive directors. In practice, a few persons play a national game of musical chairs. Each serves as a chairman in one corporation and as a non-executive director on other boards. Herman and Chomsky presented evidence to illustrate this aspect of business life. Taking ten large American media companies as an example, they reported that the same 95 non-executive directors 'had directorships in an additional 36 banks and 255 other companies (aside from ... their own firm of primary affiliation)' (Herman and Chomsky 1994: 8).

The egoistic individual is clearly the fundamental unit in the social, political and economic arena, and chaotic interactions between individuals at the local level enable Complex Adaptive Systems to assume stable but evolving global patterns. This feature, incidentally, verifies one of liberalism's cardinal tenets, the supreme importance of the individual over all other elements. Individuals are not necessarily concerned with the good of society. They seek to survive and provide their progeny with the best possible chances of survival. But, as suggested by Adam Smith so long ago, in doing so they benefit society at large, although that might not be their primary concern.

COOPERATION AND COMPETITION

In the midst of mushrooming Complexity fuelled by actions of selfish egoists, it would be unrealistic to expect anything but rampant competition. Nonetheless, contrary to that plausible expectation there is undeniable evidence of widespread cooperation at all levels from genes to nations. States wish to act as true mercantilists, but in practice they often behave differently. Politicians, certainly in democracies, find common ground for collaboration even when they feel deep-seated hostility to their political adversaries. Clearly, interactions between individuals, and states, are not haphazard events driven by blind self-interest. They show unmistakable imprints of Game Theory, imposing an added layer of rationality to self-organisation induced by Complexity.

Cooperation could be traced in the final analysis to self-interest. At one level, the incentive for cooperation is easy to comprehend; cooperation between kith and kin has rational bases, as they are survival machines for practically the same genes. Group cooperation between a few unrelated individuals could also be rationalised reasonably easily. Experience shows that they are able in that way to overcome common enemies more effectively. The same principle no doubt entices nations to form alliances against others. Under some circumstances, survival can be assured with higher probability when individuals, and states, collaborate towards a shared objective.

Spontaneous cooperation

However, the above examples do not explain numerous instances of spontaneous cooperation in situations where these considerations are not in evidence. Explanations for this paradox are emerging through the field of Game Theory. In one game, the famous Iterated Prisoner's Dilemma, there are two players and a 'banker' who pays out rewards and levies penalties. The players can choose to cooperate or compete. If one always cooperates when the other persists in competing, the former would lose badly while the latter would gain handsomely. But if both were to cooperate at all times, then there is a high probability that they would both benefit. Admittedly the rewards in this instance might be less than those derived when one competes against a foolishly cooperative opponent. Equally, there is a good chance that the rewards would be more than those arising from costly mutual competition.

Many encounters in life, including relations between states, can be shown to be variations on the Iterated Prisoner's Dilemma. Does one cooperate or compete for best results? When two parties meet for the first time the temptation to compete is high, in the hope that the other side will choose to cooperate. As the encounter is repeated a few times, it becomes clear that cooperation could lead to benefits at the expense of the banker. A constant state of competition is costly to both players; third parties – the banker, the public, and other states – benefit more in that case. Hence, when considered in purely selfish terms, it is often best for the two parties to cooperate at the expense of others. However, Game Theory defines two key requirements for spontaneous cooperation to emerge:

- There has to be a high probability of continuing future encounters, otherwise the possibility of quick once-and-for-all profit becomes a more rational policy. For cooperation to evolve without outside compulsion, the future should cast 'a large enough shadow onto the present' (Axelrod 1984: 20).
- The two sides should be able to recognise each other and recall actions in previous encounters (Axelrod 1984: 24). In this context, Game Theory recognises *reputation* and *communication* as significant factors in determining the nature of interactions between conscious partners, including nations.

Game Theory asserts that rewards do not have to be symmetric, or even of the same type, for spontaneous cooperation to emerge. For a strategy to be stable over time, a player should have only one aim: to do as well as possible irrespective of how well the other player is doing (Axelrod 1984: 24). Contrary to classic mercantilist ideology, therefore, relations between states, and of course between individuals, are not always of the zero-sum variety, where a gain by one side inevitably means a loss by the other.

Sensible regulation

In consequence, Game Theory advances practical ideas that are of pertinence to development efforts. For example, as variety and freedom for internal elements to interact and cooperate are essential for optimal performance by a Complex Adaptive System, Game Theory shows that stringent controls, by national governments and international regimes say, are counterproductive. The obsessive inclination for dictators to enforce total compliance is revealed as costly and irrational. Basically, the price of enforcing compulsion is routinely too high for it to be an evolutionarily stable strategy. Sustainable control could be achieved more efficiently by adopting rules that 'elicit compliance from a majority of the governed', because they 'find it profitable to obey most of the time' (Axelrod 1984: 150). Game Theory, in that way, throws light on the poor performance of dictators, but it also questions the heavy-handed attempts by the USA and its allies, the IMF, WTO, and the World Bank, to impose global cooperation on all nations.

International life as it is

The global system presents a hierarchy that stretches from a dominant hegemon through other powerful states to the weakest and poorest. Game Theory suggests that one side in an encounter would always compete if it were known that the other side has no option but to cooperate. Even in cases of mutual cooperation, the rewards might well be asymmetrical. All things being equal, a powerful nation faced with the possibility of interaction with a weaker nation would compete and become richer and more dominant. In addition, a prosperous state has more scope for interactions with partners at the same level in the global hierarchy. In this case mutual cooperation is more profitable for both sides. Room for manoeuvre for the weaker nation, by contrast, is strictly limited. Morality, fairness and ideology have little to do with this inevitable scenario; it is rational and predictable. Nevertheless, weaker nations are not completely powerless. They could adopt strategies, as I propose in Chapter 10, which would materially improve their performance in international encounters.

Reputations: good and bad

Reputations and labels feature prominently in Game Theory, but they also play a major role in international encounters. Knowledge of how each side might behave and, even more importantly, what they are capable of doing affects future interactions. Powerful countries strive to acquire a reputation for toughness, to ensure voluntary compliance by other players, without the need to 'fight' on each and every occasion.

They can then elect to compete while inducing others to cooperate, and thereby gain better rewards. Such a reputation can be acquired by soundly, and very publicly, defeating a weaker miscreant, as demonstrated by American continual agitation against numerous apparently highly dangerous 'enemies' such as Cuba and Iran, although in practice they are hardly worth the effort as potential threats. An elaborate edifice of weighty ideological and moral disagreements is often erected to justify action and to brand enemies with negative labels while extolling the supposed virtues of supporters.

Leading powers favour voluntary compliance with their wishes from most nations to avoid the need for overt compulsion. In that effort nothing is left to chance, including the use in sport, culture, fashion and history of *memes*, described by Dawkins as replicators of cultural transmission (Dawkins 1989). British 'fairness' in sport was a meme adopted for a long period to sell the idea that Britons are uniquely fair in all their dealings. The tactic, when used effectively, allows the countries concerned to compete while encouraging others to cooperate. Israel's masterly application of this means of acquiring a good reputation is a classic illustration of the power of that tool. Before and after the creation of the Jewish state in 1948 it managed to break every rule in the book without having to suffer any penalties worth the name.

TO RECAPITULATE

I maintain that a paradigm shift in development is necessary, and unavoidable, to enable nations to make more effective progress. As a prelude to later discussion, the present chapter described Complexity and Complex Adaptive Systems. The next chapter will reveal how linear beliefs in the practice of development have shaped local and international actions for more than fifty years. It is helpful, however, to bring together the main features presented so far:

- Complexity is a characteristic attribute of systems that present a mix of local chaos and global stability. On the whole, average Complexity tends to increase over time, and systems with the highest Complexity stand to make the most gain.
- Self-organisation, the ability of a Complex Adaptive System to achieve global stability and order without external intervention, arises from regulated local interactions by a large number of lightly connected internal elements.

- Internal variety allows Complex Adaptive Systems to survive while they adapt to changes in their habitat. Evolution in this case is a slow uphill marathon rather than a sprint to the nearest summit. It has no beginning and no end.
- Predictability in Complex Adaptive Systems is limited to global patterns rather than the chaotic local details. Specific causes cannot be linked to particular effects, and minor disturbance can produce insignificant changes or major transformations, but it is not possible to predict the outcome in advance.
- In a nation, the internal elements are egoistic persons, working individually or as groups. They have to be free to interact and capable of doing so for a nation to acquire stable, but evolving, patterns of progress; no interactions, no progress.
- And finally, it is possible for states to avoid conflict and gain spontaneous cooperation from others at home and abroad, but for that purpose the state must abide by essentially simple rules defined by Game Theory.

It is worth stressing again that 'Complex' and 'Complexity' as used here do not mean difficult or complicated. The terms apply to systems that are entirely different from the familiar linear systems encountered in Newtonian physics. These systems require different methods of analysis and management from those applicable to linear systems. The discovery that there are these two vastly dissimilar categories of systems imposes a fundamental requirement: before we rush in with solutions to problems, we have to determine first the nature of the system in question. I am prompted to labour this point somewhat in anticipation of a natural question: what is the use of pointing out the obvious, as we all know development is complex? Forthcoming sections will demonstrate why it is essential to discuss the 'obvious'.

NOTES

1. Scientists themselves helped to foster that belief. Pierre Simon Laplace (1749–1827), the French scientist and author of *Celestial Mechanics*, asserted that the universe is totally deterministic. However, Hawking (1988: 53) advanced reasons why Laplace's hopes were misplaced.
2. For a philosophical discussion of the process of transformation, including the switch from linear to nonlinear thinking, see Ferguson (1983). Hawking (1988: 1–14), on the other hand, provides an insightful technical

analysis of the way scientific beliefs and methods have changed through the ages.

3. The Uncertainty Principle advanced by Heisenberg had a pivotal impact on the future course of scientific research. For a review of developments in physics, see Davies (1987) and Peat (1991).

4. Prigogine was the first to use that expression (Nicolis and Prigogine 1989). See also Kauffman (1996: 21).

5. My principal aim is to consider development as a Complex Adaptive System and for that purpose I have to acquaint the reader with the basic concepts associated with nonlinearity without getting too embroiled in the minutiae. Those wishing to read more about nonlinear dynamics may consult Nicolis and Prigogine (1989), Coveney and Highfield (1996) and Kauffman (1993, 1996). In addition, Waldrop (1994) and Lewin (1997) present an excellent general introduction to Complexity.

6. See Arthur (1990, 1994), Waldrop (1994), Day (1994), Lewin (1997), Byrne (1998), Ormerod (1994, 1998) and Jervis (1999).

7. See also Elliot and Kiel (1997).

8. Hierarchy in science is discussed fully by Gell-Mann (1994: 109).

9. Readers may wish to read more about attractors and Byrne (1998) is an excellent point to start. Attractors are also dealt with in more technical detail in Coveney and Highfield (1996) and Kauffman (1996).

10. Obviously, there are fewer attractors than states. The number of attractors is roughly N, the number of elements in the network, divided by 2.71828, the 'e' of natural logarithms (Kauffman 1996: 82).

11. A full analysis of dynamic order and regularity is outside the scope of this book, but several authors have covered the field comprehensively. See, for instance, Kauffman (1996: 82).

12. Gregor Johann Mendel (1822–1884) did his best to overcome that drawback by studying fast-growing garden peas in 1865 to develop his laws of heredity.

13. Ray defined local rules for interaction and added a killer 'reaper' to enable fitter organisms to monopolise the available resources. The entities soon mutated into a diversity of new creatures complete with parasites. A form of community life eventually appeared (Coveney and Highfield 1996: 253).

14. Niles Eldredge of the American Museum of Natural History and Stephen Gould of Harvard University put the concept of punctuated equilibrium forward in 1972. I should point out that although the idea is generally accepted it has had its critics as well (Coveney and Highfield 1991; Dawkins 1991).

15. For a survey of the rise and fall of powers in the last five hundred years, see Kennedy (1989).

16. Gell-Mann (1994: 17) gives an illustration drawn from computer science. A binary message string in the form 001001001 and so on is highly compressible: 001 repeated so many times. A string of random 0s and 1s is incompressible: to describe it, it is necessary to repeat the whole

string. The former string represents a state of perfect order while the latter denotes chaos; an information string that describes a Complex System fits somewhere between the two extremes.

17. There is a large measure of common sense in the way Complex Adaptive Systems operate. For instance, it is natural for rich individuals to become richer, and for their offspring to do just as well. They are able to invest, and moreover they can afford to invest in risky businesses that might bring higher rewards. They have a larger network of contacts that enables them to be better informed about opportunities and risks. In short the odds are stacked in their favour.

18. For a technical discussion, including predictability in political modelling, see Kravtsov and Kadtke (1996).

19. The turn of the tide became apparent on 2 July 1997 when the Thai currency collapsed and had to be uncoupled from the US dollar (*Sunday Times*, 31 August 1997). The headline chosen on that occasion was 'Asia Crashes'. On 2 November 1997 the headline changed to 'Ten Days That Shook the World'. By 11 January 1998 the paper described the crisis as the 'Asian Plague' and followed that on 8 February 1998 with 'Japan, Asia's Sickest Man'.

20. References on the topic of elites and hierarchies are plentiful. See, for instance, Marger (1981), Bottomore (1993) and Lerner et al. (1996).

21. These phenotypes are themselves Complex Adaptive Systems. For instance, governments handpick individuals to form committees or so-called independent enquiries in the hope that the decisions will be to the governments' liking. Sometimes that policy works. However, once members begin to interact, unexpected outcomes often emerge, much to the consternation of the government concerned.

22. Informed speculation on the role of individuals in major historic events is given in Ferguson (1998).

FIVE

LINEAR RECIPES FOR
A COMPLEX WORLD

When victory in World War II became certain, the Allies decided the time had come to plan for the post-war period. There was much goodwill and idealism in the air, but the victors also wished to collect the spoils of war. In particular, the tussle over world hegemony between Britain and USA had to be brought to a formal conclusion. Meetings were held in the USA in 1944 at Bretton Woods, New Hampshire, to settle these issues, and the aftermath was a global system with 'four legs': the UN, the General Agreement on Tariffs and Trade (GATT), the World Bank and the International Monetary Fund (IMF). Although much was expected of the UN and GATT, in the context of development the Bretton Woods four-legged system hobbled 'along on the last two only' for many years (Allen and Thomas 1995: 224; Singer 1989: 8).

The Bretton Woods Conference laid the foundations for the linear paradigm that has determined attitudes to development ever since. Clear cause-and-effect relationships were taken for granted, and the process was implicitly assumed to be deterministic, orderly and predictable. Development was to be exported to less fortunate nations by means of recipes of universal applicability devised primarily by experts from abroad, and through aid, loans and expansion of free trade. Economic development, it was said, will ultimately lead to human development. This chapter is essentially a thumbnail audit of the outcome from the above decisions, but the main purpose here is to show that linear remedies and management styles were used to address nonlinear issues.

ESSENTIAL LOCAL VARIETY

Up to the present, the pursuit of development has relied heavily on analysis of the performance of so-called developed countries in the belief that there is an ultimate state of development that has been attained by these countries and a set of magic rules that enabled them to do so. Efforts were devoted, therefore, to the setting down of universal prescriptions to be adopted by one and all, with the laudable aim of helping those at the back of the trail to catch up with, or at least move closer to, the leaders. Variety and innovation are discouraged within that linear framework. However, as demonstrated earlier, development presents unmistakable parallels with the mode of behaviour of Complex Adaptive Systems in which variety is an essential element in survival and effective evolution.

Depth, in the context of Complex Adaptive Systems, implies the build-up of numerous layers of variety and redundancy over a long time. Comparison between England as it was a few centuries ago, say, and some of today's developing countries reveals a huge gap in attribute. When Charles I (1600–1649), for example, decided to fight the rebels in Scotland in 1639, 'Lords Saye and Brooke staged a damaging public protest against the non-parliamentary expedition' used by him to wage that war. There were many other challenges to the king's personal rule. At the heart of the debate were common law guarantees of personal property rights (Ferguson 1998: 97). Mengistu, for one, could not have had such an easy ride had he lived in seventeenth-century England rather than late-twentieth-century Ethiopia. His exercise of arbitrary power inflicted great harm while Ethiopians watched from the sidelines, and variety, as in the case of many other nations, was minimised. In contrast, depth allowed Britain, as a system, to accumulate sufficient diversity and flexibility to make it a better evolutionarily stable strategy.

Damaging lack of variety

When variety is minimal, most individuals, or nations, are equally suited to one set of conditions. That might not be disastrous if conditions remained unchanged, but it is abundantly clear that they are in permanent flux due to internal factors and activities by other coevolving people or nations. Sameness in this case could be positively harmful, as it does not permit the system to respond flexibly to new circumstances. The fitness landscape is reduced to a flatland that has no high spots to denote good fitness by *some* elements of the system for this or that set of conditions. If the environment were to alter radically, the averaged elements, perfectly at home in the flatlands, might not survive the shock. Britain, to continue the earlier example, laboriously accumulated variety after centuries of, at times painful, experimentation. Ethiopia, by contrast, shed most of its variety after many decades of domestic tyranny.

The answer to nations seeking development seems obvious; simply copy Britain or the USA in every detail. But life is not that accommodating. If variety were to have any meaning then it must be locally based. Technically, it is pointless to compete on someone else's fitness landscape. The diversity that a nation requires would have to be provided by internal elements that have differing levels of fitness to conditions that are relevant to that nation, and not to other countries. This point is of critical importance. As outlined in the next section, there is what is in effect an ongoing project to replace local diversity by global sameness. That drift is distrusted intuitively, but there are clear – scientific, if you will – reasons why it is a harmful policy.

IMPOSED GLOBAL CONFORMITY

The hope that in decades to come most people would acquire lifestyles modelled on a few leading nations is an absurd notion. Local circumstances are, and will continue to be, different from the global ideal, which is generally assumed to mirror conditions in the leading industrialised countries. If variety were designed out of the system, the institutions and populations of countries that depart from the ideal – in effect most of humankind for the foreseeable future – would suffer badly. It is meaningless to talk of a sensible process of learning, adaptation and survival under these circumstances: if the developed countries were to catch a cold, other nations would go down with pneumonia. This is not said lightly; history offers numerous examples of relatively minor fluctuations in the leading economies that ended in near-catastrophes in far-off lands. Positive feedback is a powerful lever on the world stage and local variety is one of the few defences available for nations to take the capricious challenges it brings in their stride. Basically, it is not possible to introduce variety on demand.[1]

The push for globalisation

The intentions behind the efforts being made by nations at the top of the global hierarchy to impose sameness through globalisation are clear. In line with Game Theory, they cooperate with their peers and compete against others to receive best rewards. To that end, they select the peaks on the fitness landscape for which they are most suited and then set out to re-engineer the world accordingly. It is wrong to think of this as being good or bad: it is rational and effective, and history confirms that it is not a recent innovation. For instance, France, Italy, Holland and Britain succeeded in acquiring concessions, known appropriately as the *Capitulations*, from the Ottoman Empire in the sixteenth century (Hourani 1991: 274). There was serious intent behind the imposition of the *Capitulations*. In Egypt, for instance, 100,000 foreigners were exempt from payment of taxes, but more importantly Egypt had to suspend local practices in favour of rules defined by the European powers. These privileges were only abolished in 1937 at the Montreux Convention (Vatikiotis 1991: 86, 323). The Ottomans, as happened elsewhere, were made to dance to Europe's tune; representatives of foreign powers assumed an ever-increasing role in steering the Ottoman political economy, local variety was replaced by imported methods that had little or nothing to do with local conditions, and the rest is history.

Asia was made to cooperate in much the same way, although the process was easier here than it was in the case of the relatively stronger Ottoman Empire. European enterprises known as the East India Companies were created to integrate and intensify European political, military and economic power abroad. Queen Elizabeth granted the charter for the British East India Company in 1600, which then effectively ruled India for over two centuries, and the Dutch and Danish equivalents appeared on the scene a little later. These companies wiped out all local diversity as being backward and unacceptable, and imposed their own unified model on the countries they administered. India is only now beginning to emerge slowly from that straitjacket.

History repeats itself

Globalisation and control by the leading powers and their institutions are not new arrivals, therefore; the difference between then and now is only a matter of scale and style. Methods used in the past are not essentially different from those employed at present, as exemplified by the Structural Stabilisation and Adjustment Programmes advocated by the IMF and World Bank. Principally, the leading powers seek to impose one common fitness landscape in which they are best equipped to occupy the summits.

Essentially, weaker nations are deprived of the essential preconditions for their Complex Adaptive Systems to function optimally. It should be pointed out again here that the governments in these countries themselves do not strive to provide appropriate local conditions for their own nations to perform effectively. Nonetheless, it is undeniable that the global regimes, and their masters, have exerted, and do exert, a negative influence on the development of nations they were ostensibly set up to help.

THE UNITED NATIONS

When the United Nations (UN) was created, idealists saw the it as the obvious world venue for setting and policing equitable international economic and political practices. After more than fifty years of disillusionment many believe it has not fulfilled that hope. Criticism is not fair though; the aspirations that lie behind the concept were founded in a linear frame of reference unsuited to a Complex world. Command-and-control from the top, no matter how well intentioned, could not impose deterministic order on all nations. More to the point, the setup was based on another equally ambitious objective that was at odds with the idealists' aspirations: to organise the world in accordance with the wishes of a small group of powerful countries.

Predictably, therefore, the structure chosen for the UN in 1945 reflected the balance of power that existed at the time. A Security Council of fifteen members dominates the organisation, but the five permanent members, USA, Britain, France, China and Russia, each have in addition the all-important power to veto any proposal that does not appeal to them. The General Assembly, on the other hand, includes all member states, each having one vote. Normally, it meets once a year and the proceedings involve in the main speeches by heads of governments beamed at their domestic audiences. In practice, a nation, or even a group of nations, would find it most difficult to advance a proposal through the UN that did not meet with the approval of the elite.

US interests come first

Boutros Boutros-Ghali, the sixth secretary-general of the UN, paid a heavy price in the mid-1990s when he seemed to challenge the dominant role played by the USA at the UN (Meisler 1995: 180). The collapse of the USSR made the position on that front even clearer than before but he misunderstood, or chose to ignore, the signs. The weakness of the UN was further revealed by its fruitless efforts to effect a settlement in Bosnia through its peacekeeping mission. A solution was found, three years and $3.5 billion later, only when the USA decided that the time was ripe for action.

For the moment, world affairs are viewed at the UN through the prism of America's interests and those of its close allies. US actions are legitimised through the UN, and that procedure is now incorporated, whenever possible, into America's rules of engagement for all overt operations. The cardinal point here concerns the imposition on a large number of diverse member states of a single viewpoint on security, politics, economics and development that perceives diversity as a challenge to world order. Control is exercised through international regimes, including the UN itself, that embody 'the interests and values of the dominant Western states, most obviously the USA as the hegemonic capitalist power' (Allen and Thomas 1995: 258).

The collapse of the USSR coincided with a worsening situation for the so-called Third World. The choice of this term to describe a large group of diverse nations was a product of the schism that divided the world after World War II into the First World, Western capitalism, and the Second World, Eastern communism. The official end of the Cold War in late 1990 did more than just make the Third World designation meaningless; it robbed that group of nations of what little independence and power they might have enjoyed at the UN. The conflict between East and West was accompanied for a while by a conflict between North, led by the USA and Europe, and South, championed by the non-aligned nations, but these groupings lost their significance in a new world order in which the USA is the undisputed leader.

Not surprisingly, Amin commented that 'the present age is one of disillusionment', but then he did not give the previous period top marks either (Amin 1990: 1). Other scholars do not challenge his assessment of past achievements. Decades of efforts made by the Third World to focus attention on its urgent development priorities and to move the medium of negotiation away from the World Bank and the IMF and to the UN did not result in many tangible improvements.[2] And since 1990 the situation has become more difficult with the shift of emphasis to the redevelopment of Eastern Europe.

UN focus on safer topics

Perforce, the UN has concentrated on uncontroversial tasks, as witnessed by its work as a relief agency at times of extreme hardship, and its role as a clearing house for issues that command ready global support. In that context, its various agencies, such as the World Health Organisation (WHO), the UN Educational, Scientific and Cultural Organisation (UNESCO), and the UN International Children's Emergency Fund (UNICEF), undertake excellent work that would otherwise be sorely missed.

In pursuing its advocacy role, the UN has adopted the format of 'world summits' in recent years, but in general observers view the summits held so far as having been good at rhetoric but short on results, as amply demonstrated by discussions on climate change.[3] The 1992 Rio Earth Summit did not yield many concrete results, although it succeeded in linking development and the environment and in establishing the UN Commission on Sustainable Development (Brown et al. 1997: 5). Those attending the Berlin conference, a follow-up to the Rio event, concluded that achievement of the moderate targets agreed in Rio for reducing carbon dioxide emissions would have to wait longer than the year 2000. The situation remained more or less the same in late 2000 when The Hague climate change conference ended in a shambles. America, responsible for a quarter of all emissions, simply refused to agree with the rest (*New Statesman,* 4 December 2000). The new Bush administration then declared, in March 2001, that the Kyoto accord on climate change is dead and buried. In Game Theory terms, the USA is able to compete in this issue area, to secure higher rewards, rather than cooperate. The UN hardly featured as an interested party in most of the discussions associated with this debacle.

Square pegs for round holes

Perceived shortcomings of the UN stem from the misunderstanding mentioned at the beginning of this section; as a presumed agency for change it is a linear response to Complex phenomena. However, the UN was set up in the first instance to assist in creating a global environment that served the interests of elite nations, and in that guise the UN did quite well, but it also went on to fulfil other tasks that did not cut across its principal role. That is the function of most, if not all, international regimes: they have a primary role and a secondary role and the two are kept well apart.

In over fifty years, the UN has demonstrated beyond question the futility of attempting to place a functional organisation at the top of the international pyramid for the purpose of handing down recipes of practical utility. An obvious question springs to mind: why could the USA do what the UN seems unable to do? The answer is equally simple. First, the USA has, and is prepared to display and use, massive military, political and economic force. Second, the USA, as the reigning hegemon, is pursuing a simple aim: to derive the best benefits for the USA first and last. Reductionist methods aided by massive clout might well work here, for a while at any rate. The USA, however, is not managing the whole global system, although it fondly thinks it is doing just that. Linear methods are powerless in this latter task; hence the world as a whole will not do better because of US leadership, or any other leadership for that matter. On the contrary, according to the rules of Game Theory humankind at large can confidently be expected to do worse.

In short, the UN, and other international regimes, serve the interests of the hegemonic in the first instance. It has found a safe niche for itself within that setup, but has had to ignore the original declarations that accompanied its creation; they were essentially window-dressing. That applies in particular to the topic of development. It operates as a facilitator rather than initiator of change in accordance with the wishes of the dominant powers. Clearly, that leaves the field open for these powers to do what pleases them, but as explained in Chapter 10 other nations are not powerless to navigate their way through that, largely inevitable, maelstrom.

THE WORLD BANK

The inaugural meeting of the World Bank and the IMF in 1946 left no one in any doubt that the USA was in the driving seat. The USA chooses presidents for both organisations. For good measure, the World

Bank is located in a building owned by the State Department, and 'the US reviews each loan proposal in detail'. Not content with that level of cooperation, 'the Reagan administration in the summer of 1983 had a "spy" software program secretly installed on the Bank computers' to make sure the US government missed absolutely nothing (Caufield 1996: 197).

The leading powers have insisted all along that the IMF and the World Bank, as opposed to the UN, should be the principal media for considering global economic and development affairs. That stance is wholly natural as these powers hold all the cards on these international regimes. Despite that vote of confidence, or maybe because of it, both agencies have met with constant criticism since their early days. In late September and early October 1998, concern that they are not succeeding in their tasks became official when heads of state, significantly led by those from the USA and Britain, met in New York ostensibly to consider ways of improving future performance. Needless to say no discernible change has come out of these meetings.

The reason for the above apparent inaction is plain to see; the IMF and the World Bank are there to serve the purposes of the leading powers. This is not a cynical viewpoint. What idealism there was at the end of the war turned quickly into realism in the hurly-burly of the Cold War and the successive economic shocks that affected Western governments and businesses. Survival of the capitalist system imposed obvious constraints on what could reasonably be done to help poorer nations. Furthermore, the enormity of the task involved in developing the rest of humankind became progressively clearer to the advanced industrial countries that were expected to foot the bill. Even if one were to accept the original proclamations at face value, the creation of the World Bank was founded on a fundamental misunderstanding of what development is all about, as I argue throughout this book.

A history of experimentation

The World Bank was initially intended as a source of long-term finance for European countries, but that changed quickly when the Marshall Plan was launched with substantially higher funding. Its interest turned to so-called developing economies. The history of the World Bank suggests that it was not entirely, or even mainly, disingenuous in pursuing that task. For the most part it tried to help countries to develop, but that activity was seen within a canvas that stuck largely to economic features, and a rigid viewpoint for that matter that appealed to the USA and its cohorts. Within these parameters, the Bank experimented, mainly in vain, with various policies which were at times diametrically opposed to each other. Significantly, these policy gyrations also demonstrated the World Bank's rigid hierarchical structure and the powerful impact its successive presidents had on its policy direction.

The first president, Eugene Meyer, lasted only six months. He left because he could not gain unquestioned control over the organisation. The second, John McCloy, who brought his team with him from Wall Street, received assurances that 'he, and not the board, would run the Bank' (Caufield 1996: 52). Under McCloy, the Bank restricted its lending to reliable clients only, in other words to European countries, until the Marshall Plan made that role obsolete. The Bank then shifted its attention to developing countries, but that was not to McCloy's liking and he resigned after only two years in office.

Under Eugene Black, the next president, the Bank continued to lend money for infrastructure projects mainly.[4] Inadvertently, however, Black resurrected the idea of the *Capitulations* imposed by Europe on the Ottoman Empire back in the sixteenth century: he insisted that borrowers should implement wide-ranging 'reforms'. That dictum was to give the Bank's officials, in later years, power to determine the internal policies of supposedly sovereign states. Several authors documented a veritable litany of blunders in that context (Rich 1994). When Black left in 1963 he handed over an organisation to Woods that was highly profitable. However, while total gross domestic product for the developing countries was growing, their foreign debts were increasing three times faster. That was an inevitable consequence of the tendency by the Bank and its backers to measure success by how much it lent, irrespective of the consequences.

The activity made perfect sense, for the creditors. Countries borrowed money for infrastructure projects that were then designed and built by firms from the lending nations. Most of the money went back to its source, but naturally the loans had to be paid back in foreign currency and, hence, debtor countries were forced to export, almost at any price. In short, the lenders could not lose and the borrowers could not win, an unambiguous illustration of Game Theory at work. The fast inflow of large sums of money had another unavoidable result: profiteering, and corruption on a vast scale by the elites in the debtor countries. Tales of the billions of dollars that were deposited in foreign banks by heads of governments have been reported well by authors and newspapers and do not merit further elaboration here. Reckless lending to impoverished nations, however, was destined to end in tears: in time structural stabilisation and adjustment programmes, by the IMF and the World Bank respectively, became inevitable to squeeze more out of the debtor nations, with drastic consequences for the populations affected (Allen and Thomas 1995: 233).

George Woods, president from 1963 to 1968, admitted in his last month in office that 'waste, inefficiency and even dishonesty have all too often deflected resources from development', and acknowledged that development, no matter how well funded, was not working out as intended (Caufield 1996: 95). He handed the reins to Robert McNamara, who promptly decreed that Bank activities up to his time had had little impact on development. Predictably, his solution was to lend even more to developing countries. By the usual yardstick of the Bank he succeeded spectacularly; during his term of office the Bank pumped just under $6 billion in loans annually. By any other standard he failed miserably. The gap between rich and poor within the developing countries and that separating these nations from the advanced economies widened significantly.

McNamara did not last long once the debt crisis came into full bloom. As Caufield (1996: 144) commented, Alden 'Tom' Clausen, the next president, introduced a new credo to the Bank: supply-side economics, 'a version of trickle-down, the economic theory that McNamara had declared a failure ten years before'. As part of the new strategy, Clausen downgraded the previous emphasis on poverty. The policies of the Bank were thus changed at a stroke, and billions of people learnt what it was like to be structurally adjusted. It is fair to say that, after some fifteen years of turmoil and billions of dollars in loans, the new experiment did not meet with unqualified acclaim either. On the other hand, the World Bank (1996: 11) argued that 'just a decade ago, only about 1 billion people lived in economies that could be called market-oriented; today, the figure is around 5 billion.' That after all was the main aim it seems, but that did not materially improve conditions for the billions whose economies were stabilised and adjusted. Undeniably, however, the policies of the World Bank and the IMF did bring the debt crisis under some control to the satisfaction of the bankers.

Barber Conable was appointed president of the Bank in 1986, and, as befits a new leader, he felt a reorganisation was in order. His method was simple: all employees had to reapply for their posts in the Bank. Selection was then undertaken in layers down the hierarchy, each person appointing those working under him or her. A Bank well known for cronyism turned overnight into an army of confirmed yes-men. Compliance in hierarchies is indeed acquired through rewards and penalties, and having or not having a highly paid job with massive fringe benefits is the ultimate lever in that process. Conable left in 1991 after five years without having achieved much, to be followed by Lewis Preston, another banker, who also left little behind. Later, the 1980s became known as development's 'lost decade'.

James Wolfensohn took over in 1995, and promptly launched a critical self-appraisal of the Bank's practices and focus. On past evidence, substantial realignment was unlikely, but there was a feeling that something more than the usual rhetoric might be in the offing. Certainly the Bank's 1996 Annual Report mentioned social topics as often as economic matters. It pointed out, rather bravely, that under its Articles of Agreement 'the Bank cannot allow itself to be influenced by the political character of a member country'. In its overview of activities, the Report kicked off with the statement that 'poverty reduction and sustainable development remain the central objectives of the World Bank', a shift from Clausen's position and back to McNamara's 'rhetoric'!

A strictly linear view of development

Judged by its policies and actions, the World Bank views the process of development as a deterministic linear phenomenon in which causes and effects are linked and detailed prediction is feasible. Once the 'appropriate' facts are gathered and analysed, problems are carved up into chunks, and solutions, largely without local deviations, are put forward that would lead in a matter of a few years to the desired end. Despite changes in emphasis at the edges, Bank officials never managed to shrug this questionable practice off and it remains therefore one of the most criticised aspects of the Bank's work. Significantly, the IMF faces similar criticisms. James Morgan, BBC economics correspondent, cited the IMF's 'one-size-for-all' policy as the main bone of contention between the IMF and its detractors (*BBC News*, 17 May 1998). More telling, Joseph Stiglitz (2000), chief economist of the World Bank from 1996 to 1999, mounted a blistering attack on the

IMF and its prepackaged recipes and methods in which he left little doubt about his views of the failings of that organisation.[5]

Emphasis on large infrastructure projects, itself a product of linear thinking, has been equally damaging to the World Bank and its reputation. Faith in the inevitability of takeoff and trickle-down that would follow capital investment and economic growth was unshakeable in the face of compelling evidence to the contrary. That obsession had disastrous effects on many nations, but it was also a godsend to consultants, suppliers and construction firms on both sides of the divide. In UNICEF's words, 'the rich got the loans and the poor got the debts' (Adams 1991: 160).

'Capitulations' of the twentieth century

Structural stabilisation and adjustment programmes, much favoured by the IMF and World Bank, attracted equally vehement criticism. For a long period the Bank estimated that conversion to a fully fledged market economy might require no more than five loans and could be completed within three to five years. After years of spectacular failure a realisation finally gained ground that life is not that straightforward. In a book published for the Bank, Zucherman (Thomas et al. 1991: 263) concluded that the efforts to effect transformations of this type 'have taken longer to implement and have proved far more arduous than originally expected'.

How long and how much? Turkey, as one example, was in a worse position after almost a decade of adjustment than it was before the process was started (Caufield 1996: 148). Its financial and economic problems continued to make the headlines in 2001. Time and money might not necessarily be the deciding influences, as factors such as who is leading the change, how, and for what purpose, might be just as important. It does seem somewhat improbable that a single process comprising a few specific steps could meet the diverse needs of all nations (Allen and Thomas 1995: 221). If nations, and their political economies, were viewed as Complex Adaptive Systems, that conclusion would become self-evident.

Predictable failure

Well-documented critiques, such as that presented by Rich (1994), have come to the conclusion that the World Bank has failed in its declared role as an agency for development. In consequence, annual meetings of the World Bank and the IMF have become occasions for demonstrations that attract representatives from almost every country and social group that these organisations were supposedly set up to help. Rich (1994: 90) reported that at the 1988 Berlin meeting 'the greatest number of police since the Second World War – some 17,000 from all over Germany – were deployed to guard against potentially violent demonstrations and possible terrorism.' In recent years the protests have become even more vociferous. Various explanations have been put forward for this level of disapproval but none is completely convincing. Puchala and Hopkins observed, for instance, that 'each regime has an elite who are the principal actors within it'. They went on to point out that regimes 'buttress, legitimise, and sometimes institutionalise international patterns of dominance, subordination, accumulation, and exploitation ... in general regimes favour the interests of the strong' (Crane and Amawi 1991: 266).

Admittedly, vested interests play a role in defining the policies of the World Bank. Nevertheless, it is also clear that the Bank has experimented with different strategies in seeking to improve its performance. Hints at a conspiracy by powerful states pose a nagging doubt: how could thousands of highly qualified individuals spend half a century and billions of dollars on numerous schemes without, at least inadvertently, transforming the lives of their clients for the better? Modest progress has been made here and there but the original basic ills are still there, and some have become more acute. And is it really in the best interests of the leading powers to inhibit the development of poorer nations so thoroughly? I doubt it. We come back to the paradox I defined in Chapter 1: why has the World Bank failed in its mission and why did it not succeed in changing course for the better?

Branding the World Bank's performance as a failure misses the point; achievement was simply immaterial. It is difficult to say whether the World Bank was a help or a hindrance, and that signifies a more radical cause for the Bank's lacklustre performance. One rational conclusion insinuates itself, almost irresistibly: the World Bank did not succeed, and could not have succeeded, because it unknowingly limited its experimentation strictly to models and ideas conceived within a linear frame of reference. Adopting such a standpoint for a Complex issue area such as development was destined to produce indifferent results. Unable to see what was really wrong, friends thought the Bank was simply not pulling its weight, and enemies thought it was incompetent, corrupt or both.

The above conclusion is not as audacious as it might appear at first glance. The evidence presented here amply supports it, but leaving that aside others have come to similar conclusions although they might not have approached the topic from the same angle. Rich (1994: 200), for instance, made much the same observations when he drew attention to the Cartesian roots that fed almost all activities undertaken by the World Bank from the start. The Epilogue to Caufield's book on the World Bank contains references that resonate strongly with an explanation of the Bank's shortcomings based on Complex Systems theory, although I hasten to add that she did not mention this theory specifically (Caufield 1996: 330). Chambers (1997), coming from yet another direction, refers to 'chaos and complexity theory' explicitly. More to the point, research work by the World Bank in recent years shows early but distinct signs of an intuitive, rather than explicit, shift to a Complex Systems viewpoint of development. I will return to this topic in Chapter 10.

SHACKLED IN DEBT

It is not unreasonable to assume that incurring debts might be inevitable in the early stages of development. Sadly, experience over a long period of time suggests that debt is a two-edged sword at best. Indebtedness, in line with other socioeconomic activities, exhibits distinct signs of nonlinearity and game playing. The selfish desires of elites and egoistic individuals in the debtor and creditor nations loom large, and the wish by those in the driving seat to induce others to cooperate while they compete is all too evident. In short, indebtedness is a chronic condition; once hooked a nation stands to pay a heavy price almost indefinitely. Admittedly, acute episodes that grab the limelight come and go but that is only because the activity follows the usual punctuated equilibrium path of periods of relative stability interspersed by major upheavals.

A permanent feature of the global system

As elsewhere, the details in this topic are unpredictable and in practice unimportant, but the overall patterns are regular and predictable. In essence, indebtedness is not a twentieth-century innovation. In ancient Greece, city-states defaulted on debts owed to the temple of Delos (UNICEF 1999: 28). The history of the debts of the Ottoman Empire should be made compulsory reading for all governments seeking loans from abroad. Better still, it should be made compulsory reading for their unwitting nations. The story is worth the telling as it reveals a repeating pattern that has endured to this day. By the middle of the nineteenth century the Ottoman sultans were in need of new money to maintain the lifestyle to which they had grown accustomed. At the same time Europe was replete with money in need of investment. Bankers, as at present, had a vested interest in lending money and the sultans welcomed them with open arms. More to the point, European powers were eager to move in on the decaying Ottoman Empire. The stage was set for what is now a thoroughly familiar operation.

The Ottomans acquired debts on a huge scale and on suitably crippling terms; in one instance 'of a nominal amount of 256 million Turkish pounds (the Turkish pound was equivalent to £0.9 sterling) [the Ottomans] received only 139 millions, the remainder being discounted' (Hourani 1991: 282). The rest of the story followed modern lines through and through; by 1875 the Ottoman Empire was unable to meet payments of interest and principal, and by 1881 a Public Debt Administration representing the European powers was set up and promptly imposed its own version of structural stabilisation and adjustment programmes on the Ottomans. The *Capitulations*, imposed on the Ottomans in the sixteenth century, were only a dress rehearsal.

Egypt followed an identical path. Muhammad Ali (1769–1849), an Albanian dictator who came to Egypt in 1801 with an expeditionary force sent by the Ottomans to fight the French, created a dynasty that lasted until the 1952 revolution. His successors, 'Abbas, Said and Isma'il decided to modernise, or more precisely to Europeanise, Egypt by borrowing from Europe. Isma'il, who ruled from 1862 to 1879, was forced in the end to sell his country's shares in the Suez Canal to Britain for what was even then a giveaway price of £4 million. Events after that again followed their normal course leading to complete control of Egypt's internal affairs by England and, to a lesser extent, France. In 1876 an Anglo-French commission, the *Caisse de la Dette*, moved in, IMF style, to make sure payments were forthcoming, and within one year 'over 60 per cent of all Egypt's revenue went to the servicing of the national debt' (Vatikiotis 1991: 129). The loans that enriched the khedives also impoverished Egypt.

The Americas were not immune from the contagion. The states of Louisiana and Mississippi defaulted on their, mainly British, loans in 1839. That event led eventually to the formation of the Council of Foreign Bondholders in 1868. About sixty years later, the next major debt crisis cropped up when several Latin American countries defaulted as commodity prices tumbled in the wake of the Great Crash of 1929. That crisis did not attract much attention because it affected mainly private bondholders from several countries (Corbridge 1993: 25). The most recent crisis surfaced sixty years later in Latin America, but in contrast to the previous event a few powerful creditors were involved. This time the crisis engaged the attention of the global elite.

The above examples are included to highlight the significance of foreign debts as a means of control and domination and to draw attention to the near-identical sequence of events the process followed then and now. In most cases a corrupt and dictatorial elite was at hand with a mixture of good, if misguided, intentions and some not so virtuous aims. Foreign banks had vast amounts of money to invest, and large-scale projects were involved, such as the Suez Canal, accompanied by madcap schemes to develop a nation quickly into some other idealised model. And in line with more recent efforts the results were most rewarding to the elites and disastrous to the populations concerned.

From those who have least

Like it or not, moneylending is an essential feature of the capitalist system. In that context personal debt is as prevalent as state borrowing. At the time of writing, personal debt in Britain has reached record levels (over £700 billion) and has inflicted burdens on millions of vulnerable individuals and families. Political parties say much when they are in opposition about the need to bring the problem under control, but they do nothing when they assume power. Essentially, lending and borrowing are integral parts of the system.

The temptation to lend money to foreign governments is irresistible as it offers opportunities to achieve broader aims. That is where the World Bank and the IMF come in, with full support by the leading powers and their banks. However, it is quite possible that the two organisations genuinely assumed that both lenders and borrowers would benefit from the efforts to offer loans abroad. External debts of developing nations took off during the 1970s and 1980s. On the one hand, investment opportunities had to be found for oil money that was flooding the banking sector in the West. On the other hand, conventional wisdom decreed that money is the prime mover in development and borrowing was the obvious answer; just what Egypt's Khedive Isma'il thought in the second half of the nineteenth century. Lessons in development are never learnt it seems. In addition, prices of raw materials and minerals were declining, while finished goods were increasing in value. Borrowing money became virtually inevitable. To compound the problem, droughts, particularly in Africa, left the nations affected with little choice but to extend the begging bowl. And finally, and above all else, weapons were being purchased on a prodigious scale, and these were frequently financed through foreign loans. As outlined in Chapter 9, the sale of arms, and conflict in general, are a godsend to the elites on both sides of the fence.

As in ordinary everyday life, loans are offered to and sought by those least able to shoulder the consequences. Sub-Saharan Africa, the most impoverished area on Earth, has a current debt of over $200 billion. At the end of 1998, its annual debt service payments to the most prosperous countries amounted to $15.2 billion. Curiously, sub-Saharan Africa paid $1.51 in debt service to foreign lenders in 1999 for every $1.0 received in aid from abroad. And since 1996, the region has paid the IMF $1.2 billion more than it has received from the Fund.[6]

Belated and limited action

The detrimental impact of debt on the poorest nations is well understood. Belatedly, the World Bank has decided to act, possibly in response to widespread criticism and the efforts of non-governmental organisations that have campaigned ceaselessly in this field. In the fall of 1998, the World Bank and the IMF proposed the heavily indebted poor countries (HIPC) initiative. The qualification criteria for HIPC illustrate the scale of debt that these two organisations consider not too burdensome. The World Bank and the IMF in association with the debtor country undertake an assessment to determine whether it is facing 'an unsustainable debt situation after the full application of the traditional debt relief mechanisms'. The cutoff level for unsustainability is a debt-to-exports ratio of 150 per cent. Predictably, and in line with age-old traditions, the debtor country must comply with stringent 'economic reform programmes'. The World Bank estimates that the countries that might qualify for the HIPC initiative, with a net present value of public debt of about $90 billion, could have their debt reduced by half after HIPC and traditional debt relief.

The heavy burden of debt endures

The debt burden is highly significant to the well-being of a country, particularly when development is treated as a Complex Adaptive System. Clearly, repayments of previous debts and opening the door for external intervention are troublesome to any nation, but that is only half the story. For a start, servicing old debts diverts resources from basic social needs such as health, nutrition and education. In the case of Ghana, for instance, 6.0 per cent of GDP is devoted to health and education, while 7.7 per cent of GDP goes into debt service. The figures for Angola, at 6.3 per cent and 33 per cent respectively, are even more disconcerting. As discussed in Chapter 8, basic services have a marked effect on the *capability* of individuals to interact. However, the impact of debts on the proper growth of civilian society and democracy is just as detrimental, and that, as described in Chapters 7 and 9, is a decisive factor in determining the *ability* of individuals to interact in the first instance.

Odious debts

An aspect relating to the last point should be underlined here. For several reasons, the most important being the wish to prop up compliant regimes, loans are often given to dictators and militarised states. Dictators do not make a distinction between state finances and their own, and for obvious reasons they tend to give top priority to spending on the armed forces and the secret services. In short, they and their cronies pocket a good proportion of incoming grants and loans, and then proceed to acquire more money through kickbacks from arms purchases. They occasionally pass some of their 'commission' to others involved in clinching the deal at the country of origin. All too often, debts play a decisive part in inhibiting the development prospects of nations because they support repression and corruption.

Sadly, the above practices are commonplace and highly sinister. Loans given in the past to known dictatorial and corrupt regimes now account for 'one-fifth of all developing country debt' (Hanlon 1998). Creditors must have known exactly what they were doing; a new word, kleptocracy, had to be invented to describe notorious regimes such as those presided over by Mobutu in Zaïre and Marcos in the Philippines. In the case of Mobutu, the IMF gave Zaïre a substantial loan shortly after the IMF's own representative, Blumenthal, resigned having advised the Fund of his very serious misgivings about the corrupt government in that country (Payer 1991).

The practice of giving loans to dictators and military rulers does not stop at the door of the USA and the World Bank. Britain, for instance, provides generous export credits to enable foreign governments to buy British goods, especially arms (Pilger 1998: 121). Nigeria, during its long period of military dictatorships that finally bankrupted that potentially rich country, was helped in that way to accumulate vast debts. Britain, furthermore, started to give loans to Algeria once the military government there annulled the open elections that nearly brought an Islamic party to power (Hanlon 1998). Promises to follow an ethical policy made by New Labour soon after it took office in 1997 do not appear to have been translated into action. As argued in Chapter 9, the dice are heavily loaded in favour of arming dictatorships.

Adams (1991) reported that Marcos pocketed almost one-third of the loans given to the Philippines during his reign, but her groundbreaking book was more significant in putting the spotlight on the questionable legal status of the 'odious debts' incurred by repressive regimes. Lawyers had started to warn their banks in the early 1980s that nations might not be responsible for repayment of such debts. A number of people have argued that case since then, including the Archbishop of Cape Town in the case of loans given to South Africa during the apartheid era. The legal argument enjoys good pedigree. The USA used the concept when it captured Cuba from Spain in 1898 to avoid payment of debts incurred previously by the authorities without the consent of the Cuban people. The principle of 'odious debts' was incorporated into international law 'in the 1923 judgement of US Chief Justice Taft in the case of *Great Britain* vs. *Costa Rica*' (Hanlon 1998). However, whether a present-day debtor state is brave enough, or reckless enough, to mount a similar case is an open question.

Indebtedness as perceived by the creditors

Naturally, creditors become agitated about indebtedness only when a threat is posed to their investments. The problem is seen as an acute episode that demands an urgent solution, and the governments concerned swing into action to do just that. In that context, indebtedness reared its head during the 1970s, at the time of the first oil crisis, and again during the 1980s. By 1983, private banks alone were owed no less than $417 billion by the developing countries. Ten years later the figure had escalated to about $750 billion. That element of international debt began to exert a significant impact on bank balance sheets and reputations. Consequently, after Gerorge Bush's election as US president in 1988 the debt problem was given top priority. The task was clear: avoid a collapse in the banking business, restore the creditworthiness of debtor countries, and lastly if possible relieve the impact of indebtedness on the poorest nations (Stallings 1995: 282). Baker, the Treasury secretary, took the lead between 1986 and 1988. The Baker Plan put emphasis on 'mobilising new lending under a more systematic program'. A new Treasury secretary, Brady, masterminded the Brady Plan between 1989 and 1994. This later plan shifted attention from new lending towards forgiveness of debt (Cline 1995: 208, 215).

Efforts were deemed to have been reasonably successful, certainly by the lenders. Net interest as a percentage of exports for the seventeen heavily indebted countries identified in the Baker Plan was reduced from 30 per cent in 1982 to just over 10 per cent in 1993. In the same period, however, the percentage for other low-income countries increased from 6 to 15 per cent. Nonetheless, it is undeniable that the crisis for the lending agencies was over; the percentage for the thirty-three countries covered by the Brady Plan was halved by 1993.[7]

Consensus within the creditor countries suggests Brady's Plan yielded good results, but there is less unanimity on how and why it worked so well. Cline summed up the situation succinctly when he wrote, 'politics and psychology are at least as important as economics in matters of creditworthiness and debt sustainability' (Cline 1995: 52). One final comment on this topic takes the discussion back to the natural 'selfishness' of individuals and nations. Volcker, chairman of the US Federal Reserve at the time, in an address to the Subcommittee on International Finance and Monetary Policy, US Senate, said, 'Our concern for maintaining a well-functioning international financial system is rooted in our self-interest, not in altruism' (Corbridge 1993: 42).

Indebtedness as experienced by the debtors

The creditors might believe the debt crisis is a thing of the past but to those at the receiving end it is a continuing saga that cripples whole nations. UNICEF's *The Progress of Nations 1999*, with eight pages devoted to debt under the title 'Debt Has a Child's Face', reported that sub-Saharan Africa 'spends more on servicing its $200 billion debt than on the health and education of its 306 million children' (UNICEF 1999: 27). The catastrophic impact on these nations, as Complex Adaptive Systems that rely for their survival on copious local interactions, is easy to comprehend. A baby starts life with a debt of $997, $1,213 and $1,872 in Mauritania, Nicaragua and the Congo respectively. The burden is shaped by factors that are in many cases outside the control of the debtors. They might run fast, but the arithmetic means they stand a good chance of going backwards. Hence, while creditor banks and governments were agonising over their investments during the 1980s' crisis, indebted developing countries 'repaid the staggering amount of $1,000 billion. Astoundingly, despite this enormous transfer of wealth, their debt burden, which was some $800 billion in 1983, reached $1,500 billion by 1990 and nearly $2,000 billion by 1997' (UNICEF 1999: 28). The debt of sub-Saharan Africa jumped from $80 billion in 1980 to its present level of $200 billion. The statistics go on and on but the picture gets grimmer all the while.

Heated debate accompanied the Brady Plan from inception to implementation. In the event, however, not unexpectedly debt forgiveness, as opposed to new lending and rescheduling, played a minimal role in managing the crisis. Nonetheless, efforts are being made at present to satisfy popular demands for the provision of relief to the most needy nations, the World Bank's HIPC initiative being a case in point. But so far progress on this score is somewhat patchy. The HIPC initiative could potentially assist forty-one countries, thirty-three of which are in Africa, but so far it has only managed to give relief to a handful of nations. Conversely, compliant leaders of heavily indebted countries were being offered additional loans soon after the crisis was declared officially over in 1993.

The IMF estimated that by 1994, the ratio of interest to exports for the seventeen most heavily indebted countries 'was back up to its 1989 level'. The World Bank gave a rosier picture of the situation, but either way the business of borrowing and lending went on as before (Cline 1995: 246). Restoring creditworthiness was, after all, one of the top aims of the Baker and Brady plans, second only to safeguarding the banking system. It would have been pointless to restore creditworthiness without securing new loans, and it would seem that objective was achieved very successfully. In 1995, debt service as a percentage of exports stood at 13 per cent for all developing countries, as compared with 11 per cent in 1970. As always, averages hide substantial local variations. In South Asia, for instance, the ratio of debt service to exports increased from 17 per cent in 1970 to 22 per cent in 1995. In the same period, Nicaragua's ratio jumped from 11 to 57 per cent (UNICEF 1998: 117).

Countries such as Nicaragua will have to endure a heavy burden for the foreseeable future even if their governments were to decide not to borrow another penny, but for many nations the problem of debt continues to worsen. This is particularly the case in sub-Saharan Africa, excluding South Africa, where external debt increased from 76 per cent of gross national product (GNP) in 1985 to 108 per cent in 1997 (UNICEF 1999: 31). The Middle East, North Africa, East and South Asia, and the Pacific did better but they, nevertheless, showed a similar trend in mounting debt.

The impact of debt on domestic policies is devastating. Subsistence agriculture, for instance, would not do; cash crops that have a market abroad have to be cultivated at any cost, up to and including malnutrition. Moreover, allocation of available finance is heavily compromised to favour debt repayments. Hence, in Tanzania about 16 per cent of the budget was devoted to all basic social services in 1998 as opposed to 46 per cent for repayment of external debts (UNICEF 2001: 55). The corresponding figures for Zambia were 8 and 40 per cent respectively.

The tragic consequences for the development of these countries, as Complex Adaptive Systems dependent for success on uninhibited interactions between members of their populations, are all too obvious. At base, the debt habit is difficult to kick: surplus funds have to be invested somewhere, loans are helpful to growth when taken in moderation, indebtedness delivers compliant client states, and above all else the opportunities for corruption presented by easy foreign money are simply too tempting.

THE 'SHAMEFUL CONDITION' OF INTERNATIONAL AID

Gro Harlem Brundtland called aid-giving a 'shameful condition' when she voiced her concern about the level of aid given, the conditions attached to donations and the way recipients and causes are selected (UNICEF 1995a: 45). 'Selfish' individuals, elites and game playing are conspicuous elements in handing out loans, but one would have expected aid to poorer nations to follow more altruistic lines. As always, evidence shows that this sector is not different from any of the other issue areas considered earlier.

A shrinking pool of goodwill

Two years after Brundtland made her remarks, UNICEF declared that aid was 'in the doldrums'. An international target by which 0.7 per cent of donor nations' GNP was to be allocated for aid remained unfulfilled over a quarter of a century after it was agreed in 1969. The figure for twenty-one members of the Organisation for Economic Cooperation and Development (OECD) was 0.34 per cent of their combined GNP in 1990. That went down to 0.22 per cent by 1997, with the USA devoting a mere 0.09 (UNICEF 1999: 33). However, UNICEF suggested that there was a halt in the decline of aid in 1998 'due in part to short-term support in the aftermath of the Asian financial crisis and the decision by several countries to re-emphasise or rebuild aid programmes after cutbacks in the 1990s'.

Shrinkage in the volume of aid has been attributed to many causes. The USSR was a donor until its collapse. Some of its past members themselves turned overnight into clients in need of help.[8] In any case, the need to buy favours through aid was also reduced with the ending of the Cold War. At present, the main element of aid that could be clearly labelled as being purely political is the disproportionate amounts allocated by the USA to Israel and Egypt. When all elements of overseas aid are put together, the USA donates about $7.5 billion annually, of which Israel and Egypt receive $1.2 billion and $0.8 billion respectively. The leading economies also suffered some reverses that affected their ability or willingness to offer assistance, the recession in

Japan in the late 1990s, the top donor in 1995 at $14.5 billion, being a case in point.

Aid is not a free lunch

Significantly, the World Bank (1998) attributed the fall in aid to 'a sense that aid does not work well'. There seems to be much truth in that statement in the context of how aid has been dispersed in the past. As defined by the World Bank (1994), Official Development Assistance (ODA) 'consists of loans and grants made on concessional financial terms by all bilateral official agencies and multilateral sources to promote economic development and welfare'. Nothing could have been more helpful to needy nations, particularly for sub-Saharan countries unable to attract investment or loans in the open market, but in the untidy world of international relations deeds hardly ever accord with intentions.

Primarily, the distribution of aid between supported causes and between recipient nations does not necessarily follow a pattern dictated by needs. Reflecting once again the 'selfish' activities of egoistic nations and individuals, high priority is routinely accorded to the donor's interests. This bias is not an oversight or a closely guarded secret, but the manifestation of consistent policies and practices. USAID, the federal government agency that administers American aid, for instance, recognises openly that one of its main objectives is to further 'America's foreign policy interests'. For that purpose, USAID 'receives overall foreign policy guidance from the Secretary of State'. Furthermore, the agency has close working relationships with more than 3,500 American companies and offers an extensive range of business and procurement services to its US clients. Naturally, giving priority to the donors' interests has a painful downside: less than one-third of ODA in 1993, for example, was allocated to thirty-nine countries that comprised the most impoverished region on Earth: sub-Saharan Africa.

To make matters worse, the granting of aid does not reflect the most urgent needs. These were defined, yet again, at the 1995 World Summit for Social Development as: nutrition, primary healthcare, clean water and safe sanitation, basic education, and family planning. UNICEF (1997: 63) viewed these factors as the 'foundation for sustainable human development'. As I argue in Chapter 8, UNICEF's stance accords closely with one of the most fundamental conditions that have to be met if development, as a Complex Adaptive System, is to proceed satisfactorily.

The 1995 Summit called for the target set in 1969 – 0.7 per cent of donor nations' GNP to be channelled into aid – to be met, and then went on to recommend that on average 20 per cent of ODA and 20 per cent of the budget of recipient countries should be earmarked for basic social programmes. This has become known as the *20/20 formula*. It is highly significant that the figure was pitched as low as 20 per cent, reflecting the realities of how and why aid is currently given. The figure says just as much about the priorities of the local elites in poorer countries. Two years after the 20/20 formula was adopted, UNICEF (1999: 33) was only able to record 'a glimmer of hope' in the disquieting aid picture, and implementation of the formula continues to be patchy at best.

Aid with strings

Misallocation of aid is caused in part by the foreign policy priorities of the donors. However, that is only one of several factors that skew the direction of funds into less obvious avenues. The need to promote the sale of products and services abroad, particularly military exports, is a significant element in this context. For readily obvious reasons, ODA is more amenable to the application of demanding conditions than straightforward commercial loans. *Conditionality*, therefore, has become an indispensable feature of aid-giving; on average about one-third of foreign aid is tied to purchases of goods and services from the donor country. As reported by Stallings (1995: 361), it increased substantially during the 1980s 'from macroeconomic policy (on the part of the IMF) and specific project feasibility (the World Bank) to structural adjustment policies'. Conditionality reduces the value of the assistance provided as it limits choice and competition. The belief that aid 'does not work well' becomes quite reasonable when it is remembered that another third of the aid provided usually goes into administration or corruptly disappears into private bank accounts.

The understandable wish of donor nations to get something in return for their money has a pronounced bearing on the selection of countries to be given aid. For instance, assistance from one government to another might be linked to the purchase of weapons, as reportedly happened in the case of British government financial subsidy to the building of the Pergau Dam in Malaysia and the construction of roads and a new power station in Samarinda in Indonesia (*Observer*, 13 November 1994).[9] Not unexpectedly, aid is also most useful when political favours are required. Egypt's support during the Gulf War was secured in 1990 by judicious application of the stick of political pressure and the carrot of 'generosity'.[10]

Regional preferences

As discussed in Chapter 10, a 'triad' consisting of the USA, Europe and Japan (possibly in alliance with China and Southeast Asia) seems to be slowly replacing the previous bipolar system that was based on the USA and USSR. Members of the 'triad' have their own historic, political and economic preferences when it comes to aid. That again tends to produces an overall allocation of aid that does not correspond to the most pressing needs of recipient nations. In the early 1990s, the largest slice of ODA originating in the USA went to Israel, Egypt and Latin America. In Japan's case, more than half of ODA was allocated to Asia, mostly to East and Southeast Asian countries. Europe, on the other hand, favoured past colonies in Africa with almost half of its ODA devoted to that continent (Stallings 1995: 359). Clearly, the global political economic structure has a regional bias that determines to a large extent the distribution of aid. Absolute need is a secondary consideration.

Remnants of altruism

The picture of aid is not all black. Dissatisfaction led some members of the UN to seek approval at the General Assembly in 1952 for the setting up of a Special UN Fund for Economic Development (SUNFED). To retain control over funding for development, however, the World Bank with US encouragement created instead the International Development Association (IDA) in 1960 to provide interest-free credits to qualifying countries. Undoubtedly, the creation of IDA was an encouraging sign in the search for some alignment between aid-giving and social needs (World Bank 1994: 149). Though short of the SUNFED ideal, the multilateral nature of the assistance given overcame some of the bias associated with bilateral aid.

IDA expanded faster than the World Bank: between 1961 and 1993 the Bank's resources grew by a factor of almost twenty-eight and those of IDA by a factor of sixty-seven. Nonetheless, the Bank's commitments in 1993 were still two and a half times those of IDA. Significantly, a 1998 report from the World Bank (1998) on the subject contrasted aid-giving overall with that provided by IDA. It concluded that the latter awards aid to countries with environments that favour effective use of resources, especially in terms of maximising poverty reduction.[11]

Despite the above encouraging signs, aid in general is in a mess. Countries would have to be seriously desperate, or highly reckless, if they were to depend on shrinking global generosity as a significant factor in their effort to make progress. The developing countries received about $65 billion in aid in 1995, as compared with $159 billion in loans and foreign investment, and that balance of preference by the donors will not change. It is a rewarding setup for those in the driving seat, and as such has become a frozen accident in the global system. Nonlinearity and the interplay between cooperation and competition in this field are as evident here as they were in the other topics discussed earlier.

INTERNATIONAL TRADE

The Bretton Woods Conference held at the conclusion of World War II led in time to the establishment of the General Agreement on Tariffs and Trade in 1947. GATT provided a forum for the promotion of international trade, the reduction of barriers to trade, and the settlement of trade disputes between countries. Its work took the form of lengthy *trade rounds* of negotiations, the last, completed in 1993, culminating in the replacement of GATT by the World Trade Organisation.

Global trade engineering

The WTO, as was and is the case with the World Bank and the IMF, became the focus of increasingly bitter criticism from day one. If anything, it has fared worse than its sister organisations. It has emerged as the main driving force behind the effort mounted by the leading economies to impose globalisation on one and all. In consequence, some in the developing world perceived the WTO 'as global trade engineering promoted by developed states who realised that GATT no longer served their economic needs' (*Arab–British Trade*, November 1999). The WTO ministerial summit held in Seattle in November 1999 resulted in highly disruptive riots. Security considerations, it seems, forced the WTO to hold its next ministerial meeting in November 2001 in relatively remote Qatar.[12]

Deserved or otherwise, hostility to the WTO is understandable. The UN, the World Bank and the IMF shrink into insignificance when compared to the power wielded by the WTO. By November 2000, 140 countries had signed up as members. That might be considered a resounding vote of confidence, but in truth it reflects the realities of life: a country that does not join places itself in jeopardy. When a country finally decides to take the plunge it is met with an equally disadvantageous situation; the rules as defined by the founding members are not negotiable. Then comes the ultimate in linear thinking built on order and command-and-control from the top: the agreement a country has to sign is about 500 pages long and caters for every eventuality. Variety is out and compliance is in, WTO officials settle disputes between states, and a WTO panel, whose decision is final, hears appeals. In short, the WTO is fast becoming a global government, certainly as far as trade is concerned.

Eagerness by the leading powers to engineer world trade to their satisfaction is perfectly understandable. There has been a phenomenal growth in international trade since the end of World War II; by the mid-1990s cross-border imports and exports stood at some $5 trillion. Following a period of relative stagnation, trade picked up in the late 1990s; world merchandise exports alone amounted to $5.5 trillion in 1999, while commercial services exports added a further $1.35 trillion (WTO 2000a). In sum, this huge and fast-growing business is at the heart of global capitalism, and WTO is the engine that drives it in accordance with the wishes of the main stakeholders.

In creating the WTO, the elite led by the USA did not set out to penalise poorer and weaker nations, they simply wished to promote their interests and to maximise their rewards. Furthermore, the elite are genuinely convinced that they are working for the common good of all nations. Clare Short, British Secretary of State for International Development, for instance, considers the WTO a 'more democratic multilateral organisation than any we have in the world system' (*Newsweek*, 25 January 2001). Interestingly, she contrasted the WTO with the UN, the IMF and the World Bank on that score. The first has a Security Council, she said, while the other two operate on the basis of 'a-dollar-a-vote'. Undeniably, the global elite believe that growth in trade will deterministically lead, through trickle-down, to prosperity for all.

GATT's uneven playing field

Hostility to the WTO stems from events prior to 1995 when the organisation came into being. GATT, and its interminable trade rounds, did not endear the setup to many people, particularly those in the developing world. Reducing barriers to trade was the fundamental mission for GATT and that, so the scenario went, would assist all economies. Theory and practice did not go hand in hand though. In outlining the origins of dissatisfaction and distrust, I will confine my comments to the seventh and eighth rounds, the Tokyo and Uruguay Rounds.

In the Tokyo Round of GATT negotiations concluded in 1979, tariffs were reduced by 25 per cent on industrial products to 'liberalise trade', but the reduction on agricultural products was held at 7 per cent. The distinction reflected the balance of power and rewards between developed and developing nations, and contradicted the proclaimed intention of the Round of giving preferential treatment to poorer nations. Not content with that, the industrialised powers reserved for themselves the right to invoke the so-called safeguard clause they wielded regularly against imports from the rest of the world that could be considered disadvantageous to their businesses.

The Tokyo Round achieved a decrease in tariffs, but it was accompanied by distinct moves towards the erection of more sophisticated protective measures. Krugman (1995: 263) pointed out, for instance, that four important bills were 'passed in 1978–79 attaching Buy-American strictures to federal purchases totalling $18 billion ... six more procurement bills with Buy-American restrictions have become US law, covering even more trade'. Emphasis during the Tokyo negotiations on tariffs was itself considered discriminatory by many observers. Governments of some of the poorest nations see tariffs as a source of revenue rather than an intentional hindrance to trade, and they, moreover, do not have the administrative resources to apply nontariff barriers to trade.

The Tokyo Round was followed by the Uruguay Round, initiated in 1986 and concluded in 1993. The long time taken underlines the obvious fact that international negotiations, involving on that occasion 117 states, demand considerable horse trading and arm twisting. Despite the large number of participating countries, negotiation was essentially between the rich and poor nation blocs. The World Bank, in commenting on the outcome of the Uruguay Round, noted, 'industrial nations didn't forget one another. They cut tariffs on trade with one another proportionately more than they did on imports from the developing world.' Overall, 'the results of the Round reflect realities – the leverage of the main contracting parties, particularly the United States and the European Union, with the European Union resisting even a modest liberalisation of agricultural trade.' Agriculture was not the only activity in which lack of progress was detrimental to weaker participants. Textiles and clothing, ideal exports from less industrialised nations, continued to face 'significant barriers in industrial countries'.[13]

SUPPORTING EVIDENCE FROM AN UNEXPECTED SOURCE

A recent study published by the WTO on trade, income disparity and poverty makes interesting reading. The research was clearly meant to highlight the virtues of trade, and in many instances the final report managed to achieve that aim. In other respects, however, the report contained revealing glimpses of WTO thinking. The doubts centred on trickle–down, the solid foundation on which the free market, and in fact the push for globalisation, is built.

Facts presented by the WTO study showed that the number of people living on less than one dollar per day has remained the same at about 1.2 billion from 1987 to 1998, while those who had to live on less than two dollars per day increased by 250 million over the same period to 2.8 billion people (WTO 2000). Basically, a massive increase in trade failed to help over one-fifth of the world's population to earn more than one dollar per day, and failed to enable half of the world's population to climb over the two dollars per day barrier. Expressed in the language of Complexity, the cause – increasing trade – did not lead to the desired effect, a reduction in utter poverty. Put another way, economic development does not necessarily lead to human development.

The WTO study underlined the lack of direct and immediate linkage between trade and poverty. As in a typical Complex Adaptive System, causality is difficult, in most cases impossible, to establish, contrary to the linear assumptions that pervade the practice of development at present. In addition, the WTO study went further by recognising that the gap between rich and poor has increased in recent decades and that it is likely to continue to do so in future; the rich will get richer, an unmistakable sign that nations, individually or in groups, behave as Complex Adaptive Systems. This conclusion was lent further support by facts presented earlier in respect of debt and aid. Nonetheless, the development industry, particularly the World Bank in the present context, perseveres in treating nations and their development as linear phenomena. Under these conditions, failure of the most needy nations to develop was inevitable.

NOTES

1. A shift to the microscopic level helps to illustrate the point. The introduction of antibiotics would have eradicated all bacteria had it not been for the fact that a few bacteria here and there were not as badly affected as the rest. It is wrong, therefore, to think that new resistant bacteria somehow appeared on the scene; they were there waiting in the wings.
2. Space is not available for full discussion of this topic but more detailed analysis is given in Amin (1990) and Allen and Thomas (1995).
3. See, for instance, comments on the 1992 Earth Summit and 1995 World Social Summit in Brown et al. (1997: 1, 129).
4. The World Bank's Articles of Agreement allowed 'general purpose' loans only in special circumstances.
5. Stiglitz felt that people have a point when they suggest that the IMF does not 'listen to the developing countries'. He added, 'Critics accuse the institution of taking a cookie-cutter approach to economics, and they're right. Country teams have been known to compose draft reports before visiting.' Stiglitz's article, appropriately titled 'The Insider', is well worth reading as it reveals starkly, and unintentionally, the workings of Complexity, Game Theory, elites and hierarchies.
6. These figures were obtained from Jubilee 2000 Coalition (www.jubilee2000uk.org).
7. An account of the history of that debt crisis and its later management, as well as theories related to the topic, is given in Corbridge (1993).
8. Fred Halliday, professor of international relations at the London School of Economics, suggested that the 'greatest single anxiety expressed about the impact of the end of the cold war on the third world is that it will

lead to a displacement of the developing world in terms of aid and trade' (Stallings 1995: 62).

9. The subject is dealt with more broadly by Pilger (1998: 115).

10. Heikal (1992: 22) observed, 'President Bush's decision to forgive Egyptian debts of US$7 billion helped [President] Mubarak convince his public that Egypt's involvement was worthwhile. Ironically, Bush's generosity cost Washington nothing, as it was offset by donations collected from Gulf oil producers, Japan, and Germany.'

11. See also World Bank *Policy and Research Bulletin*, vol. 9, no. 4, October–December 1998.

12. The intentions of the government of Qatar were somewhat contradictory. On the one hand the authorities declared that they would permit the organisation of protests. On the other hand, the Qatari minister of finance informed media representatives attending a conference on tourism held in January 2001 that Qatar would not allow people into the country if they intended to demonstrate. In the event, the meeting went off without a hitch, much to the relief of the organisers.

13. The quoted remarks come from the World Bank *Policy Research Bulletin*, vol. 6, no. 1, January–February 1995.

SIX

THE WEALTH AND POVERTY OF NATIONS

A conundrum of critical importance has to be settled by any plausible development theory: could Adam Smith's invisible hand help the least developed communities to satisfy their basic needs and social priorities, or would improvements in these fields empower the invisible hand to kick in? This is not the traditional conundrum about the chicken and the egg. I aim to show in this chapter that there is a fundamental difference between economic development and human development, and that for nations that require human development most desperately the economic route is largely irrelevant, and possibly wasteful. Complex Systems theory provides robust scientific explanations to substantiate these assertions, but the history of today's developed nations provides equally compelling evidence in that respect. Basically, and as demonstrated in Chapters 7 to 9, repressed, diseased, illiterate and malnourished people are neither free nor capable of interacting locally to energise the Complex Adaptive System we recognise as 'nation', and they are certainly not in a position to bring the invisible hand into action.

HUMAN POVERTY

We are all aware of what wealth and poverty mean when applied to nations. Or are we? Wealth is relatively easy to discern; there is no doubt that Switzerland and Luxembourg are rich in every way. There is only one detail that needs clarification: wealth is very exceptional. Most people on Earth in comparison are excessively poor, which brings us to the thorny question of poverty. Economists define poverty as a level of income that is 'necessary to maintain a subsistence level of consumption' (Samuelson and Nordhaus 1995: 362). That definition poses obvious conceptual problems associated with what is understood by 'subsistence level of consumption'. Hence, the 1992 poverty line set in the USA at an income of $14,000 means little or nothing when it is applied to nations in the developing world. Expressing poverty in terms of income in itself is problematic, as own production would not be included.

We therefore need to look at something that is more meaningful. Ben Crow defined poverty 'in terms of capabilities rather than command over goods ... capability to get enough food, adequate health care, access to clean water and sanitation, and to be a functioning member of society' (Allen and Thomas 1995: 28). The last item on the list draws attention, albeit unintentionally, to the need to view nations as Complex Adaptive Systems in which interactions between all members of the community are of pivotal importance for sustainable progress. The United Nations Development Programme (UNDP) refers to this definition of poverty as *human poverty* to distinguish it from income-based definitions of *extreme poverty*, lack of income necessary to satisfy basic food needs; and *overall poverty*, lack of income to satisfy essential non-food needs (UNDP 2000: Box 1.1).

Treating poverty as human poverty is most appropriate when development is seen as a Complex Adaptive process. UNDP suggested that lack of basic capabilities signifying human poverty involves illiteracy, malnutrition and disease, and that suitable measures to assess its severity include access to goods, services and infrastructure such as energy, education, sanitation, drinking water and communication. Denial of access could also be the result of repression, war and social conventions. That vision of poverty suggests a situation in which most personal effort is expended in simply staying alive: a low-interaction low-energy mode that might permit subsistence but hardly anything else.

For the many millions of diseased, malnourished and illiterate people, as well as for oppressed nations, women and ethnic and religious minorities, exploration of the local envelope of opportunities by interacting individuals is pie in the sky. Believers in the current conventional wisdom on development would quickly point out that to-day's leading nations disprove this assertion. Did they not 'truck, barter, and exchange one thing for another', in the words of Adam

Smith, to acquire all the trappings of development, including health, food and education? As I argue below, that contention is a myth. The rise of these nations took a very lengthy period of time and was the cumulative result of modest, and unplanned, incremental progress on many fronts.

A BRIEF HISTORY OF EXCEPTIONAL WEALTH

It is useful to begin by underlining four key attributes of governments of the leading nations. According to Samuelson and Nordhaus (1995: 278), they 'tend to tax and spend a larger fraction of GDP than do poor countries'. IMF figures show, for example, that in the mid-1990s Italy's government expenditure was over half its GDP, while that of Paraguay was less than 10 per cent of GDP. They also redistribute income from richer to poorer sectors of the nation on a huge scale. In addition, they devote a higher proportion of their budgets to an impressive array of basic programmes, particularly education and health. And finally, the state in successful countries distances itself from tactical day-to-day issues. In essence, level of government intervention 'means virtually nothing', but type of intervention is all-important. Therefore, the state permits citizens to act freely in all matters that do not impinge on strategic issues (Chandler 1997: 525, 534). But the question remains, how did they get to this privileged position in the first instance?[1]

Long-term steady accumulation of wealth

It is essential to understand that current members of the select group of prosperous nations have been exceptionally wealthy for a very long time: their gross national product per head of population in the early nineteenth century, converted to 1990 international dollars, seems more than acceptable by present-day standards. For instance, GNP per head in 1820 was $1,756, $1,561 and $1,287, for Britain, the Netherlands and the USA respectively (Chandler 1997: 6). The wealth gap is given scale when these figures are compared with the GNP per head in 1999 of $870, $1,010 and $1,230 for Albania, Bolivia and Kazakhstan (UNICEF 2001). More striking examples, from sub-Saharan Africa, say, could have been given but there was no need to be selective as the picture is clear whichever way one looks at it.

Moreover, it is important to point out that today's wealthiest nations maintained steady but relatively modest rates of growth for lengthy periods of time, a strong indication that their progression followed an evolutionary course. Maddison calculated the rate at mostly over 1 per cent from 1820 to 1992 (Chandler 1997: 7). The same evolutionary process was at work in the build-up of other facets of life such as education and public health. As a result of these and other improvements, the nations concerned accumulated higher levels of productivity; modest annual rates of growth allowed sixteen leading industrialised countries to raise their labour productivity by 1,150 per cent over eleven decades from the nineteenth century. Baumol (1989: 12) called this the 'tyranny of compounding'. Fundamentally, nothing happens overnight in the course of the evolution of nations.

Gateway events and punctuated equilibrium

Gateway events, leading to the sudden appearance of unforeseen opportunities, played a decisive role in the surge forward by present-day elite nations. The Industrial Revolution was such an event. Engels coined the name in 1844, but the transformation started in Britain about a hundred years prior to that date and involved gradual progress in a wide cross-section of issue areas. New possibilities for creating, and using, capital on a large scale emerged and Britain was propelled into the limelight. But success relied heavily on a reasonably healthy, well-fed and skilled workforce. However, that was not the only gateway event of its type. Historians cited at least two earlier industrial revolutions in Europe; one straddling the twelfth and thirteenth centuries and another in the sixteenth and seventeenth centuries, underlining the significance of continuous evolution and the passage of time (Baumol 1989: 11).

The above and other gateway events were unplanned and unexpected. Individuals simply pursued what they took to be unremarkable everyday activities.[2] Basically, life had been sedately going along in its familiar manner for many decades when all of a sudden circumstances became right for it to fall into a substantially different pattern. The Industrial Revolution was here and life was not the same as before, but the new conditions soon became the norm. Yet another change came about at the close of the nineteenth century on the American side of the Atlantic. The latest gateway event, the Second Industrial Revolution, introduced new forms of high-volume production, distribution and marketing. Again, the Second Industrial Revolution was unplanned. Other major upheavals followed, including the development of computers and the revolution in information technology. However, the salient point here relates to the significance of unexpected gateway events to the development of leading nations and the pattern of punctuated equilibrium that marked their move forward.

Japan's path to development

The rise of the Japanese economy also illustrates key facets germane to the principal theme under discussion. As in the case of the USA and Europe, its rise through the ranks did not happen suddenly. Japan's GNP per head in 1820 was a respectable $704, when converted to 1990 international dollars (Chandler 1997: 6). It should be noted that the country has few natural resources and its local market is limited. Consequently, the key to its 'building a solid economic foundation while maintaining its independence under the impact of the West was industrialisation' (Chandler 1997: 307).

Growth was well in evidence at the end of the nineteenth century. The zaibatsu, a diversified business group owned by one family, was in control at that time. At national level attention was focused on education and training. Japanese exports were restricted to labour-intensive products such as silk, cotton, sugar and papermaking. The picture changed during World War I: capital-intensive industries began to appear in embryonic form, but limited domestic markets and poor quality did not encourage fast growth on that front. Most significantly, Japan limited itself to dealing with nations in its region, and concentrated on products based on indigenous knowledge and skills. It widened its circle of trading partners only when it was ready to offer products that could compete without imperilling its freedom of action. These preferences survive to this day throughout East and Southeast Asia. In the early 1990s, over 40 per cent of Japan's imports and about one-third of its exports were from and to Asian countries. Japan's success lies in its appreciation of the need to be selective in choosing trading partners, an intuitive recognition of the fundamental principles of Game Theory.

World War II ended in catastrophe for Japan. However, punishments by the occupying forces, such as the sacking of pre-war managers and company owners, helped to rejuvenate Japanese businesses; actions often lead to unexpected results. Nonetheless, it took Japan only a few decades of hard work to re-emerge once again as a leading economic power: the basics of literacy, native skills, health and nutrition were already in place. But the vital twist in Japan's fortunes was triggered accidentally by the war in Korea in 1950. The Allies designated Japan as supply base for the war effort, and the Japanese took full advantage of that gateway event. Reinvestment was put in train on a massive scale, and an aggressive form of managerial capitalism, controlled by younger business leaders, replaced the defunct zaibatsu system.

As in the case of all the latecomers – France, Italy, Spain and, later, South Korea being prime examples – the state played a critical role in Japan's early stages of recovery and its later ascendancy to the top of the world hierarchy. The Ministry of International Trade and Industry (MITI), restyled in January 2001 as the Ministry of Economy, Trade and Industry, orchestrated the transformation. Essentially it provided protection against foreign competition, especially in the fragile initial period; it discouraged inward investment, apart from that needed to acquire the latest technological know-how; and it guided Japanese businesses painstakingly up the ladder of increasing added-value, from basic low-value exports to sophisticated high-technology high-value innovations. Above all else, MITI was not allowed to interfere in tactical business matters; an example of effective state intervention at the correct level.

In sum, appropriate action by governments, steady long-term incremental evolution on a wide front, punctuated equilibrium and gateway events featured prominently in the rise of today's leading nations to the top of the league. Most importantly, people as individuals and groups were free to interact in business and social events without undue interference from the state. They were also able to take part because they were reasonably well-fed, healthy and literate. Trial and error over the centuries allowed these countries to evolve modes of behaviour that corresponded to the nonlinear nature of national and international affairs. Recent discoveries about Complex Adaptive Systems provided scientific explanations of why these policies worked so well. In short, theory merely explained and supported successful custom and practice.

NOT BY DOLLARS ALONE

In the course of the last five decades, super-rich nations were held up as models of ultimate achievement to be copied by the 'underdeveloped' countries. More specifically, economic growth was unquestionably assumed to be the key, and the single escalator, to success. Development itself was seen as strictly 'economic development'. The scenario was simple to follow: the leading nations performed miracles in the early part of the twentieth century and have gone on to consolidate their position, and it is now the turn of other nations to repeat that performance. Washington's missionaries preached that economic gospel zealously to anyone who cared to listen, and many did.

The rest is history. Classification of nations in the 'development league' was made easy through use of a yardstick based on GNP divided by mid-year population. Increase in that single parameter from year to year, it was claimed, would measure overall progress. Life could not have been more linear in that conception. Start and finish are known. If specific prescriptions of universal applicability were faithfully followed, then GNP per head would grow steadily, leading eventually, and inevitably, to the blessed state of development. All a nation had to do was to reduce imports, increase exports, borrow a little, open its borders to trade, welcome foreign investment, and generally behave in a manner that did not pose a threat to the 'world order' as defined by the dominant powers and their international minders. Some managed to do just that and in some cases GNP per head showed impressive growth, but the basic ills and inequalities refused to disappear. Economic progress was not enough, and in certain situations it was shown to be irrelevant.

Yardsticks reflect visions of development

Per capita GNP was an appropriate measure as long as development was taken to mean economic progress and nothing else. But that was not a sustainable stance: it defied logic as well as the sheer weight of mounting evidence to the contrary. People could starve, die young of treatable diseases, be illiterate, and live on less than a dollar a day in a country where the economy was doing tolerably well.

The search was on, therefore, for a better way to gauge progress on the path to development. UNICEF advocated the under-five mortality rate (U5MR), possibly in combination with GNP per head, as a more appropriate tool. It measured the probability of dying between birth and five years of age expressed as number of deaths per 1000 live births. UNICEF (1998: 123) recommended U5MR on three grounds: it involves an output rather than an input to the development process; it 'is known to be the result of a wide variety of inputs', including health, education, nutrition, safe water and sanitation as well as the state of a nation's economy; and it is less susceptible than per capita GNP to the fallacy of the average.

Human Development Index

U5MR and GNP per head together might well be a sound basis for comparing nations, but they still do not convey a full picture of the varying circumstances that confront nations while they attempt to move forward. The UNDP (1999: 85, 87) has taken that topic a step further. It concluded significantly that, 'although there is a strong link between trade and [economic] growth, there is no automatic link with human development.' Similarly, it argued that 'the link between foreign direct investment, [economic] growth and human development is not automatic.' In line with that viewpoint, the UNDP has published since 1990 various composite indices to measure different aspects of human development and these have been modified over the years to reduce overreliance on economic indicators. The gender-related development index (GDI), the gender empowerment measure (GEM) and the human poverty index (HPI) are specific examples (UNDP 1999: 127). However, the principal yardstick continues to be the human development index (HDI), combining life expectancy, educational attainment and income ('as proxy for a decent standard of living'). The HDI ranged in 1997 from a low 0.254 for Sierra Leone to a high 0.932 for Canada. The averages for the world, developing countries and industrialised countries were 0.706, 0.637 and 0.919 respectively (UNDP 1999: 137).

Adoption of the GNP per head measure, which is still in use, reflected a linear view of development as a one-dimensional activity with a distinct beginning and end, and linked causes and effects. The moves to broaden the yardstick to embrace other criteria recognise the variety of parameters that come into play in assessing and pursuing development. The UNDP's approach is highly significant in two respects. First, it has consistently stressed that no single measure is sufficient to give the full flavour of the process of development. Second, bringing matters such as gender and poverty into the equation begins to focus attention on the pertinent drivers of the development process: a multitude of egoistic actors free and able to interact at the local level.

The UNDP comes very close to considering development as a Complex Adaptive System, although it is obvious that the organisation has not yet crossed that Rubicon in its evolving view of development. Nonetheless, it is clear that even at this stage the UNDP approach veers towards local action in which the main aim would be to increase interactions within the community by tackling its most pressing social needs. There is no end to that developmental journey, and there is no clear route either. Twists and turns, accidents and opportunities, self-reliance and learning, are essential components in that unending process of evolution. However, the wider viewpoint brings into focus an inevitable question: could significant progress be made on basic needs at low levels of economic growth? That question is answered later in the chapter.

AN IMPOSSIBLE GAP TO BRIDGE

It is necessary on a purely rational basis to take a broader view of development, but there is a simpler, one could say almost mundane, reason why a focus on economics misses the point. Basically, it poses impossible, and possibly wasteful, targets for many nations desperate to make meaningful progress. To substantiate this view, it is useful to consider briefly the wealth attributes of the two world blocs: the haves and have-nots. One element is perfectly clear: ranked in order of their GNP per head, nations are vastly dissimilar; but it is necessary for the present purpose to quantify the scale of the wealth chasm separating the two principal factions.

The present structure of a few exceptionally wealthy nations forming an exclusive elite at the top of a hierarchy that embraces many poorer nations appeared in embryonic form during the fifteenth and sixteenth centuries. Explicitly or implicitly, interactions between the haves and have-nots follow the normal rules of Game Theory. The elite are free to compete, but might choose to cooperate, while the rest are obliged to cooperate at all times. Rewards from interactions reflect that balance of power. Given the chance, any nation would operate in precisely the same manner, and historic parallels over the millennia support that assertion unambiguously. Good or bad intentions are to a large degree irrelevant in that pattern of behaviour. The key point is that wealthy nations stand a good chance of becoming richer still.

In 1992, average GNP per head was $21,364 for the highest 22 nations and $191 for the lowest 22 (UNICEF 1995b). On that basis, the richest were 111 times more affluent than the poorest. By 1999, the averages had changed to $26,376 and $200; and the wealthiest had become 132 times richer than their poorer cousins (UNICEF 2001). In that year, out of 193 countries, 141 had a GNP per head less than $4,000, and 48 had to manage on less that $500. To make matters worse, 56 nations experienced a decline in their GNP per head between 1990 and 1999. Needless to say, almost all of those who lost ground were in the so-called developing world. These statistics show that being wealthy is the exception not the rule, that development efforts when measured by economic indicators failed a substantial number of nations, and that the gap between haves and have-nots has a tendency to increase.

Cruelty of numbers

Poorer nations have an Everest to climb in arithmetic terms even when all the practical hindrances are discounted. An increase of one percentage point in GNP per head would lead to an increase of $383 for Switzerland, but only $3.60 for Kenya. But the matter could be illustrated more forcefully by looking at what a poor nation needs to do in order to draw closer to the leaders. Nigeria, a country blessed by many natural resources and cursed by awful governments, had a GNP per head of $310 in 1999, while Greece, a developed country that is not particularly rich, had a GNP per head of $11,770. Nigeria enjoyed an excellent average growth rate of 4.2 per cent from 1965 to 1980 (it only managed 0.2 per cent from 1990 to 1999). By comparison, the compound annual growth rate between 1820 and 1989 was 1.27 per cent for the United Kingdom and 1.83 per cent for Japan (Chandler 1997: 529). At an unusually high compound annual rate of 4.2 per cent, it would take Nigeria eighty-eight years to equal Greece's present GNP per head. It might even enjoy the same standard of living providing that there was no inflation and the rest of the world failed to grow at all in that time. I set impossibly favourable assumptions for Nigeria and defined unusually harsh conditions for the rest of the world simply to highlight the drawbacks piled against poorer countries.

In summary, high levels of GNP per head are exceptional; the rich are more likely to become richer; and the gap in wealth between rich and poor nations could not be closed, or even reduced, in a meaningful period of time. At base, growth is achieved through small but steady accumulation over very lengthy periods. Preoccupation with the wealth gap between nations, therefore, is irrelevant for practical purposes. This takes the discussion back to Complex Adaptive Systems and the differential evolution of nations. Comparisons between nations on the basis of economic criteria are relatively meaningless as the real test is how well or badly a nation performs within its own fitness landscape, a medium determined by both internal and external factors. Nigeria failed exceedingly badly on that score because it allowed itself to become bankrupt despite its considerable potential resources. It did not fail because it did not measure up to Greece, or any other country for that matter.

INCOME DISTRIBUTION IS NOT IRRELEVANT

Much could be done to address basic needs even at the lowest rungs of the economic ladder. With or without a paradigm shift to Complexity, poverty reduction is now seen as the 'top priority of international development co-operation' (OECD 2001). A substantial portion of the World Bank's current research work is focused on that topic. Similarly, UNICEF identified poverty as 'a merciless foe' of development. The primary intention here is not to lament inequality in incomes as a manifestation of unfairness and deprivation but to examine influences that help or hinder the performance of nations as Complex Adaptive Systems. In all circumstances, elites strive to acquire the largest slice of the wealth and incomes cake. However, governments in successful economies have always appreciated that a degree of equity is desirable to enable all strata in the community to contribute to wealth creation, which helps the elite more than anyone else. Conversely, elites in less successful economies do nothing or little to raise the incomes of the lowest sectors of society to a level that brings them into the frame as active participants in the life of the nation.

Critical thresholds

At the heart of incomes lies the balance between consumption and investment. When income is exceedingly low, people spend it all on food, clothing, primitive forms of energy, and shelter. At lower levels of income, shelter or clothing, say, might have to be dispensed with. As incomes increase beyond the *human poverty* level, people arrive at a point where they gain access to healthcare, education and training, and possibly transport and recreation. Activities by members of the community move at that stage beyond the demands of sheer survival to capabilities that energise interactions, in the context of Complexity, which could lead to self-organisation and sustained evolution. Ultimately, higher incomes might permit some savings to be made. These regular patterns of spending are known as Engel's Laws, after the nineteenth-century Prussian statistician (Samuelson and Nordhaus 1995: 422).

The portion of income spent on each category increases with income but there are limits. For instance, regardless of income a family can only consume a finite amount of food. Therefore, beyond a certain level of income, savings rise rapidly. By contrast, at low levels people 'tend to dissave' (Samuelson and Nordhaus 1995: 424). In other words they are forced to consume their basic assets to stay alive, as happens when firewood is burnt beyond a sustainable level; capital depletion is observed as opposed to capital accumulation. A few facts about consumption and savings in the USA will demonstrate how incomes determine personal capability to interact. Consumption embraces spending on *nondurable goods*, food, clothing and energy for instance; *durable goods*, such as household equipment; and *services*, including housing, transport, education, and health. In 1993, Americans spent almost twice as much on services as they did on nondurable goods, 57 per cent and 31 per cent of total consumption respectively. At the end of World War I, they spent 41 per cent of their income on food and drink alone. That figure has now shrunk to 19 per cent (Samuelson and Nordhaus 1995: 423).

Americans in effect were able to broaden their consumption to include services, especially health, education and training, and to acquire the means for higher levels of mobility and communication. Under these circumstances, citizens were empowered to participate as much or as little as they wished in all aspects of life. In other words, interactions by elements of the Complex Adaptive System known as the USA were optimised, and ideal conditions were created for self-organised Complexity to emerge from the apparent chaos of disparate actions by millions of individuals and groups. In more traditional terms, the invisible hand was unleashed to increase wealth in the USA. The contrast with the situation in an impoverished country could not be plainer. Consumption is restricted to food, energy and shelter. Little, and often nothing, is left for physical and mental self-empowerment. Capital assets are sometimes depleted in the effort simply to stay alive. In that way, both Complexity and wealth are lost.

Slicing the incomes cake

The above comments, it might be thought, apply to rich governments that can afford to be generous, but I will argue in Chapter 8 that governments of poor countries are not powerless to help their nations to perform better as Complex Adaptive Systems. For the moment, I will cite income distribution as an instance where such governments fail to play a constructive role.[3] Basically, sufficient income for people to progress from bare subsistence to capability, no matter how modest, is of critical importance. Tellingly, there are significant differences between developed and developing countries in the way incomes are distributed within their populations. The share of household income for the top 20 per cent and bottom 40 per cent for the developed countries are 41 and 19 per cent respectively, while those for the developing countries are 51 and 15 per cent. Disparity in incomes within populations of the sub-Saharan countries is even more pronounced at 58 and 11 per cent (UNICEF 2001: 81). Irrespective of absolute levels of income, which are influenced by wealth, the link between the proportional distribution of income and performance is perfectly clear.

Disparity between income groups follows the standard format defined by Complexity and Game Theory. Plainly, in the normal course of events the rich stand a better chance of becoming richer. There are technical reasons for this phenomenon, as discussed previously, but one can say that their status allows them to be in the right place at the right time. But the distribution of incomes is governed by other factors, such as the presence or absence of democratic checks and balances. Clearly, the distribution of income follows conscious policies set by

the ruling elites in many countries. The elites in the leading economies decided, on the basis of trial and error, that their vested interests
are served best when most members of the population take part in the
overall effort to increase wealth. That policy is also affected by the
prevailing view on the stability of the elite. Repressive regimes consider
their hold on power to be transitory, and in consequence they seek to
gather wealth quickly. The elite in democratic states are reasonably
stable and can, therefore, afford to take a longer-term view over the
sharing of income.

Disparities in wealth

Clearly, distribution of incomes within any nation is skewed, and that
feature is more evident the further one goes down the ladder of
development. Moreover, the gap separating richer and poorer individuals is widening in a similar manner to that shown in international
comparisons. In the year 1999, the 500 top earners in Britain 'notched
up more than £5 billion'; an average of £10 million each (*Sunday
Times*, 19 November 2000). The top earners in the USA, according to
Forbes Celebrity 2000, did even better. However, income disparities
shrink into insignificance when compared with wealth inequalities. In
1989, one-third of wealth in the USA was owned by 1 per cent of
households (Samuelson and Nordhaus 1995: 204).

The *Sunday Times* publishes an annual survey of the richest persons
or families in Britain, resembling the *Forbes* list of the richest people
in the USA. In addition to the concentration of wealth in a few hands,
the British survey, first produced in 1989, highlighted over the years
two indicative trends. First, the rich are getting steadily richer. In
1995 the cutoff for inclusion in the list was £25 million. To keep the
list to 500 names that threshold has had to be raised by £5 million
each year. The inevitable happened in 1997: the list was enlarged to
1,000, and by 2001 the cutoff was set at £35 million. In that year the
wealth of the richest 1,000 in Britain was a record £150 billion (*Sunday Times*, 21 January 2001). Second, the elite in Britain is becoming
more eclectic. Newcomers, including women and persons from ethnic
minorities, are joining the select few. In effect, there is a noticeable
broadening at the top of the pyramid.

In terms of exceptional wealth Britons are almost impoverished
when compared with those in the USA or Europe. The *Rich List 2000*

featured no one from Britain within the world's richest fifty. Americans dominated that group with twenty-seven names, including Bill Gates of Microsoft at a personal fortune of £53 billion, while Germany dominated the European billionaire league. *Forbes* estimated that in 2000 the 400 included in its list shared $1.2 trillion between them. In other words, the world elites also come in the shape of a well-defined hierarchy.

Forbes also publishes a rough estimate of the wealth of 'Kings, Queens and Dictators'. As expected the top ten names in the 2000 list come from oil-rich countries in the Middle East and Brunei. Significantly, however, Saddam Hussein, after ten years of UN sanctions against Iraq, appears as sixth with an estimated fortune of $7 billion. Exceptional personal wealth is not restricted to the West and to leaders of oil-rich states though. The open-door policy launched by Deng Xiaoping in 1979, for instance, has already produced a crop of Chinese multimillionaires; the wealth of the top 50 amounted to $10 billion in 2000 and their wealth and numbers are expected to increase rapidly in future (*Forbes Global*, 27 November 2000).

INEQUALITY BY GOVERNMENT DECREE

It is useful to delve a little further into the role played by governments in encouraging, or discouraging, their nations to optimise their performance as Complex Adaptive Systems. Unquestionably, the absolute levels of resources available to governments are important, but the allocation of funding to the different programme areas is of even greater significance. In general, the proportion devoted to basic services and the transfer of income from the relatively rich to the poorer sections of society is higher in developed than in developing nations. Once again, it is important to point out that governments in the former group are not overtly working within a nonlinear paradigm; centuries of empirical experience has convinced them that transfer of money on a large scale and concentration of spending on basic programmes produces better results.

The biggest enterprise on Earth

The only possible word that could be used to describe the American government is colossal: Federal Government receipts in 2001 were just over $2,000 billion, and spending amounted to some $1,800 billion; about $6,500 per head of population.[4] These figures are undeniably impressive in absolute terms, but it is the way the money is raised and allocated that is of critical interest in the present context. Over 90 per cent of US government receipts are raised through taxes and charges levied on individuals and corporations who are in a position to pay. Conversely, social security absorbs 23 per cent of spending, Medicare and Medicaid 19 per cent, and other means-tested entitlements for people with low incomes 6 per cent. In addition, another 18 per cent of spending goes to an array of programmes that include education, training, science, technology, housing and transportation. In sum, two-thirds of the budget is focused on measures to assist individuals, including those in the lower income groups, the disabled and pensioners, to be active rather than passive members of society.

But the story does not end there; the US government directly employs one-fifth of the labour force. Fundamentally, the state seeks to create the right conditions for the majority of American people to perform optimally as freely interacting elements in a Complex Adaptive System. Few escape the safety net. A most important feature must be highlighted at this point: the pattern of spending does not change materially from one US administration to the next. Party politics might involve some window-dressing, but flexibility and pragmatism define the fundamentals of the budget from year to year.

Other developed countries present the same pattern; big government is the norm. The budget presented to the British parliament in March 2000 estimated public spending to be around £370 billion.[5] Well over two-thirds goes into basic programmes and income transfer, 27.8 per cent to social security, 14.6 per cent to health, 12.4 per cent to education, and 15.7 per cent to other sectors such as housing and transport. Yet again, the structure of the budget hardly alters with periodic changes in administration. The vociferous arguments between the political right and left rarely stray beyond the details.

Ineffectual governments in the developing world

It is interesting to note that income redistribution on the scale exercised within the US, British and other supposedly liberal economies would be branded as distinctly 'socialist' if it were adopted anywhere else. However, there is little danger of that happening, as governments in the developing world practice, in the main but with some notable exceptions, policies that differ substantially from those described above. Clearly, their revenues and hence their budgets are more modest than is the case in industrialised countries. More to the point, repayments of debts absorb much larger proportions of the available resources.

Nonetheless, it is undeniable that in general the governments concerned give a lower priority to basic needs. One reason for that policy orientation relates to the systems of government prevalent in these areas. More often than not, corruption and inefficiency are rife, the states are undemocratic, there are serious security problems in the cities, and the governments have to rely on the support of client groups of richer and more influential people, particularly army officers, to stay in power. These factors have a direct bearing on national budgets. The effect on receipts is especially punishing as collection of taxes and charges for services fall far short of what could be raised from these sources. Up to 60 per cent of treated and pumped water in the developing countries, for example, never reaches its intended customers because of illegal tapping and leakage. Worse still, those responsible for running electricity, water and other utilities 'remain largely unaccountable to the community at large, and often they make little effort to go after customers who fail to pay their bills' (UNICEF 1997: 7).

As discussed in Chapter 9, military spending is a significant item in the budgets of some of the most impoverished countries on Earth. The average for all countries in 1996 was 2.4 per cent of GDP and in general governments usually come close to that. However, there are surprising exceptions, such as Angola where $1.14 billion was spent on defence in 1995; this was a major improvement on 1993 when it allocated $7.2 billion or about 32.4 per cent of its GNP to that purpose (SIPRI 1997: 192).

Ruinous policies

It is no exaggeration to say that the impact on the monies that are actually devoted to basic services is ruinous, and health and education bear the brunt. The world averages for the proportion of government expenditure allocated to health, education and defence in the late 1990s were 12, 5, and 9 per cent respectively. The corresponding figures for the industrialised countries were close to the average at 14,

4, and 9 per cent. By comparison, those for South Asia were 2, 4, and 17, and those for the least developed countries as a group were 5, an impressive 13, and a disastrous 14 per cent. As usual, there were notable exceptions. Albania allocated only 4 and 2 per cent of government expenditure to health and education, Azerbaijan 1 and 3 per cent, and India 2 and 3 per cent (UNICEF 2001: 98). Individual figures should be treated with caution, but the general picture is perfectly clear: basic needs are not given the same *relative* priority in the most needy countries that they receive in more prosperous countries. Basically, in too many cases the limited financial resources are used primarily to subsidise the richest 20 per cent of the population at the expense of the poorest 20 per cent (UNICEF 2001: 95). The inevitable result on development, as a Complex Adaptive process dependent for success on local interactions, is consistent failure, as argued in forthcoming chapters.

HUMAN DEVELOPMENT FIRST

For too many years the noise made by the World Bank, the IMF, the WTO and their masters in their push to focus attention on economic development drowned voices that called for focus on human development. The two forms of development are far from being the same and the distinction between them has to be explicitly identified and then kept to the fore. Fundamentally, a decision has to be made right at the start as to which development is being sought by a nation. In truth, the real failure in development in the last half-century was a lack of success on the human development front.

I have to return, therefore, to a pivotal question posed earlier: can significant progress be made on basic needs such as disease, malnutrition and illiteracy in the absence of economic growth? Put another way: is it sensible to adopt a policy based on the premiss that action on a nation's most pressing social needs must await economic growth? More to the point, is there any guarantee that these needs will receive due attention once the economy is put right, even if one assumes that sustainable economic growth is possible in the absence of social progress? The answers to these questions are a definite yes, a certain no, and not necessarily.

The above answers are not as challenging as they might seem to be. They will not come as a surprise to anyone who has even a nodding acquaintance with development. However, there is something of a gentlemen's agreement that these answers should not be uttered so starkly in polite company. Regardless of what frame of reference is used to tackle development, this quaint reticence will have to be overcome if needy nations are to focus on what really matters – in the words of the UNDP (1990: 1), the primary task of enabling 'people to enjoy long, healthy and creative lives'. The subject is put beyond debate when development is treated as a Complex Adaptive System, as the issue becomes clear-cut: sustainable economic progress can only be made once most people become free and capable of interacting, and that can only come about when basic needs are met. Now that is a challenging stance.

Progress in the absence of economic growth

Botswana enjoyed an average annual growth rate in its GNP per head of 9.9 per cent from 1965 to 1980 and 1 per cent from 1990 to 1999, but life expectancy fell from 52 years in 1970 to 45 years in 1999 (UNICEF 2001: 98, 94). Uganda's economic performance was less impressive but life expectancy fell all the same. Zimbabwe and Zambia, by contrast, were losers on all counts. Other countries made good progress in human development or in economic development, but direct correlation between the two is difficult to establish.

A cursory glance at the various indices designed to gauge progress in the different issue areas that impinge on development is sufficient to illustrate the above point. UNICEF suggests that U5MR, as an indicator of the performance of nations, should be used alongside GNP per head, as the economic yardstick. The UNDP, on the other hand, advocates a number of composite indices to measure performance, including the human development index (HDI) and the human poverty indices (HPI–1 and HPI–2 for developing and industrialised countries respectively). Predictably perhaps, the few countries that appear at the very top and bottom of the league on the basis of all these indices are practically the same; Switzerland and Luxembourg do exceedingly well, while Mozambique and Afghanistan do very badly on all counts. Outside these extremes, however, nations present a mishmash of statistics that do not reveal a discernible relationship between economic growth and progress in meeting basic needs.

The UNDP has repeatedly drawn attention to that feature. For example, it reported 'different human progress', 'same starting point, different outcomes', 'same outcomes, different paths' and 'same HDI, different HPI–1' (UNDP 1999: 131). These conclusions are of critical importance to the theme argued throughout this book. Sacred ideologies, universal laws, imported wisdom and single economic escalators to success are moonshine. Nations, as Complex Adaptive Systems, develop under their own steam along an uncertain evolutionary path.

The discrepancy between human and economic development

Statistical analysis to compare the distribution of all nations on the basis of GNP per head and U5MR, I consider, would be a reliable test for the hypothesis that high growth rates on the economic front do not necessarily guarantee good results in relation to basic needs. The figures given in UNICEF's *The State of the World's Children 1998* were used for that purpose and the results were revealing: excellent under-5 mortality rates could be, and are, achieved at relatively low levels of GNP per head.

The analysis showed that the figures for GNP per head fell off rather rapidly down the table of nations, while under-5 mortality rates build up noticeably more slowly. The *median* for the GNP head index was $1,390, a relatively low level. In other words, exactly half the UN member states have a lower GNP per head than $1,390; wealth is exceptional while relative poverty is widespread. The median is a more useful indicator in this instance as the *mean*, $5,108, is distorted by the few nations with very high GNP per head. When the median and mean have the same value the sample is said to have zero *skewness* but as the values diverge skewness increases. The distribution of GNP per head between nations has a high skewness of 2.35; wealth is shared between nations in a highly lopsided manner. On the other hand, the median for U5MR, 38 deaths per 1,000 live births, is reasonably close to the mean value of 66. In effect, half the nations have a lower U5MR than 38, and the overall list has a moderate skewness of 1.37 only; the spread of U5MR values are not as lopsided as those for GNP per head. It might not be enough, but most nations seem to have made some social progress despite being exceedingly poor, but the reverse is not always true.

IS HUMAN DEVELOPMENT AFFORDABLE?

This topic is addressed more fully in other chapters, but it is appropriate to make a few introductory remarks on affordability in the context of the wealth and poverty of nations. Lack of progress is often blamed on the presumed high costs of remedial measures and on shortage of funds. Pain today and gain tomorrow is the usual promise but the scenario is a sham. For instance, health and poverty are not mutually exclusive. Cuba achieved an enviable record in healthcare despite the sanctions that crippled its economy after the 1959 coup. Life expectancy at birth increased from 64 in 1960 to 76 in 1999 and the under-5 mortality rate is now only 8 (UNICEF 2001: 77, 78). In both cases, Cuba's figures are indistinguishable from those applying to the leading industrialised economies. The same can be said about its achievements in literacy and nutrition, and similar examples could be cited from other parts of the world.

The absolute costs involved in tackling basic needs are not an insurmountable hurdle either. Timberlake (1991: 40) for instance wrote, 'African countries can expect the greatest improvement in life expectancy from health investments in maternal and child health services in rural and urban slum areas, costing less than $2 per capita.' Often, the cost is so low it could not possibly affect decision-making, as described in Chapter 8 in relation to vitamin A and iodine deficiency.

Actions that make sense locally

Occasionally, governments need to have sufficient confidence in their knowledge of local circumstances to try something different. In that context, Ordonez, director of Basic Education at UNESCO, suggested that 'where the unreached are a majority, principally in sub-Saharan Africa and South Asia, conventional systems are often not only unaffordable and irrelevant but also alienating to those they are intended to serve' (UNICEF 1995a: 19). That takes some doing, though, at a time when governments are being bombarded with advice and pressure from abroad to buy the latest healthcare and educational systems, especially when these imported services also offer the added incentive of lucrative commissions.

Allocation of scarce resources

Remedial measures might not be costly, and governments might adopt broad-minded policies, but where does the money come from? Against expectations, shortage of funds is not a critical problem. It was concluded at the 1995 Copenhagen Summit that an additional $30 to $40 billion a year, allocated properly, could have a dramatic effect on the well-being of the poorest communities in the world. The scale of that level of investment is simply negligible: 'the world spends more than this on playing golf' (*The Economist*, 8 January 1994). Moreover, twice as much is spent on wine and three times as much on cigarettes (UNICEF 1995a: 59).

As mentioned previously, governments of the so-called developing world spent about $440 billion annually in the 1990s, of which only about $50 billion was earmarked for nutrition, healthcare, primary education, family planning, and clean water and sanitation (UNDP 1994: 7). Profligate military spending is another sizeable drain on the scarce resources of impoverished countries, as explained in Chapter 9. Apart from biased allocation between budget heads, most of the modest resources available for top social needs are channelled into towns and cities with not unexpected detrimental effects on rural communities. Hence, 75 per cent of government health spending in India, for instance, is directed to urban areas where 25 per cent of the population live, and of the 12,000 doctors who graduate annually, mainly at public expense, over 9,500 go straight into private practice in the cities (UNICEF 1995a).

Furthermore, in 1998 Official Development Assistance (ODA) from richer to poorer countries amounted to $51.9 billion. That would have gone a long way to finance basic programmes. However, as detailed in the previous chapter, donors are just as perverse in distributing their aid as states are in allocating funds within their budgets. In practice, it is not uncommon for only about 10 per cent of all international aid for development to be specifically devoted to the main human priorities. That was one of several conclusions reached by a study of sixteen countries published by UNICEF and the UNDP in 1998. It was reported that the proportion of aid given to basic needs varied widely over time but it exceeded 20 per cent on only a few occasions (UNICEF 1999: 33). Taking all the above factors together, it is possible to say that finding the additional finance for basic social needs might not be easy but it is hardly impossible.

PAST FACTS AND PRESENT MYTHS

I sought in this chapter to establish a few facts and to challenge a few myths. The way today's developed countries achieved their status was considered in detail to highlight long-term evolution on a wide front that took in more than just economic development. In addition, the role of big government in enabling most people to play an active part in the evolution of their country was emphasised. However, my principal aim was to make the point that sustainable economic development is dependent on achieving reasonable progress in human development in the first instance. Putting the emphasis on economic growth too early in the process would be technically ineffective, harmful to national morale, and a waste of time and effort in the long run, as experience in the last fifty years amply demonstrates.

NOTES

1. A well-documented record of how and why prosperous nations attained their unique position is given in Chandler (1977) and Chandler et al. (1997).
2. For instance, James Hargreaves (1720–1778) invented the spinning jenny, Richard Arkwright (1732–1792) explored waterpower, James Watt (1736–1819) perfected the steam engine, and Samuel Crompton (1753–1827) developed the spinning mule. It is most unlikely that any of them thought they were taking part in an industrial revolution.
3. Studies of inequality now form an important part of economics. *Lorenz curves* are commonly used to give a graphical illustration of inequality in income and wealth. A straight line at 45 degrees indicates perfect equality. The *Gini coefficient* measures these aspects quantitatively. Basically, it expresses deviation from absolute equality as a percentage of total inequality (Samuelson and Nordhaus 1995: 359).
4. Most of the US budget statistics were obtained from publications of the Office of Management and Budget.
5. The budget information for Britain was based on figures released by H.M. Treasury.

SEVEN

FREEDOM TO INTERACT

The main strands of the arguments I have advanced so far can be summed up in a few sentences. Nations behave as Complex Adaptive Systems, and their development, therefore, should be seen as an endless evolutionary trek through a fitness landscape with few signposts and shortcuts. In that concept of development, stable but evolving global patterns are dependent on local interactions by members of the population. In other words, people are, or should be, active participants rather than mere passengers on that journey of life. At heart, development cannot be imported or gifted from abroad: it is what a nation does for itself. In consequence, economic development makes sense only when it is set within the more fundamental context of human development.

Nothing happens in the absence of local interactions; the nation grinds to a virtual halt. On the other hand, haphazard interactions without appropriate rules that command general support produce chaos and little else. Both forms of wasteful existence can readily be observed in many of today's so-called developing countries. They are going nowhere and will go nowhere until and unless they manage to turn most of their populations into willing actors in social, political and economic events. The essential distinction that sets a successful nation apart, therefore, concerns the *freedom* and *capability* for most of its people to interact, in accordance with sensible rules, in a wide spectrum of activities that in total add up to a state of development.

The first precondition, freedom, is a function of the institutional setup – democracy, human rights, rules and regulations and so on; while the second, capability, depends on whether people are physically able to interact – their state of health, education, nutrition and security. The present chapter deals with freedom of interaction. Clearly, it is futile to pore over hindrances to capability, such as illiteracy, if individuals are not permitted to exercise their right to interact peaceably with others in the first instance.

DEMOCRACY: TOO VAGUE FOR THE PRESENT PURPOSE

'The thick masses of foliage', in the words of Richard Crossman (1907–1974), that add up to the concept of democracy, as seen in Britain for instance, are too broad and convoluted to be of much use in considering the more specific topic of the freedom for people to interact. Basically, the idea of democracy has been abused and misused from ancient times to the present. It is traditional, for example, for the man or woman in the street, as well as scholars who should know better, to talk of ancient Athens as the cradle of democracy; 'rule by the people'. The fact that less than a quarter of adults were able to enjoy the fruits of that democracy is forgotten or ignored. Three-quarters of adults were reduced to the status of spectators at best, and slaves at worst. As discussed below, the trappings of democracy do not necessarily guarantee to turn most people into free actors in the development project.

A movable feast

Modern politicians from left and right hold equally fluid views of democracy as those espoused by their counterparts in ancient Athens. For a start, international relations seem to fall outside the scope of common democratic conventions. It cannot be assumed that a democratic state will act democratically abroad, especially when it is powerful enough to please itself. In that sense the world is still a jungle where might is always right. Hence, the British defence secretary, in announcing wide-ranging reforms to the armed forces in July 1998, based the case for Britain to continue to be a major military power partly on the premiss that 'people like Saddam' should not be allowed to dominate regions of interest to Britain. Not unreasonable, but the other side of the argument – the dominance of British over Iraqi interests – was implicitly taken as being sacrosanct without the need for tedious explanations. In fact the whole saga of the invasion of

Kuwait, the Gulf War, and the UN sanctions is a sorry tale of violation by one and all of the rights of ordinary people throughout the region. In a similar vein, a state of democracy, or lack of it, often judged by little more than the whim of the leading powers, is now regularly cited as justification for assisting or penalising nations. Hence it is permissible to strangle Cuba, for example, on the grounds that it is a communist dictatorship, but the same yardstick is not applied as vigorously to Indonesia. In its heyday the USSR was just as active in that form of ideological abuse. And weaker states are even more ambivalent when it comes to democracy. As a rule, the mere mention of 'democratic' or 'peoples' in the name of a country is a sure indicator of highly undemocratic practices by the state.

Oppression by the majority

Democracy suffers from other practical problems. Taking 'rule by the people' first, one is confronted by the need to be more specific. Do we mean the majority? That seems fair, but what about the minorities and their rights? 'The subjection of the minority to the majority' – Lenin's description of democracy in *State and Revolution* – could, and often does, lead to oppression and violent clashes, as happened regularly throughout Nigeria's so-called democratic period. Heavy-handed treatment of the Kurdish minority in supposedly democratic Turkey is another case in point. A valued ally of Western powers, Turkey persecuted, to the point of genocide, the Kurds, and the Armenians before them, for many decades with total impunity.

One might opt for inclusive democracy in place of one based on majority rule, but instances where that has been tried are few and far between. How would it work in practice? And does the system deal with more subtle forms of violation that command popular support? Religious and social conventions often invade and restrict a person's democratic space. Moreover, and as discussed in later chapters, nutrition, health, education and security are additional influences that determine limits to the fundamental right of people to interact peacefully with others. In combination, these factors set the height of the hurdles to be negotiated by a nation in the process of exploring its fitness landscape; low in developed countries and higher in the case of other nations.

Democracy is not always welcome

There is a natural, but unwarranted, assumption that democracy commands approval from all sides and that nations taking their first steps towards democratic reforms will be helped, or at least left to manage their affairs without intervention by others. In ancient Greece, and in the eighteenth century when the word started to be used again, democracy was often referred to with disapproval. Plato and Aristotle were certainly no fans; the first because he felt democracy 'handed control of the government from experts in governing to populist demagogues', and the second because 'government by the people was in practice government by the poor, who could be expected to expropriate the rich' (McLean 1996: 130).

It is only to be expected that local elites and dictators would hold similar views about the virtues of democracy, but certain governments and corporations, with excellent democratic credentials at home, also share misgivings about the onset of democracy elsewhere as it could pose a threat to their interests. As history amply shows, this is more of a distinct probability than a remote theoretical possibility. It is almost certain, for instance, that the US government viewed the referendum held in Bahrain in February 2001, which resulted in a large vote in favour of constitutional multiparty monarchy, as a risk to 'stability' in neighbouring Kuwait and Saudi Arabia. A change in style of government in these countries, through revolution or popular plebiscite, would simply not be permitted. Democratic or otherwise, the new government might not be as accommodating of American vital interests, period.

Concerns regularly led to action in the past. Algeria is one example among many. Army officers, supported by France, promptly seized power when the 1992 elections looked set to bring the Islamic Salvation Front to power. The country has been unstable, with daily massacres of innocent civilians, ever since. French action was based on good precedents. Chile attracted the attention of America's CIA throughout the 1960s and 1970s because the US government did not approve of policies advocated by certain politicians, such as Salvador Allende (1908–1973).[1] Large American corporations were involved locally and that translated into 'vital national interests'. Allende was repeatedly voted to Chile's Senate from 1945 until 1970, when he was elected president. Effort was made by the CIA under orders from the White

House to topple him, but General Schneider, commander of the armed forces, was a democrat and that was viewed as a major hurdle. Various coup attempts were made, including one in which Schneider was conveniently killed, but a coup in 1973, which cost Allende his life, was successful, reportedly at a cost to the CIA of only $8 million. Chile, one of the few democratic countries in Latin America, was handed over to brutal military dictatorship for many years to come.

Secret services, the CIA included, are powerful weapons in the drive against the emergence of democracy abroad wherever and whenever that presented potential harm to national, or commercial, interests. Iran provides a good illustration of the procedures and excuses used to justify covert, and occasionally overt, intervention. During the latter days of the Shah's reign it became clear that he and his regime were on their way out. After decades of doting admiration, the message from the West changed overnight to one of criticism of his autocratic rule. When Mussadegh came to power in the 1951 election, he tried to introduce reforms in response to similar concerns about the Shah's misuse of power. However, that was perceived as a threat to Western oil interests. The CIA set Operation Ajax in motion in 1953 and it is reported that it took only two months and $200,000 to topple Mussadegh and bring the Shah and his ruthless clique back to power. The action also succeeded in stopping budding democracy in its tracks. Obligingly, the Shah 'poured money into armaments and industrialisation but [he also] drove the masses into the arms of the ayatollahs' and the Islamic revolution in 1978. Curiously, President Carter told the Shah six months before his overthrow that 'Iran was an island of peace and prosperity in a sea of trouble and poverty' (Heikal 1992: 53).

Democracy in the eye of the beholder

Attitudes to the democratisation of developing countries have not changed in recent decades. Nigeria was racked by ethnic and religious rivalries since independence in 1960 and the military 'had to step in to restore order'. In 1993, however, the Armed Forces Ruling Council was disbanded in preparation for elections. Abiola, a businessman with liberal attitudes, was duly elected president in June of that year. After many years of corrupt rule by the military that event was not welcome by senior officers. Certain foreign governments and corporations, who supported and benefited from previous regimes, liked the new setup even less. The elections were eventually declared null and void, Abiola was imprisoned, and that was followed in November by an inevitable coup that brought Abacha to power. The most populous country in Africa with good agricultural land and massive petroleum and natural gas deposits was led in short order into bankruptcy. Abacha died in June 1998 and his successor, Abubakar promised reforms, but Abiola had to renounce his claim to the presidency first.[2] Fortuitously, Abiola died suddenly on 7 July 1998, during a meeting with a 'democracy team' led by the US undersecretary of state. Nigeria was restored to some sort of democracy in May 1999, but, in the words of President Obasanjo, that is 'a process and not a one-off event', and it remains to be seen how that process pans out in future.

It is indeed a rare dictator who does not claim to be the ultimate democrat with interest in nothing more than the good of the people. The ambiguity is just as pronounced when foreign policy comes into play. A blind eye is turned to excesses by regimes friendly to powerful governments and their interests, as suggested by Carter's remarks about Iran under the Shah. Similarly, little is said about the state of democracy in Brunei Darussalam or Saudi Arabia, say, although, in the words of the UNDP, both countries have 'never had a parliament' (UNDP 1999: 220). Libya and China, by contrast, are castigated for being undemocratic. The aim here is not to judge these countries but to underline the point that labels, accolades and brickbats from abroad are worth little, particularly in connection with democracy. As in all social, political and economic phenomena, democracy comes in all shapes and sizes. As befits a Complex Adaptive System, it is also an uncertain process that has no beginning or end.

No quick fixes to democracy

Al-Gosaibi, at the time Saudi Arabia's ambassador in London, does not harbour any ill will towards the West, but in a 1998 lecture he had some forthright words to say about the importation of business and political ideas from abroad. Democracy as defined today, Al-Gosaibi said, 'is a Western product, part of a long-evolving Western history.... Yet the attempt to impose democracy on all and sundry is relentless.' He felt that there were prerequisites for that particular brand of democracy that might not necessarily be on tap in other societies. Interestingly, Al-Gosaibi expressed similar reservations about trends in international trade when he added, 'the slogan is globalisation. In short, it means that the rest of the world must do business à la America.'[3] The thrust of his comments was not directed against the generalised concept of democracy. Difficulties arise, however, when attempts are made to transplant an intricate system that evolved over many centuries to other cultures. When the effort is prompted by factors that have little to do in reality with personal or human rights the results become inevitable. In recent decades, calls for liberal political attitudes were mainly intended to convince target states of the need to adopt liberal economic policies, especially in relation to international trade. Incessant pressure on China to 'reform' might well fall in that category.

In any case, liberal systems of state do not necessarily lead to perfect societies. For example, it took social upheavals caused by two world wars for Britain finally to embrace the welfare state. The move was a long time coming, but when it finally did the transition was swift. Britain was in the grip of a new *attractor*, and it all happened in the life of one parliament following the 1945 elections. It took just as long for injustices to be rectified in other societies. Despite a constitution that was amended regularly since it was adopted in 1874, women in Switzerland were allowed to have a voice in choosing their government only as recently as 1971. Equally, the American Declaration of Independence might intone that 'all men are created equal' is a self-evident truth, but somewhere on the way black people missed out on that lofty principle. Equality arrived on the scene as late as the 1960s. Finally, the ability of an American president or a British prime minister to take his or her country to war without a democratic vote by the people's representatives might be considered undemocratic by some, but that does not make the arrangements in the USA and Britain wrong or unacceptable. They simply reflect historic local choices.

Additionally, Western-style democracy has not stopped states or their agents from committing atrocities against foreign nations and citizens. Purely for business reasons, 200 of Switzerland's elite convinced the government that secret cooperation with Nazi Germany was desirable. Switzerland not only discouraged persecuted Jews from finding a haven within its borders but it also turned against Swiss Jews. Possibly the most disturbing accounts of that period related to the purchase of assets held by German Jews at knock-down prices in exchange for safety. Furthermore, democracy did not save some citizens from barbarian practices by their own governments, as was the case when Australia decided to 'civilise' the Aborigines. That project turned into a huge experiment in social engineering that lasted from 1910 to 1970. During that time, about 100,000 Aboriginal children were taken away from their families and put in the care of white people. Many were abused or simply died from neglect. Britain adopted complementary practices; orphans were exported to Australia to populate the continent, and that scheme lasted up to the 1960s (*Sunday Times*, 31 August 1997).

In short, Western-style liberal democracy might be superior in many ways, but it does not come with guarantees. As in all matters relating to Complex Adaptive Systems, an ultimate model does not exist; evolutionary change in democratic norms is continuous and requires a long time to unfold. Learning from others is useful, but imitation is not a substitute for exploration of local constraints and possibilities.

THE FUNDAMENTAL RIGHTS OF THE INDIVIDUAL[4]

In consequence, it seems more helpful, in looking at development as a Complex Adaptive System in general and freedom of people to interact in particular, to consider the topic from the perspective of the social, civil, economic and other fundamental rights of the individual. The intention is not to consider the subject in depth, but to give an outline of the state of individual rights in the developing world in order to show that, while progress is undoubtedly being made, the overall picture is most unsatisfactory. Essentially, the aim is to highlight the link between human development and individual rights: the former is a dependent variable of the latter. In other words, progress cannot be delayed, as there is more at stake than questions of fairness and morality.

Well-trodden subject

Individual rights are a popular topic of discussion at conferences, especially those attended by government leaders. Impressive declarations, backed by detailed treaties, covenants, conventions and monitoring arrangements, are promulgated on almost an annual basis. The 1992 Rio Declaration, for example, proclaimed 'human beings are the centre of concerns for sustainable development. They are entitled to health and productive life in harmony with nature.' That was clear enough, but it was followed in 1993 by the Vienna Declaration, agreed at a world conference devoted entirely to human rights, which concluded that these rights and freedoms are 'the birth rights of all human beings and should be treated as mutually reinforcing'. The 1994 Cairo Declaration was appropriately more specific by declaring that 'the principle of gender equality and women's right to reproductive health are vital for human development'. Then the 1995 Copenhagen Declaration arrived at the scene to address another specific right by announcing that 'eradicating poverty is an ethical, social, political and economic imperative of mankind'.

Global preoccupation with human rights is not a new phenomenon. The Universal Declaration of Human Rights was agreed as far back as 1948. In a handful of articles written simply but eloquently, the UDHR left nothing more to be said about the basic principles. The Declaration is now enshrined in the International Bill of Rights, which also includes the International Covenant on Civil and Political Rights and the International Covenant on Economic, Social and Cultural Rights; both agreed in 1966 and implemented in 1976 (UNDP 2000: 44). Other agreements embrace the 1969 Convention on the Elimination of All Forms of Racial Discrimination (ICERD) and the 1981 Convention on the Elimination of All Forms of Discrimination Against Women (CEDAW). Substantial progress in the last half-century has been made in establishing institutional and monitoring arrangements to define accepted norms and the means by which states can signify their adherence to these conventions.

Modest real progress

It would seem, therefore, that every eventuality has already been catered for most adequately, but effort did not stop there. Procedures were enacted, in the form of standing commissions and courts, to keep close watch on violations and to bring the guilty to account. In addition, UN-sponsored systems have been augmented by regional arrangements. Those in the Americas and Europe come as no surprise, but Africa has its own elaborate setup comprising an African Charter on Human and Peoples' Rights (1981), an African Human Rights Commission (1987), and an African Human Rights Court that was created in 1998 although it has yet to begin its work (UNDP 2000: 47).

In short, the effort devoted to the promotion of human rights, if the written and spoken word were used as a yardstick, is on a par with that lavished on development. The results are just as disappointing: progress is made here and there but has not yet gained sufficient momentum to turn it into a self-sustaining activity. On paper everything is perfectly acceptable, as clearly demonstrated by the statistics provided by most countries and published periodically by the UN and its agencies. But in practice violation of human rights is as widespread as ever. Essentially, repressive regimes and societies have become more sophisticated. As happened before in the case of overt colonisation, subtler practices have substantially replaced the outdated naked repression model. Experience in Africa illustrates this point. During the 1990s, Africa's one-party states gave way to multiparty regimes and everyone applauded the move. However, a pattern has emerged whereby government 'fixes the election; the opposition boycotts it or rejects the result; the government ignores the opposition'. Cynics, *The Economist* reported on 23 November 1996, call that sham 'donor democracy'; it offers 'just enough to keep aid-givers happy', or at least quiescent.

STATE REPRESSION

The most obvious and prevalent form of violation of people's rights centres on the exercise of brute force by the state over civilian populations through the display, and ready use, of weapons provided with alacrity by the international arms industry. The final stage in oppression is of course death: during the twentieth century governments murdered about 170 million people – men, women and children. That situation is not accidental and did not come about overnight. Oppression by the state is an ancient phenomenon that did not disappear in these supposedly enlightened times. On the one hand, colonisation, particularly in Africa and Asia, had to be replaced by something that was equally beneficial to the colonial powers. On the other hand, a new contending political philosophy arrived on the scene with the avowed intention of converting the whole world to communism at any price.

The developing world in organised agitation

In consequence, the developing world suffered well over a hundred successful military coups between 1960 and 1990. It is appropriate to call them coups to distinguish them from the traditional popular revolutions that took place, for instance, in England, France and the USA a few centuries before. There were at least three stages to that succession of coups. First, newly independent nations had to be kept under the control of their past, mainly European, colonial masters. That was easily accomplished; they appointed their chosen puppet rulers before they left. In some cases, the previous colonial powers were mandated by the League of Nations to oversee the affairs of their past colonies for several decades. Next, the two superpowers organised military coups to overthrow some of the vassal rulers in order to install client regimes that were entirely to their liking. And then the two superpowers themselves began a long process of unseating each other's local dictator, mainly by violent revolutions that masqueraded as liberation movements of various hues.

Obviously, some coup leaders were honest but most were little more than willing pawns in a profitable global game of chess. In practical terms, it is difficult and costly to mount a coup, and that applies even more so to prolonged civil wars. Foreign logistic and financial help is indispensable if coup leaders, well-intentioned or otherwise, are to meet with success. Materials and funds are easily transferred through secret services and third parties and the new regime is hooked. The process is not only dependable in achieving results, but the mere threat of such action to unseat a leader is sufficient in most cases to acquire compliance from the government of the day. Above all else, these activities are highly rewarding to individuals on both sides of the fence. Untraceable suitcases of money used in clandestine operations are notoriously difficult to audit, and receipts are never asked for or given.

Democracies nurture dictatorships abroad

Rhetoric apart, modern history is littered with examples of powerful countries with impeccable democratic traditions that expended money and effort in order to install or maintain dictatorial regimes abroad. The case of Mobutu in Zaïre provides a classic illustration. He came to power in 1961 after a coup backed by America and Belgium, and went on to become a ruthless tyrant. When Kabila, 'inspired by a Chinese version of communism', managed to occupy Stanleyville, now Kisangani, in 1964, Belgian paratroopers were transported in American aircraft to restore Mobutu's grip on the town (*Sunday Times*, 11 May 1997). Zaïre was thus made to endure Mobutu and his clan up to 1997 when Kabila took over, this time with help from Rwanda and Uganda, and encouragement from the USA. In August 1998 his allies turned against him to support a new rival; Kabila, they belatedly discovered, was unreliable. He was finally killed in early 2001 in a mysterious event that brought his son to power.

There are many other instances of that ilk, as was the case in Indonesia. President Sukarno became the focus of attention in Washington in the mid-1950s. He committed two sins: he courted the Indonesian communist party to offset the influence of his army generals, and decided that as the communists had won about one-quarter of the vote in the 1955 elections they should also be given a place in the cabinet (Ranelagh 1992: 105). The CIA was ordered to take steps to bring Indonesia back to the straight and narrow, and action was taken on all fronts, including rebellion on the island of Sumatra and the release of a pornographic film with a Sukarno lookalike! The operation was inconclusive but Sukarno moved closer to the USA, which was the object of the exercise in the first instance. But that promptly resulted in a failed coup attempt, organised this time by the Chinese communists, that resulted in the death of about half a million people.

Ambivalent attitudes to human rights

The leading democratic powers are, at best, indifferent to human rights abroad. Basically, they are not against democracy or human rights, but they certainly put their interests first on all occasions. Remarks made by one of the top people at the CIA during a conference convened to discuss Latin America illustrates this stance perfectly. He declared: 'we should not hesitate before police repression by the local government. This is not shameful … it is better to have a strong regime in power than a liberal government if it is indulgent and relaxed and penetrated by communists' (Lafeber 1983: 107). The conference was held at the height of the Cold War, but in a 1993 update of his book on *Inevitable Revolutions* Lafeber was able to demonstrate that

American policy has not changed much in more recent years. At the end of the day, the 'policy' of any country is the sum total of the desires of a vast number of egoistic individuals and interest groups. Evil conspiracy or ill intent is not part of the process.

As such it should not be thought that the USA is alone in subverting human rights abroad in the cause of promoting its national interests. The French, Belgian and Dutch colonial record in this field is inglorious to say the least. British history is only marginally better, and current actions continue to put national interests above the rights of people abroad despite assurances that Britain now has an ethical foreign policy. The USSR, as was seen in Ethiopia and Somalia, was of course a major player in the growth of repression within the developing world, on the principle that the ends justified the means. As discussed in Chapter 9, the provision of weapons, on a commercial basis or as gifts, was the principal channel chosen by the USSR, and other powers, to change the destiny of humankind into their chosen image. Invariably, the main outcome was oppression of civilian populations by greedy tyrants; intervention by foreign powers rarely results in anything else.

There has been a relative lull over the last few years in violent revolutions and the growth of overt military dictatorships. However, the lull does not suggest a move to representative government and respect for human rights. In 1960, less than one-third of the population of all developing countries were ruled by military-led dictatorships. Fifteen years later the proportion had grown to a half (Ohlson 1988: 18). Nowadays, the drift is towards civilian governments dominated directly by retired army officers or indirectly by serving officers. The new element since the late 1980s has been the emergence of the USA as the sole hegemonic power. There is no need for military takeovers, as any change would require the prior approval of the USA and that can be arranged more decorously by other means.

It depends on the repressor and the repressed

World reaction to repression depends very much on the parties involved and, yet again, whether the interests of the leading powers are affected. Over 200,000 people, a third of the population, were killed during Indonesia's occupation of East Timor starting in 1975 (*New Internationalist*, November 1994: 14). The invasion of Tibet by China had roughly similar effects, and in both cases systematic efforts were made to wipe out the cultural, as well as the social and political, heritage of whole nations. Although these violations attracted some noisy protests from human rights groups and certain sectors of the media, hardly anything was done at the official level to bring the aggressors to account. Trading and cultural relations, including of course the sale of weapons, were maintained without interruption.

The contrast with what happened when Iraq invaded Kuwait is striking. Here, vital oil interests were at issue and the response was swift and comprehensive; the so-called world community, meaning the USA principally, simply could not tolerate the aggression. When the Gulf War was over, the allies declared a no-fly zone in the north of Iraq, ostensibly to protect the Kurds. Combat missions are regularly undertaken by allied air forces from military bases in Turkey for that purpose. Simultaneously, the same bases are used by the Turkish air force to mount attacks against the Kurds in southern Turkey and northern Iraq. The allies, and in fact the UN and the world community, seem oblivious to the irony of the situation. In simple terms, oppression of the Kurds by Iraq is unacceptable, but it is tolerated when exercised by Turkey.

In theory, the situation is perfectly clear

The above anomalies are very common, but what do the numerous conventions, declarations, commissions and courts that have grown as masses of foliage around the topic of human rights say about the subject? They all have one perfectly simple and clear view: human rights are *universal, inalienable and indivisible*. They are universal because they have the same weight and have to be respected in relation to each and every individual. They are inalienable because they cannot be withheld from and given up by any individual. And they are indivisible because they are all of equal value; economic rights are not more or less important than social or cultural rights, and certain rights cannot therefore be promoted at the expense of other rights. Governments and large corporations routinely violate these principles all over the world, but the UN and its agencies continue to act as if all is reasonably well on the rights front.

The softly softly approach might avoid embarrassment and confrontation, and it might well provide a degree of moral palliation that something is being done, but it has failed to produce the desired results. The effect on human development is as clear as it is devastating. Fundamentally, violation of individual rights imposes a set of conditions that are the exact opposite to those needed by Complex Adaptive Systems to function optimally. Oppressive regimes, local and foreign, are interested first and foremost in control. Diversity in actions and behaviour, and free exploration of possibilities are disallowed, and often harshly punished. The effects are debilitating as they reduce the ability or even willingness of individuals to participate in social, cultural, political and economic affairs.

Put simply, oppression, in all forms and at all times and places, has disastrous effects on the ability of nations to make progress on human development. The state might be 'generous' in providing food, shelter and healthcare, but the structure cannot be an evolutionarily stable strategy (ESS) without the voluntary input of energy by individuals through day-to-day interactions with others. Sooner or later, largesse has to stop due to 'economic difficulties', as seen in the USSR and as experienced by many nations in the so-called developing world. Tragically, repressive states hardly ever realise that they create their own problems by curtailing interactions that would not have challenged the privileges of the ruling elite. Leading powers have the same blind spot; most of their actions abroad come back to haunt them with a vengeance in later years.

APARTHEID OF GENDER

The late UNICEF executive director James P. Grant coined the provocative, but apt, phrase 'apartheid of gender' to describe repression directed at women. In the words of Bunch (UNICEF 1997: 41), 'violence against women and girls is the most pervasive violation of human rights in the world today. Its forms are both subtle and blatant and its impact on development profound. But it is so deeply embedded in cultures around the world that it is almost invisible.' Other sectors of the community chosen on the bases of ethnic origin or belief also find themselves at the receiving end of serious violations of human rights. These forms of selective abuse are insidious as they frequently command a measure of consensus that lends them a veneer of legitimacy. In numbers, women are the most significant targets for systematic repression; comprising half the population, their active participation in national life is pivotal in achieving optimal performance.

Prejudice against women is commonplace, but it is on an altogether higher plane in certain parts of the developing world. The essential difference lies in the absence of institutional safeguards that might help to alleviate the problem. Quite the reverse, in fact, as traditions in some regions condone practices such as 'honour' killing, female genital mutilation (FGM) and dowry deaths. However, other less brutal restrictions on women's freedom of interaction are more widespread, and just as harmful to development efforts. For example, whenever a choice has to be made it is standard practice in certain countries to give priority in education to males at the expense of females. It would seem, yet again, that human rights are alienable and divisible irrespective of what a stack of conventions might have to say on the matter.

Difficult barriers to overcome

Complicity between state and society is a major hurdle. Certain religious traditions lend support to the view that women should be hidden away and watched over to a degree that in effect stops them from being active members of the community. In some cases zealous focus on women does not extend to taking care of their health and other needs. In Afghanistan, Guinea, Sierra Leone and Somalia, for instance, a woman faces a 1-in-7 risk of dying due to pregnancy or childbirth during her lifetime. In Spain, by contrast, the risk is 1 in 9,200. Prejudice against females is doubly costly. First, it limits the contribution that women can make to the well-being of their community. Second, young children receive their first helpings of learning and healthcare from the females around them, normally their mothers. Ill-informed, oppressed and illiterate women are of little value on that score.

Women receive a particularly raw deal in some Islamic countries. This is perplexing, as they are accorded a valued place in that religion. A whole section in the Koran is devoted to their rights and their status in society. However, the Shari'a, Islamic law, continued previous practices in some respects. Some Islamic sects, particularly Shiism, took the matter further. Hence, while it is perfectly clear that the Koran does not require women to cover themselves from head to foot, that stipulation is followed strictly in a number of Shiite communities. It has been suggested that women in high society began to wear the veil after the elite acquired concubines, in order to set themselves apart from courtesans, and the fashion then spread to other households (al-Wardi 1996: 56).

The picture is not the same everywhere and for all time periods. In the early days of Islam women played a decisive role in the life of their communities that went well beyond domestic chores. Muhammad himself married Khadija, a widow engaged in running a successful trading business. There were also famous female poets, whose works are admired and studied to this day. Others took an active part in the many campaigns that marked the early growth of the new religion. And women continue to enjoy similar status to men in many Islamic countries. Vocal feminists, such as 'Anbara Salam in the Lebanon and Huda Sha'rawi (1878–1947) in Egypt, performed a valuable service in that respect (Hourani 1991: 344). In these enlightened locations highly educated and emancipated women are an integral part of society.

Nonetheless, there are glaring exceptions. Women in Afghanistan were ordered by the Taliban government to work only in a few occupations such as nursing, while women college professors and those involved in business had to resign and stay at home. Moreover, although it is unwise to generalise, it is noticeable that Islamic countries on the whole are slower in ratifying international agreements relating to women's rights (UNICEF 1997: 48). And where progress is made it is painfully slow. Hence, female genital mutilation and 'honour' killing continue to be widespread in too many locations. The rate of FGM in Djibouti, for example, is a startling 98 per cent although that country adopted legislation against it in 1994 (UNICEF 2000: 31). Three-quarters of all cases are found in Egypt, Ethiopia, Kenya, Somalia and Sudan. Sadly, the record on 'honour' killing is equally bad.

A dilemma for some cultures

A word of caution is necessary here. Islamic nations observe the liberation of women in Western societies with some concern on grounds that are not easy for more liberal societies to comprehend. For example, they are baffled by the need for women participants in sporting events to take part wearing the briefest of outfits. The International Volleyball Federation, for example, requires female competitors to wear bikinis. Undoubtedly, the needs of television viewers and of sponsors are a major consideration in that policy. Volleyball is not alone in this; emphasis on sex and minimal dress is evident in other sports, particularly in track and field events (*Sunday Times*, 6 June 1999). But looked at from the perspective of more traditional cultures these practices appear threatening and to an extent gratuitous. They perceive a dilemma, which is not treated with sympathy in the West: once the process of liberation starts it cannot be trimmed.[5] However, there is a considerable difference between these understandable concerns and efforts to oppress women. In addition, discounting the input of half the population itself exacts a heavy toll in development terms.

Forgotten rights of the child

Children comprise another significant sector of society that is oppressed in ways that hold the development of some societies back. The subject is not unconnected with violation of the rights of women, as oppression is particularly rife in relation to young girls. In its mildest form, this can be illustrated by the disparity in the treatment of girls in education. In the late 1990s, the ratio of girls to boys enrolled in primary schools in Afghanistan was 9 per cent. The ratio for secondary schools in Yemen was only 26 per cent. Nevertheless, that seems tolerable in comparison to more extreme kinds of abuse. Apart from underage marriage to older, and often unknown, men, who can divorce them at a stroke, young girls are put to prostitution and often exported abroad for that purpose. In consequence, certain countries have earned themselves a terrible reputation as they attract paedophiles in large numbers as sex tourists.

Other forms of violation of girls and boys are equally prevalent. An estimated 250 million children between the ages of 5 and 14, roughly equal in number to the population of the USA, are economically active (UNICEF 2000: 27). About 50 million of these work in particularly awful occupations as child soldiers, bonded workers in sweatshops, and prostitutes. As many as 15,000 boys, some as young as 6, served as soldiers in Liberia's seven-year civil war that ended in 1997. Similarly, during Iran's war with Iraq in the 1980s, youths spearheaded attacks at the war front in response to a promise that if killed they would go straight to heaven. Clearly, children while they are involved in these activities are beyond the reach of the education and health systems; they are effectively barred from the development project for the rest of their days. In combination, and regardless of the moral and legal issues that are undoubtedly involved, the oppression of women and children has a practical and direct effect on the development process. Fundamentally, there can be no human development in the absence of these human rights.

ETHNIC AND RELIGIOUS OPPRESSION

Oppression directed at ethnic groups does nothing to improve prospects for progress by any community. The same mechanisms apply as in the case of women and children: interactions are curtailed, thereby reducing the input of self-organising energy to the nation as a Complex Adaptive System. In this instance, however, oppression often leads to local strife or all-out civil war; ethnic tensions open the door for domestic as well as foreign mischief-makers. Waste in material assets is added to loss in human resources.

Collier (1998: 5) suggested that ethnic divisions have 'various detrimental microeconomic effects, tending to reduce public sector performance, increase patronage, and lower the level of trust among individuals'.[6] However, he challenged the assumption that diversity would lead to conflict in all circumstances. Collier showed that societies most at risk are those in the middle of the range of ethnic diversity. Homogeneous societies do not have a problem *per se*, but more to the point those with high levels of diversity are just as stable. Conflict arises when there are a few ethnic groupings, especially when one monopolises most of the rewards. In practical terms, it costs less to initiate and coordinate conflict when there are a few large groupings.

Africa fails on all counts

Ethnic and religious fractionalisation in Africa is greater than that seen in the rest of the developing world. On that score, oppression and the incidence of civil war should be lower (Collier 2000: 6). On the other hand, democracy and personal income also play a major part in whether conflict can be successfully initiated. Democracy helps in the resolution of disputes before external or internal interest groups can exploit them, while income determines the opportunity costs as perceived by individuals when they consider an invitation to fight under the banner of an aspiring leader or a foreign power. Once civil war commences, though, the picture changes. In that situation, resolution of conflict hinges more on ethnic composition and less on income and political rights. Hence, Horowitz (1998: 11) pointed out that 'some peace settlements may need to change borders so as to increase (or reduce) the ethnic diversity of the state'.

Africa scores badly on most counts. Consequently, it comes as no surprise to read that 'Africa is the most conflict ridden region of the World and the only region in which the number of armed conflicts is on the increase' (SIPRI 1999: 20). There are clear historic reasons for ethnic tensions in that continent. National borders were determined by past colonial powers to suit their purposes and the ambitions of their local puppet dictators. As mentioned before, that would not have been a serious problem but for the fact that the lack of democratic institutions combined with low incomes to provide ideal conditions for local factions, foreign governments and clandestine groups to exploit the situation. Collier (1998: 13) makes the point that resolution of tensions 'might be sufficiently easy in homogenous societies that it does not depend upon democratic institutions, whereas in diverse societies these institutions make the difference between zero sum and cooperative solutions.'

The continent presents an assortment of instances to illustrate the tragic consequences of these factors. Sudan, as one example, has suffered from a debilitating civil war between the Muslims in the north and the Christians in the south for many years. Ethiopia and Somalia are equally illustrative of the stimuli that cause oppression and, therefore, hinder development efforts. In the course of negotiations for the independence of Ethiopia, Menelik convinced the colonial powers to extend the country from its original highlands region to twice that area by incorporating Eritrea and Tegre in the north and the Ogaden to the east. In that way, religious as well as tribal tensions were made unavoidable and they did not take long to materialise.

A 1969 military coup in neighbouring Somalia brought Mohammad Siad Barre to power. He was determined to advance his country's claim to the Ogaden. Impoverished Somalia had previously accepted a Soviet offer to equip and train its army immediately after independence, and by the time the coup took place the armed forces were among the largest in Africa (Johnston and Taylor 1986: 248). Yet again, the familiar pattern of arms from a foreign power leading to a military takeover repeated itself. Ethiopia followed a similar path, but in this case the USA was the source of weapons up to the 1974 'socialist' revolution. After that, the Soviets stepped in to give Ethiopia massive military help. This enabled it, in 1978, to attack Somalia and to re-establish control over Eritrea, which prompted the USA in turn to assist Somalia. The two superpowers helped both sides. The unavoidable outcome was a long history of violation of human rights, massacres, famines and a permanent state of strife. There were no winners among the players, domestic and foreign, but the ordinary people had to suffer deprivations for many decades.

NO DEVELOPMENT WITHOUT BASIC FREEDOMS

I will return to interstate and civil war in Chapter 9, but the topic had to be outlined here to give a rounded picture of the impediments that curtail the freedom of individuals to participate in social, political and economic affairs. The discussion concentrated on two key aspects. On the one hand, for a nation to evolve efficiently as a Complex Adaptive System individuals should be free to interact. That is inescapable. On the other hand, powerful forces sometimes set out to curtail the freedoms of individuals, significant groups of people, or whole nations. When they succeed the performance of the nation is compromised to a lesser or greater extent depending on the proportion of people written off.

The link between basic freedoms and good overall performance is hard to miss. Admittedly, debate has raged for some considerable time on which comes first, liberties or progress in economic and other issue areas. However, if it were accepted that nations evolve as Complex Adaptive Systems in which members' interactions determine overall performance – and, as argued so far, the evidence for that is overwhelming – then debate is essentially irrelevant. The two are inseparable.

Allowing time for change and recognising the linkage between all action areas are paramount factors in achieving sustainable progress. There is an ever-present temptation to jump to the conclusion that if only this or that parameter was improved a nation would be able to take giant steps that could short-circuit the tedious process of natural evolution. In that sense, the next chapter, dealing with capability and the factors that limit it, is a continuation of the present chapter. Clearly, freedom and capability are inseparable. They must be treated, therefore, as being indivisible and inalienable if nations on both sides of the divide are serious in their intention to succeed.

NOTES

1. According to Ranelagh (1992: 177), Secretary of State Kissinger, while chairing the anti-Allende campaign committee, is said to have commented, 'I don't see why we need to stand by and watch a country go communist due to the irresponsibility of its own people.'
2. When UN Secretary General Annan visited him on 1 July 1998, he found him 'very realistic' (*Sunday Times*, 5 July 1998). His wife Kudirat was assassinated in June 1996 and he evidently did not want to meet a similar end.
3. *Journal of the Arab–British Chamber of Commerce*, vol. 5, nos 7 and 8, March/April 1998.
4. Country Reports on Human Rights Practices published by the Bureau of Democracy, Human Rights and Labor US Department of State, available on the Internet, give revealing glimpses of conditions in many countries, some supposedly democratic, as in the case of India.
5. See al-Wardi (1996) and al-Ghazali (1994), which deal with the subject in depth and from differing viewpoints.
6. See also Horowitz (1998) for analysis of this issue area.

EIGHT

CAPABILITY TO INTERACT

A multitude of august gatherings have concluded after much delibera-
tion that the top social imperatives are still the same as those revealed
by St John the Divine two millennia ago. He identified Four Horsemen
of the Apocalypse as agents of the world's destruction on Judgement
Day: famine, disease, war and civil disorder. Destruction is an appropriate description even in the modern context: about 100 million
people die from hunger and hunger-related diseases annually, and 'from
1914 to 1991, over 180 million people were killed or allowed to die by
human decision' (Stephens 1995: 46).

The developing nations are well acquainted with the Four Horsemen and their cohorts. The present chapter features two of the original
Horsemen: famine, or more generally *malnutrition*, and *disease*. It also
presents *illiteracy*, or more broadly ignorance, as a newcomer to the
field of battle. Chapter 9 is set aside for the other two Horsemen, the
agents of war and civil strife. The biblical vision of destruction is
modified here to assess the impact of malnutrition, disease and ignorance on the capability of people to interact effectively. Basically, I
argue that development is not possible in a nation where most of the
people are badly fed, diseased and illiterate. In addition, I also set out
to show that cost and affordability are in many cases little more than
excuses for unwillingness to change course radically.

It is indisputable that malnutrition, disease, ignorance and war are
closely linked. They hunt as a pack and they share a common ancestry
of poverty. Simple diseases, easily shrugged off by the well fed, become outright killers when associated with malnutrition. Illiteracy
provides an added punch to these threats. As Timberlake (1991: 39)

pointed out, 'the killers in Africa are conditions which ... in the North are trivial inconveniences (measles, diarrhoea), or which have been virtually eradicated by hygiene or cheap injections (diphtheria, poliomyelitis and tetanus).'

By the same token, a small improvement in one component tends to diminish the ferocity of the others. Hence, the returns from modest actions can be, and frequently are, spectacular: collaboration between the Horsemen magnifies opportunities as well as perils. Income levels and economic growth are important but not essential factors. Evans et al. (1981: 1122) demonstrated that China, Sri Lanka and the state of Kerala in India 'are examples of countries that have attained a life expectancy close to the level in the industrialised world, with income levels in the range of the least developed countries'.

FOOD SECURITY: THE MOST FUNDAMENTAL THREAT

Nothing is as important or as in need of concerted action as food and water security. They provide the input of energy needed to keep living systems going; the self-organised stasis achieved by these systems is wholly dependent on that process. It is not surprising, therefore, that the 1.2 billion people who have to manage on one dollar a day spend almost three-quarters of that pitiful sum on food. The parallel with the mode of behaviour of Complex Adaptive Systems is unmistakable. Nations in turn depend on the energy provided by local interactions between people to achieve the self-organised but evolving pattern we recognise as 'development'. Therefore, the link between nutrition and national performance is clear in technical as well as commonsense terms.

Gathering clouds of food scarcity

There was a time in history when humankind was able to rely on plentiful availability of food and water. Overall, land and water were plentiful, and rivers and seas were brimming with fish. Land under irrigation increased over the millennia up to the end of the nineteenth century when the area amounted to some 40 million hectares, but that increased sharply to 94 million by 1950 and to 248 million by 1993 (Brown et al. 1997: 29). Consumption increased rapidly during the nineteenth and twentieth centuries due to faster growth in populations and a move up the food chain driven by rising affluence, but new demands were met by more intensive fishing, by the cultivation of new lands that required special irrigation methods, and by heavy reliance on fertilisers.

There are indications, however, that future expansion might not be as easy. For instance, the amount of fish caught increased from 19 million tons in 1950 to 88 million tons in 1988, but the catch seems to have hit a ceiling as it has remained roughly at that level ever since (Brown et al. 1997: 24, 29). Clearly, much can be done with the help of advanced technology but cost of production – in other words, price of food – begins to be a limiting factor. Additionally, other factors have conspired to make future prospects less promising. Increasing use of chemical fertilisers has become less effective; in many instances fertilisers now make little difference to yield. Water for irrigation is another major headache these days. Levels are falling in even the great rivers of the world, such as the Yellow River in China and the Colorado in the USA. In addition, the water table is falling fast in many parts of the world that rely on underground supplies for agricultural purposes.

And it seems global warming is becoming an established fact that few venture to dispute. A few areas have suffered floods, but in the main drought and desertification are on the increase. To make matters worse, demand for food is escalating due to rapidly increasing populations and growth in consumption per head. In short, the candle is burning at both ends. It is now generally accepted that there is a serious problem of food and water shortage, which is likely to grow worse in future, particularly in Africa.

Population growth

Food scarcity poses fundamental threats and challenges to the developing world. To an extent, it is driven by factors that are largely beyond the control of the nations concerned, but in many ways local trends and practices contribute substantially to the severity of the situation. Sheer numbers mean the developing countries start with a considerable burden. The world's population is just under 6 billion, of which 4.8 billion live in developing countries. Almost as many people live in sub–Saharan Africa, some 600 million, as in all the industrialised countries, at 850 million. That itself is not a critical factor; many of the developing countries do not have large populations.

Rate of population growth, on the other hand, is most certainly a major concern. While the industrialised countries now have virtually static populations, people in the developing world are increasing at an unsustainable rate of about 1.7 per cent annually. As always, sub-Saharan Africa is in the lead at 2.6 per cent. At this rate there are expected to be some 1.45 billion mouths to feed in that region of Africa by 2030. However, Afghanistan tops the league with a staggering 4.5 per cent rate of growth (WHO 2000: 156). High death rates and short life expectancy are known to lead to high birth and fertility rates. In simple but nonetheless accurate terms, parents attempt to counterbalance these factors by producing more babies. In the absence of provision for unemployment, sickness and old age outside the family, the offspring are relied on to provide all these social benefits in future years. Clearly, advocacy of birth control and education are, at best, of secondary importance, as they do not address the primary stimuli for population growth.

The 'population explosion' within the so-called developing countries is frequently cited, with a fair measure of justification, as the biggest hurdle to sustainable progress. In that context, the number of years it takes the population of a country to double provides a useful indication of the severity of the situation. *Doubling time* for the developed countries is in the range of 80 to 100 years. By contrast, the equivalent figure for countries in the developing world hardly ever exceeds 30 years. The population of Zaïre, for example, doubles every 22 years. The resulting burden on shaky economies is abundantly clear. Standards of living will deteriorate unless the economy grows at the same fast rate as the population, a tall order indeed.

Drift to the cities

Not unexpectedly, increasing population when coupled with urbanisation produces an amalgam of problems that is devastating to fledgling nations. Again, while urban populations are more or less static in the industrialised countries, they are growing by some 4.7 per cent each year in sub-Saharan Africa, and only a little less for the rest of the developing world (UNICEF 2001: 78). Urbanisation in that part of the world has now turned into a flood. It is no exaggeration, therefore, to say that the Apocalypse is just around the corner. In 1950 there were more urban dwellers in the developed than in the developing countries; in 1970 there were equal numbers; but by 1980 the picture was reversed with more people in developing countries living in the cities, and the upward trend continues unabated (Elliott 1996: 83).

Urbanisation, industrialisation and economic growth are significant factors in creating food scarcity, possibly the most damaging, and least obvious, element being the loss of agricultural land. Lands previously used for food production are paved over to provide housing, factories and roads. In Java, for example, fast urban and industrial expansion 'claimed 20,000 hectares of cropland in 1994, an area large enough to supply rice to 330,000 Indonesians'. On a larger scale, China's rapid industrialisation has been achieved at the expense of agricultural land. Rough estimates suggest that between 2.6 million and 6.5 million hectares of arable land might have been lost in that way in just six years from 1987 to 1992 (Brown et al. 1997: 46). And the drift continues.

The transition to city life in today's developed countries was prompted by increased productivity on the farm and growth of new jobs in town brought about by the Industrial Revolution. Economic gains offset the social costs. By contrast, urbanisation now taking place elsewhere in the world has few positive features; migration is from decaying rural areas to cities unable to provide food and shelter for the newcomers, let alone offer them employment. The topic was considered at the 1996 UN Second Conference on Human Settlements held in Istanbul. World leaders, it would seem, are resigned to escalating urbanisation, with consequential emphasis on tackling the worst problems at the receiving end in the cities. Hence, actions adopted by governments and by bodies such as the World Bank are aimed mainly at solving urban problems rather than tackling the forces that drive the rural populations to urban slums. The skewed patterns of spending seen in the budgets of the countries involved are the inevitable consequences of this policy of despair.

Major projects: illusions of progress

Possibly the most appalling, and exceedingly harmful, outcome of the focus on solving urban problems relates to the implementation of major infrastructure projects. The declared aim is in most cases simple: to generate electricity to meet increasing demands from industry and urban dwellers. So far so good, but there are also hidden agendas.

The projects are designed and built by foreign firms with only a passing interest in human development. Their fees, and at least some of the construction costs, are met from the aid programme sponsored by their country of origin. Local elites have every reason to welcome these activities. Apart from the claim that they are looking after 'the public interest', there are genuine security problems in the overcrowded urban areas and no government can ignore that lobby. In addition, the elite include the local agents and firms who benefit directly from large projects. Above all else though, these projects are golden opportunities for kickbacks at all levels within the private and public sectors (Caufield 1996: 17).

Major projects are damaging in other respects. The Sardar Sarovar Dam in India, part of the $5 billion Narmada Valley Project started in 1961, is a case in point. It has been described as 'an environmental catastrophe, a technological dinosaur and an example of flagrant social injustice' (Elliott 1996: 48). The dams included in the projects will ultimately 'displace 200,000 people, submerge 2,000 sq. km. of fertile land and 1,500 sq. km. of prime teak and sal forest'.[1] The results are not consistently positive even when the project is specifically designed with irrigation in mind. India again provides a good illustration. With the coming of independence, the national government with enthusiastic support from the international community in general, and the World Bank in particular, set out to put India to rights. Appropriately, food was the primary concern, agriculture the target, and irrigation the vehicle for achievement. More than 1,500 large dams were built, Nehru's temples of modern India, and in the words of Catherine Caufield India became 'one of the most dammed nations in the world'. Three-quarters of the irrigation projects remain uncompleted or have been abandoned altogether. Interestingly, Rajiv Gandhi, the prime minster who finally gave the go-ahead to the Sardar Sarovar Dam, lamented in 1986 that 'almost no benefit has come to the people from these projects ... no irrigation, no water, no increase in production, no help in their daily life' (Caufield 1996: 16).

The role of foreign experts

'Is Africa getting the right advice?' asked Timberlake (1991: 3). He concluded that it is not. He estimated that there were normally about 80,000 foreign experts working in sub-Saharan Africa alone for the specific purpose of helping local people to overcome their problems. With consulting firms charging some $180,000 per year for each expert this is a big business that consumes over half the aid donated to the area. Nonetheless, 'in the two and a half decades since African independence, Africa has plunged from food self-sufficiency to widespread hunger.' But Timberlake also pointed out that the same conclusion was reached by a senior vice-president of the World Bank, who admitted 'we have not fully understood the problems. We have not identified the priorities. We have not designed our projects to fit.' One wonders how long it will take for the overpaid and overstaffed World Bank to learn from past experience.

THE GLOBAL AGRICULTURAL MAZE

Is there a food shortage and why? These are not unreasonable questions at a time when farmers in the UK, for example, are going out of business because they cannot sell their produce at economic prices. Similarly, the casual visitor to the USA cannot but be amazed by the amount of food wasted. And high standards common to all the industrialised countries require the immediate destruction of any produce that is not perfect in every way. The average person in these and other countries where food availability is not an issue might well conclude that the situation is more or less the same everywhere. Would a visit to a country where food scarcity is a problem shed light on the subject? Not necessarily. The five-star hotels tourists frequent offer the same quantity and quality of food available at home. Maybe a visit to the countryside would help? Not necessarily again. Fields cultivated with tea, coffee, cotton and exotic fruits can be seen in abundance. Where is the problem?

I presented earlier a few instances of local conditions or actions that exacerbate food scarcity. It is appropriate to complete the picture by considering briefly the wider issues that impinge on the topic of food production and consumption. Two points should be kept in mind in this context: domestic and foreign forces frequently combine to drive the system towards scarcity, and even when food is generally available many people simply cannot afford to buy it. It is common experience that plentiful supplies of food are on display in cities that are only a few miles away from areas of famine. Similarly, severe malnutrition was caused by the UN sanctions imposed on Iraq although food, for those who had the magic dollars, was not in short supply. Essentially, food scarcity is not only a function of land, water and farmers. When looked at globally, these factors are important but not decisive. All too often, nutrition and economics are inseparable.[2]

Distant fallout from domestic policies

Governments in the industrialised countries provide substantial subsidies to their farmers and then buy enormous amounts of food for storage, destruction or export. Surplus food is stored as strategic reserve and as carryover stocks into next season. Food is a trading commodity like any other, but governments view it also as a strategic asset. Hence, in 1972, a year of widespread starvation associated with the Sahelian drought in Africa, the American government paid farmers $3 billion to take 50 million hectares out of production. The government also encouraged huge sales of produce to the Soviet Union to feed cattle. Decision-makers in Washington perceived some advantages in cooperating with the USSR at that point (Johnston and Taylor 1986: 233). Taking land out of production was not a perverse policy either; it was a necessary conservation measure to combat falling productivity and soil erosion. Starvation elsewhere was hardly a consideration in these decisions; the US government was merely looking after American interests.

The European Union's notorious Common Agricultural Policy (CAP) was instituted with similar objectives in mind. It was designed to create stable markets and give European farmers a reasonable standard of living. It grew into one of the most expensive systems of agricultural protectionism in human history, but has not been abandoned. In the mid-1990s, CAP provided export subsidies, local price support and paid for the collection and storage of tens of millions of tons of excess food, at an overall annual cost of $45 billion; about 60 per cent of the European Union's budget (Malcolm 1995: 52). In addition, the European Union destroyed two and a half million tons of fresh fruit and vegetables of perfect quality in 1995 alone (*Sunday Times*, 17 March 1996). And the European Union has similar policies to the USA so far as conservation is concerned; farmers are paid to leave some of their land uncultivated.

Protection measures and subsidies in Europe and the USA distort the world's food markets, making it difficult for farmers in poorer nations to compete, even in local markets saturated by cheap exports from abroad. To make matters worse, industrialised nations have set up effective barriers to discourage imports. For instance, the Uruguay Round of GATT, completed in 1993, left agricultural protection virtually untouched. Poorer nations were hit twice: once by cutbacks in barriers to industrial goods, a sector favouring elite nations, and then again by retention of barriers on agricultural products, a sector which could have helped weaker economies (World Bank 1995a). Sub-Saharan Africa was expected to show an overall loss as a direct result of that round. In other words, proliferation of so-called free-trade principles globally might not help the most needy region on earth to feed its people (World Bank 1995b).

Aid and debt make matters worse

Ironically, richer nations spend a great deal more on agricultural subsidies and other actions that impede poorer countries' ability to produce simple foodstuffs than they give in aid. But aid itself can be just as damaging. For instance, as Timberlake (1991: 32) reported, 'of well over $1.2 billion in food aid shipped to the Third World every year, about 70 per cent is sold at subsidised rates to Third World governments, which usually resell it [locally] to help balance their budgets.' The impact on the viability of domestic agricultural production is patently obvious. The capability of nations locally to meet at least part of their demand for food is compromised through this apparently well-intentioned effort to help. As seen in other cases, aid often acts against the long-term interests of the recipient nations.

The global agricultural maze does not end there. Not unexpectedly, governments in need of foreign exchange to fund imports and to pay for past debts encourage the move from staple foods to cash crops, such as tea and coffee. The World Bank and the IMF condone that shift for obvious reasons. Hence, Ethiopia, as an example, suffers regular bouts of famine and a permanent state of malnutrition but still manages to be one of the top ten world exporters of coffee, producing no less than 180,000 tons annually. The same applies to Bangladesh and its tea industry. The circle is now complete. In addition to the natural and human factors that degrade agricultural lands and water resources, local and foreign forces come together to impose their own burdens; the inevitable result is a chronic state of food scarcity, dependency and severe malnutrition.

Could they produce food for themselves?

Naturally, the question will be asked as to why farmers in the developing countries do not cultivate their lands simply to grow food to satisfy their own needs. For a start most farmers in that part of the world do not own 'their' lands. They pay rent to, typically, a few rich and powerful landowners and they can only do so by selling some of their harvest. Additionally, they require cash to meet the cost of other necessities such as transport of crops, medicines and household goods. Again, they can only do so by selling or bartering produce from the land. It goes without saying that they lack the funds to invest in machinery or in efficient irrigation and drainage systems. Selling produce locally is not an option, as that market is too limited. Crops have to be packed and transported to larger towns and cities, and in some instances this is done successfully through farming cooperatives. However, the same urban areas are targeted by foreign and large local agribusinesses offering better quality and quite possibly lower prices.

Inevitably, a point is reached whereby the small-scale farmers are priced out of the setup. They leave voluntarily or are evicted from the farms, the next stop being urban slums or refugee camps and humanitarian aid from abroad. Frequently the land reverts to wilderness or, in certain climes, is surrendered to the inexorable process of desertification, making agricultural land worthless through human misuse. In short, even those lucky enough to start out with some land soon join the landless. But of course others are not so lucky.[3]

Larger agricultural units, owned by governments, wealthy families or domestic and foreign companies, survive and in fact do quite well in many developing countries, but then they mainly specialise in cash crops with a ready market overseas. In response to well-understood economic pressures, even simple peasants with minute plots of land are forced by the state to move from staple foods to cash crops. Ironically, 'the main drawback to cash crops is that over the last decade they have produced less and less cash' (Timberlake 1991: 57). Timberlake's analysis is well worth reading as it highlights the significance of *indigenous knowledge* in agriculture. As in other situations, ill-informed experimentation by the World Bank is much in evidence. Early in the

1980s they believed strongly that benefits of cash crops would solve many problems, but that policy was later dropped: cash crops themselves, it was found, might be partly responsible for deterioration in soil quality.

DEPENDENCY ON IMPORTED FOOD

Clearly, availability of food is being increasingly outstripped by consumption. On the one hand, population growth and urbanisation are excessive, and, on the other hand, local and global responses are inadequate, counterproductive or irrelevant. In truth, the impoverished countries themselves should rightly shoulder some of the responsibility for their dire situation. Nonetheless, the mix of negative factors has elevated the situation in that part of the world to a degree of seriousness that has turned it into a question of 'food security' (UNDP 1999: 211). Africa, as mentioned earlier, nose-dived from self-sufficiency in food in the 1960s to endemic hunger. Stephens (1995: 46) argued that globally 'fewer than 20 nation states can now provide for a stable domestic food supply within their own borders compared with 100 at the turn of the [twentieth] century.' Consequently, many nations have lost what little independence they might have enjoyed in the past, as they are now reliant on a food production system that is controlled by a handful of countries and global agribusinesses. Annual food aid in cereals given to sub-Saharan Africa alone amounted to about 2.6 million tonnes in the mid-1990s (UNDP 1999: 214). Significantly, the USA controls 'a larger share of grain exports than the Saudis do of oil' (Brown et al. 1997: 36). In strategic terms, reliance on the ability, and often the whim, of one country to provide such a large proportion of the grain needed to feed the rest of the world verges on folly.

Beggars can't be choosers

Hunger and malnutrition reduce interactions and reflect badly on the performance of a nation as a Complex Adaptive System. That is a very serious constraint on the ability of any nation to develop. However, food insecurity has another sting in the tail that accord with the dictates of Game Theory: countries in need of food have to cooperate on all occasions, while those who have food security can compete. The sharing of rewards follows the usual pattern, with most going to the latter group. In essence, the developing countries are disadvantaged whichever way the topic of food is considered.

THERE IS MORE TO MALNUTRITION THAN SHORTAGE OF FOOD

Having made the point about dependence, I intend to concentrate henceforth mainly on the impact of chronic malnutrition on nations' performance. Deficiency in the intake of proteins and carbohydrates is an obvious cause of malnutrition, but poor feeding practices are just as important as shortage of food itself. For instance, according to WHO (2000: 57), malnutrition in central and eastern Europe 'is often "poor calories" rather than a "lack of calories"'. As discussed later, safe water and sanitation are also significant components of both nutrition and hygiene. However, an equally critical but less obvious element relates to lack of vital micronutrients in the diet. This is particularly significant in certain regions such as sub–Saharan Africa and South Asia where low intake of vitamin A, iodine and iron combine to inhibit the capability of people to take an active part in the social and economic life of their communities.

The silent and invisible emergency

Chronic malnutrition generates little public interest; hence UNICEF's reference to the 'silent and invisible emergency'. By contrast, dealing with famines associated with acute food scarcity attracts all the headlines. This dichotomy of response detracts from global efforts to address the more fundamental issues that leave 1 billion people, or one in six of the Earth's population, at the mercy of debilitating chronic malnutrition. Lack of focus on the big picture also obscures a deeper cause for alarm; namely the impact on infants, children and women. UNICEF (1998: 9) highlighted this aspect on two counts. On the one hand, malnutrition is 'implicated in more than half of all child deaths worldwide, a proportion unmatched by any infectious disease since the Black Death'. On the other hand, it leaves millions of survivors 'crippled, chronically vulnerable to illness, and intellectually disabled'. The impact on interactions by members of the population as elements of a Complex Adaptive System is self-evident.

Cheap and efficient remedies

In 1994, there were 652 million children under 5 in the developing world, of which some 231 million received an inadequate intake of vitamin A. As a result they stood a 23 per cent higher risk of death from common diseases. The deficiency also resulted in half a million cases of severe eye damage or blindness, more than 3 million cases of xerophthalmia and well over 13 million cases of night blindness. Half the children who go blind die within a few months (UNICEF 1995: 18). The solution to vitamin A deficiency, UNICEF (1995: 19) pointed out, has been known for decades: 'daily diet can be changed, usually at little cost, to include small amounts of green leafy vegetables; or 2 cent vitamin A capsules can be given three times a year to children over six months of age, or vitamin A can be added to sugar or cooking oil.'

Lack of iodine is even more brutal in inhibiting capability. In 1993 the World Health Organisation (WHO) estimated that over 1.5 billion people, or 30 per cent of the world's population, were at risk. The deficiency caused about 6 million cases of cretinism, 26 million cases of brain damage, and an 'increasing risk of mental impairment' to 655 million people. In short, one in ten people on earth are affected to some extent. Again, UNICEF (1995: 14) reported that an inexpensive remedy to iodine deficiency disorders has been known for most of the twentieth century: iodine can be added to the common salt used in food, at a cost of 'about 5 cents per person per year'. Nevertheless, there are 34 countries, with a combined total of 1 billion people, in which 50 per cent or less of the population use iodised salt. That shortsighted policy has 'serious economic and social consequences ... an overall reduction in the mental capacities' of whole communities (UNICEF 2000: 16). Ultimately, however, proper attention to diet and cooking methods are the first line of attack in tackling the problem of malnutrition in terms of both shortage of 'food' and deficiency in vital components.

MALNUTRITION AND DISEASE JOIN FORCES

The young, in particular, succumb to infections such as measles and diarrhoea before death occurs due to lack of food. As mentioned earlier, the WHO estimates that the 231 million children under 5 years of age with inadequate intake of vitamin A stand a 23 per cent higher risk of death from common diseases. In that sense, the often-repeated statistic that 8 million of the 13 million annual deaths of children under 5 can be attributed to diarrhoea, pneumonia, malaria and vaccine-preventable infections does not give the full picture. Over half of the 13 million deaths strike children suffering from mild to severe malnutrition (UNICEF 1995a: 14).

Incidence of anaemia, especially among children and women, caused by low absorption of iron from food, underlines the link between nutrition and health. About a quarter of a billion children in the developing countries are anaemic to a lesser or greater extent, and it is estimated that over half of pregnant women in that part of the world also suffer from this easily, and cheaply, treated condition. In the context of capability, the effects of anaemia are truly crippling. The WHO reported that the condition 'lowers the productivity of entire populations'. In the words of UNICEF (1995: 17), 'mental growth can be retarded by neurological damage, and there is strong evidence to show a measurable loss of IQ points in anaemic children.'

The toll of malnutrition and disease

The impact of disease, aided by malnutrition, is considerable and easily observed. Basically, the two 'Horsemen' are good at their jobs. Average life expectancy in 1999 was 64 years for the entire world and 78 years for the industrialised countries. But it was only 49 years for sub-Saharan Africa. Life was, and is, even shorter in Afghanistan, Bangladesh and Benin. In the case of Botswana, Malawi and Sierra Leone people could count themselves lucky if they were to survive to their fortieth birthday (WHO 2000: 156). And it should not be assumed that progress is being made in all cases. Life expectancy in Zimbabwe, for instance, decreased between 1993 and 1999.

Death rates – expressed as annual deaths per 1,000 population – of 14 and 16 for the developing countries and sub-Saharan Africa respectively, as compared with the global average of 9, tell their own story. And as usual Sierra Leone is at the head with 24 deaths per 1,000 population. The infant mortality rates – the probability of dying between birth and one year of age expressed as a percentage of 1,000 live births – are a cause of even greater concern. In 1999 the rate was 31 for the industrialised countries and 141 for the developing nations.

As expected, the situation is worse for the least developed countries and sub-Saharan Africa (UNICEF 2001: 78). High infant death rates and short life expectancy are known to lead to high birth and fertility rates. As outlined before, under these conditions family planning advice on its own is of marginal benefit.

Women and children first

The groups most susceptible to malnutrition and disease are infants, children and women, in that order. Beyond feelings of pain and grief, national economies pay a heavy price. Keeping the majority of the population below the capability divide means in effect that their Complex Adaptive System would operate at well below its optimum energy level. Self-organised patterns are not achievable and the system oscillates between wasteful chaos and deathly stasis.

Short lives and high infant mortality are the more obvious outcomes of malnutrition and disease. Conversely, the effects on mental aptitude and stamina often go relatively unnoticed. However, stunting of children – inadequate growth of the long bones in the body – is one noticeable mark that is left after the two Horsemen have done their work. Low weight at birth, caused by malnutrition and disease afflicting mothers, insufficient food and micronutrients, and repeated episodes of illness in the early years combine to produce children whose height is less than children who are fortunate to live under a different set of conditions.

It would be wrong to assume that stunting is just a physical condition. Because it is the outcome of deprivations that affect children in the critical first years, 'cognitive development and learning ability' are impaired, and 'once established, stunting and its effects typically become permanent ... the damage is often irreversible'. In several countries in South and Southeast Asia about half the children are stunted, and those in sub-Saharan Africa fare only slightly better (UNICEF 2000: 14). This incapacitating condition exists in more than 200 million children within the developing world. Stunting signals ongoing problems in adulthood and parenting. It is a cyclical process: stunted parents produce stunted children. The problem is more serious for girls, as smaller pelvic size increases the likelihood of serious medical difficulties associated with childbirth, a major problem for women in the developing countries at the best of times (UNICEF 1997: 21).

The latest reapers

Discussion of disease would be incomplete without mentioning the recent spread of tuberculosis and HIV/AIDS throughout the developing countries. Both conditions are efficient as outright killers and as inhibitors to capability. The former is difficult but not impossible to treat, while a cure for the latter has not yet been found. HIV/AIDS causes special concern in other ways. On the whole, it is a condition that mainly afflicts the young. Just as significantly, it has now assumed the scale of an epidemic in Africa. Drugs to control it are expensive, but critically it is a disease that thrives on ignorance.

Nowadays, the 'HIV/AIDS epidemic kills over two million people in Africa every year – more than 10 times the number that perish in wars and armed conflict' (WHO 2000: 58). There were over 10 million young people, between 15 and 24 years of age, suffering from HIV/AIDS in 1999, of which almost two-thirds were females, and half the cases were in sub-Saharan Africa (UNICEF 2000: 5). At present, the best defence is prevention and that relies heavily on education. In short, success is difficult in countries where illiteracy is high. To make matters worse, social customs, and particularly attitudes to women, present a big hurdle to efforts to address the raging epidemic. Additionally, expense is a powerful incentive for governments to seek to minimise the scale of the threat, as was the case in South Africa.

WATER: THE FOUNDATION OF DEVELOPMENT

Water has a dual role in hygiene: as a carrier of infection and as a cleansing agent. Scarcity of safe water is now a strategic problem confronting most countries, including those in the developed world. In the early 1990s, twenty-six countries were listed as suffering from critical water scarcity: those that had annual supplies of less than 1,000 cubic metres per person.[4] The situation is becoming progressively worse due to global warming, and to pollution and overexploitation of sources of water. In the USA, for instance, about one-fifth of the total irrigated area is 'watered by pumping in excess of recharge' (Brown et al. 1997: 119).

Rivers, lakes and seas are regularly used as dumps for waste material, from sewage to, astonishingly, radioactive substances and unstable surplus military weapons. And yet seawater represents no less than 97 per cent of the Earth's water resource. More and more water is being drawn from available sources and at the same time these assets are being actively polluted, a typical case of burning the candle at both ends. Western industrialised countries were for many years the main culprits, but not any more. The USSR, with its manic concentration on industrial production, came to occupy a special place in that league of wanton polluters. The record of the developing countries is not much better.

Demand for water doubled between 1940 and 1980; it was expected to double again by the end of the twentieth century; and it could double yet again in the decade after that (Tickell 1993: 38). Water availability to people in the developing countries, however, varies from place to place. Some have water piped to their homes with only occasional interruptions of supply. Others, still comparatively fortunate, have their water delivered by tanker, or communal standpipes, on a reasonably regular basis. For the rest, the search for water involves travel on foot for miles to the nearest well, and as usual women in these areas end up being saddled with that unwelcome task. That continues to be the case despite the fact that the UN designated the 1980s as both the International Drinking Water Supply and Sanitation Decade and the Decade for Women!

Water insecurity

Lack of safe water is a critical factor in increasing sickness and disease. The WHO attributes well over three-quarters of the incidence of illness to this single agent alone. Predictably, the dependence of any country on water resources located outside its borders is a sure sign of trouble. That subject features prominently in the negotiations between Israel and the Palestinian Authority, for example. Similarly, there are gathering clouds in relations between Turkey, Syria and Iraq caused by Turkey's intention to dam the Euphrates River flowing through all three countries. In sum, water, as with food, is becoming a major security problem for many nations.

Efficient reapers

Shortage of safe water for agriculture and other uses is an obvious difficulty, but inadequate sanitation is an even bigger threat. In 1999, about a quarter of the population in the developing world, some 1 billion people, had to manage without safe water supplies. In the same year half the population, more than 2 billion people, lacked access to adequate sanitation (UNICEF 2001: 89). As always, rural areas suffer more badly on both counts. For instance, three-quarters of people in rural areas are denied adequate sanitation.

The combination of unsafe water and bad sanitation is devastating. One outcome, diarrhoea, illustrates the scale and nature of the fallout. On the face of it diarrhoea does not seem too alarming, but according to the WHO it kills almost 2 million under-5s within the developing nations annually. It is one of the five top child killers, alongside perinatal conditions, respiratory infections, vaccine-preventable diseases, and malaria. Just as tragically, diarrhoea 'leaves millions more children underweight, mentally and physically stunted, easy prey for deadly diseases and so drained of energy that they are ill equipped for the primary task of childhood: learning' (UNICEF 1997: 5). The partnership between the Horsemen of malnutrition, disease and ignorance in impeding capability is revealed here to perfection.

Remedial costs are not prohibitive

It might be thought that dealing with the problem of shortage of safe water and inadequate sanitation is too costly, but that is not necessarily the case. All too often the real problem with respect to water is conservation and accountability. Up to 60 per cent of treated and pumped water in the developing countries never reaches its intended customers because of illegal tapping and leakage. Such losses 'cost Latin Americans between $1 billion and $1.5 billion each year – the amount needed annually to provide water and sanitation services to all the region's currently unserved citizens by the year 2000'. With a very small customer base, 'most sanitation utilities remain largely unaccountable to the community at large, and often they make little effort to go after customers who fail to pay their bills' (UNICEF 1997: 7). Basically, the cost of meeting some, if not all, of the demand is already embedded in the system.

The above problem has another critical dimension: there is no glamour in maintenance, and even less personal profit, legitimate or otherwise. In brief, there is little incentive to audit performance and improve efficiency. Therefore emphasis is placed instead on costly capital projects; they serve the middle classes in the cities and attract foreign investments and grants into the bargain, but they also offer better opportunities for kickbacks. As UNICEF (1997: 8) suggested, using 'the right technology for the job is another affordable way to provide modern sanitation', and no doubt safe water as well. 'Designers and engineers, wedded to traditional construction methods and often caught in a tangle of questionable bidding practices, insist on using large-width piping and installing it deep in the ground. These costly procedures are appropriate for intensively developed areas and heavy vehicular traffic.' Predictably, perhaps, foreign experts with little knowledge of local conditions often opt for familiar products and techniques more appropriate to their home countries.

What are we talking about in overall cost terms? Well, it is estimated that it would cost about $6.8 billion a year to achieve universal coverage of safe water and adequate sanitation. That is a very small fraction of military spending by the developing countries. Interestingly, India and Pakistan, proud owners of new atomic weapons, are typical offenders in this respect. In New Delhi, for example, less than 40 per cent of households are connected to sewers. Less than one-third of the population in India enjoy adequate sanitation, and one in five do not have access to safe water. Pakistan is not much better (UNICEF 1997: 7; UNICEF 1998: 104).

Desalination of brackish and sea water

Fundamentally, lack of access to safe water and adequate sanitation continues to be a potent threat to nations' capability to develop because decision-makers refuse to change tack. At the end of the day, however, there is a need to find new sources of water and it is generally assumed that poorer nations could not afford the costs involved. Naturally, there is an element of truth in that assumption, but it is not always correct to ascribe lack of action to cost. The most expensive source, desalination of seawater, used in areas of extreme shortage is a good illustration. The cost is higher than for conventional methods, but it is far from being unaffordable. For instance, production of water at the desalination plant in Buckeye, Arizona, costs about 0.02 cent per litre; only twice the cost of using conventional sources. It is interesting, incidentally, to compare that with the price of a litre of petrol.

The technology is not new by any means. Buckeye in Arizona and Key West in Florida were among the earliest towns in the USA to obtain fresh water from the sea. They converted to that system in 1962 and 1967 respectively. Units are also in operation in the Bahamas and in Saudi Arabia. A reverse-osmosis method is used in Oklahoma, while an electro-dialysis system provides water for Port Mansfield, Texas. In essence, desalination is now seen as a practical and inevitable source of potable water. The Water Desalination Act of 1996 in the USA put that issue beyond doubt. The Desalination and Water Purification Research and Development Program (DWPR) was set up under the Act to develop more cost-effective and technologically efficient means of obtaining water from that source. However, effort on that front is not confined to the USA. Similar organisations are in existence, such as the European Desalination Society (EDS) and the Middle East Desalination Research Centre (MEDRC). And the initiatives are bearing fruit; progress has been made, for instance, on plants using seawater reverse osmosis (SWRO) to achieve economies in capital and running costs.

However, the most promising aspect of desalination lies in the ability to build units to provide potable water to small and isolated communities. For example, while a Japanese firm is building a plant in Saudi Arabia capable of processing 720,000 cubic metres per day, mobile units that process less than 60 cubic metres per day are being tried in Jordan. More to the point, these units, previously used by the American forces during the Gulf War, are being modified to use renewable energy sources such as wind and sun. Apart from the obvious environmental advantages, the units can thus save up to 80 per cent of the cost that would have been spent on diesel fuel.[5]

Inaction is not an option

Water tankers currently supply villages in the area that will be served by the mobile desalination units mentioned above. In other words, providing water to that community is at present inefficient and costly. It is often the case that even the direct costs of existing arrangements are not accounted for fully when considering alternative methods of extraction and supply. In addition, providing safe water and good sanitation might be perceived as costly undertakings, but the problems created by lack of provision of these basic necessities are decidedly costlier. The loss in productive capability and the cost of remedial services such as additional healthcare are quantifiable and known.

At base, water and sanitation are indivisible factors in both malnutrition and disease. They exert direct and substantial influence on the performance of nations as Complex Adaptive Systems. Capability for individuals to contribute to the well-being of their community could be enhanced, and hence Complexity increased, through improvements in meeting these basic needs. Conversely, lack of action imposes an escalation in financial and other costs, leading ultimately to an inability to make any headway in human development terms. Yet again, cost is not the principal impediment; good progress could be made at reasonable costs as long as inefficiencies are discovered and reduced, and remedies then selected to reflect local needs and possibilities.

There is, in effect, a vast gap between the 'potential of public spending to improve health status and the actual performance', and that applies to spending in other issue areas as well (Filmer and Pritchett 1999: 1309). The WHO (2000: 10) reported in this respect that 'many deaths of children under 5 years of age could be averted for $10 or less ... but the average actual expenditure in poor countries per death prevented ... is $50,000 or more.'

ILLITERACY JOINS THE FRAY

Chapter 4 described the evolution of Complex Adaptive Systems as a cyclical process that links adaptation, survival and learning. A developing system, as an individual, community or whole nation, perceives its environment, evaluates the inputs, identifies regularities, and determines responses that help it to survive long enough for the next step in adaptation to take place. If that process is impaired, through illiteracy say, the whole system will be affected negatively. This sums up the case for identifying illiteracy, or on a broader level ignorance, as a major barrier in inhibiting capability for nations to help themselves.

Ignorance has three key components: illiteracy, disregard for indigenous knowledge, and lack of reliable information. UNESCO has defined illiteracy as the inability of people to read and write a simple statement relating to their everyday life. By that definition, one in six males and one in three females throughout the world are illiterate. The global distribution of illiteracy follows a familiar pattern, with sub-Saharan Africa and South Asia leading the field. In the late 1990s, adult literacy rates in Chad, Sierra Leone and Afghanistan were 44, 45 and 46 per cent for males, and 22, 18 and 16 per cent for females, respectively (UNICEF 2001: 90). Fundamentally, illiterate people cannot put their collective foot on the first step of the ladder to development. They are excluded from participation in even the most mundane activities that can be classed as an input into the affairs of their communities. They are, also in part as a result of their illiteracy, malnourished and unhealthy. Therefore they are not only exploited and disadvantaged, but they lack the means to break out of their miserable existence.

The situation with respect to illiteracy among women is a major handicap to optimal performance by nations as Complex Adaptive Systems, but the case of illiterate children is just as bad. More than 110 million children of school age within the developing nations do not attend any form of school; most are in full-time employment in any case. As always, lofty pronouncements by the movers and shakers never fail in putting the cart before the horse. The Convention on the Elimination of the Worst Forms of Child Labour, for example, suggested that the long-term solution 'lies in sustained economic growth leading to social progress, in particular poverty alleviation and universal education'. I will deal with the question of 'what education' later.

Forgotten coping strategies

Traditional life skills, including tried and tested coping strategies that have served many generations well, are often discarded in favour of the promise of modern ways from abroad. There is, or should be, no conflict between science and indigenous knowledge, which itself could be just as scientific. Elliott (1996: 72) pronounced the two as being 'complementary and mutually reinforcing'. Problems crop up when supposed experts convince the local population haphazardly to substitute so-called modern methods for the knowledge accumulated over the centuries. Undoubtedly, people in the developing countries, particularly their foreign-educated leaders, are themselves eager to replace indigenous knowledge by imported know-how. I must stress that this is not a call for second-rate technology for poorer nations: the accent is on *appropriateness*.

Denied reliable information

In addition to illiteracy and loss of indigenous knowledge, poorer nations suffer badly from lack of reliable information, and lack of access to what little information is available. Timberlake (1991: 30) highlighted this factor as making planning and monitoring 'extremely difficult' in the developing world. Badly informed and hence readily misled people are easy prey for dictators. Predictably therefore, radio and television stations are designated in military coups as targets to be captured early in the day. The monopoly of knowledge by priests in ancient times is another illustration of the same feature. And denying women the right to become better informed is yet another example; al-Ghazali (1994: 17) described women in some Islamic societies as being 'hostages in two prisons: ignorance and poverty'.

What education?

Improving the standards of 'formal education', embracing graduation from primary and secondary schools to vocational training and higher education, is a sensible aim in general. Clearly, it is apt in situations where formal job opportunities are the norm. But following that track rigidly in all cases can be misleading in the context of the most immediate needs of some nations. Basically, education as it is perceived within the developed countries does not always match the practical requirements of the most needy people. It diverts attention and resources from actions to create the appropriate skills necessary to tackle pressing social and economic problems on a self-help basis in informal settings. This remark might be interpreted as a call for 'second rate' teaching practices. Nothing could be further from my mind. Again, the suggestion merely advocates the application of a test of appropriateness to find optimal means to achieve best progress within local constraints.

Appropriateness, incidentally, is an issue that is now debated within the leading industrialised nations as well. The topic has added significance in the developing world, however, as the scope of the discussion changes from one of fine-tuning to radical analysis. For instance, it is not unusual to have in one and the same country a thriving and sophisticated higher education industry and rampant illiteracy and ignorance. India, where only 71 per cent of men and 44 per cent of women are literate, has an abundance of persons with doctoral degrees. Debate is ongoing about the role of specialised higher education in development. Conventional wisdom decrees that a few highly educated individuals are necessary to provide leadership and stimulate economic takeoff. That makes sense in a linear conception of the process of development founded on a top-down command-and-control management style; the few can pull the rest up the ladder of success.

A diametrically opposite viewpoint emerges when development is viewed as an evolutionary process associated with a Complex Adaptive System. In this case interactions by individuals throughout the population provide the energy that drives the system forward. A few specialists are unable to make much difference, no matter how clever and highly qualified they happen to be. In absolute numbers, their interactions are limited, as they have to seek and then link to other appropriate partners. The often-observed pattern of small isolated islands of excellence and refinement in a large sea of deprivation and misery is a familiar feature within less developed communities.

Governments try to open more primary and secondary schools, at least part of the aim being to produce suitable candidates to feed the higher education machine. The results are universally disappointing. Many drop out after a year or two. Those who stay the course frequently fail to go back to their rural communities. Graduates from colleges and universities do not succeed in finding suitable employment and soon set their eyes on work elsewhere. In a bewildering turn of events, poorer countries frequently end up spending their limited resources on educating their most promising young citizens to fill posts in more prosperous countries. The case of the glut of Indian, Pakistani and Middle Eastern doctors in the USA and Europe is too well rehearsed to need further elaboration.

The dilemma is understood, however, by those directly involved in the search for solutions. Victor Ordonez, director of basic education at UNESCO, considers that the traditional educational system, in terms of both content and structure, 'is a poor preparation for life in the 21st century; it meets neither the personal needs of individuals nor the development needs of their societies'. He added, 'the problem is the exclusion of so many children by barriers of language ... culture, or geographic inaccessibility ... where the unreached are a majority, principally in sub-Saharan Africa and South Asia, conventional systems are often not only unaffordable and irrelevant but also alienating to those they are intended to serve' (UNICEF 1995a: 19). Timberlake (1991: 40) voiced the same concerns. He advocated a shift to primary health care, a move away from doctors and hospitals and into the community. Timberlake preferred 'education and the hardware of health (piped water, protected wells, sanitation systems, safe food storage) rather than the hardware of disease'. Reflecting this approach, he pointed out that more than a hundred community health workers can be trained and equipped for the cost of educating a single doctor. And yet the developing countries continue to put their limited resources into poor imitation of Western systems.

Education is under the microscope in richer countries

This topic is not of relevance only to poorer nations: Western experts are beginning to question long-established ideas and methods. In Britain, for instance, moves are afoot to put emphasis on primary care and on 'nurse-practitioners' to ease the financial and operational pressure on the National Health Service and the higher education establishments. There is also a growing belief that students fortunate enough to proceed to higher education should pay for their education, in the reasonable expectation that they will earn more than others in the future. By contrast, most of the developing countries are still wedded to the concept of free, or subsidised, higher education in the belief that the process will lead to development and progress.

On the broader front, the process of learning is under intensive scrutiny. 'Does Education and Training Get in the Way of Learning?' was used by Stephanie Marshall, executive director of the Illinois Mathematics and Science Academy as the title of a 1997 lecture she gave at the Royal Society of Arts, Manufactures and Commerce in London. She argued that the crisis of education should be seen as a crisis 'about learning and the structures we have designed to develop it'. The reason for reformulating the problem was given as the 'discoveries in fields as diverse as quantum physics, chaos mathematics, evolutionary biology, systems theory and the neuro and cognitive sciences'.[6] She called, in effect, for learning structures to be examined from first principles. Essentially, debate about which format is superior misses the point: the best system of education for any community is the one that produces the best results in meeting its own needs.

Can they afford literacy?

I argued earlier that the notion that 'wealth determines health' might be a ready excuse for inaction. Similarly, an assumption is regularly made that literacy depends first and foremost on finance. That is a reason regularly given by decision-makers in developing countries for doing little to cope with basic needs within available resources. China helps to illustrate that literacy and poverty are not mutually exclusive. That nation could not afford to lavish money on education in line with practice in wealthier nations. Nevertheless, by the late 1990s, in that vast nation 91 per cent of males and 77 per cent of females were literate. Comparison with India, at 71 and 44 per cent respectively, is instructive. China decided to seek local solutions, while India depended on imported ideas. A near obsession with basic needs, indigenous remedies, and communities that function as supportive units has enabled that country to cross the capability divide. Having moved up the human development ladder, China is now ready to tackle economic development. The only danger on the horizon concerns its ability to maintain its independent approach to problem solving in the face of pressure from the USA.

There are evidently lessons for poorer nations to learn in distinguishing between so-called science and indigenous knowledge to help citizens across the board achieve capability as opposed to educating the few. But the task is not straightforward. There is always a temptation to stick to internationally accepted models rather than to think through educational programmes and methods of delivery from the bottom up. Additionally, there is much at stake in terms of career prospects for the educationalists themselves, as well as national prestige as viewed by politicians and other leaders of the community.

HOW, RATHER THAN HOW MUCH

It is useful in concluding this chapter on the Horsemen of malnutrition, disease and ignorance to highlight three cardinal points. First, the capability for most people in a nation to interact effectively is determined to a large extent by their state of nutrition, health and knowledge. Without that capability they will be powerless to take an active part in the natural evolution of that nation as a Complex Adaptive System. Second, the Horsemen are more powerful when they hunt together, but because of that interdependence even modest *integrated* measures to control their ferocity as a pack give outstanding returns overall.

And third, progress is not a function of cost. Efforts should focus on finding locally appropriate solutions to the most pressing problems within the opportunities and constraints existing at that particular time and place. The danger in isolating wealth as the primary impediment is the temptation to conclude that little can be done until the economy has been uplifted substantially. That, fortunately, is not the case. The *New England Journal of Medicine*, for example, published an article on this topic back in 1981 to suggest that Africa could expect the greatest improvement in life expectancy from investments targeted at rural and urban slum areas, at a cost of less than $2 per head (Evans et al. 1981).

Waste, corruption and military spending were highlighted earlier in the chapter as activities that absorb much-needed funds that should be devoted to basic social programmes. As mentioned in Chapter 6, governments of the developing countries spent about $440 billion annually in the early 1990s, of which less than $50 billion was earmarked for nutrition, basic health care, primary education, and clean water and sanitation. The picture remained essentially the same at the turn of the century. Sadly, little change in this lopsided view of the top priorities will take place unless public demands are articulated forcefully: the link between malnutrition, disease, ignorance and lack of human rights is plain to see. William Beveridge (1879–1963), the father of the welfare state in Britain, observed that 'ignorance is an evil weed, which dictators may cultivate among their dupes, but which no democracy can afford among its citizens.' That sums up the situation admirably.

NOTES

1. See discussion of the project in Elliott (1996) and in Caufield (1996). Involvement by the World Bank is of particular interest.
2. This point is illustrated by what happened to water and sanitation when the developing countries were subjected to the shock therapy of the structural stabilisation and adjustment programmes during and after the debt crises of the 1980s. In Nairobi, for instance, capital expenditure for water and sewerage fell by a factor of ten from 1981 to 1986, and in

Zimbabwe about one-quarter of village pumps fell into disrepair (UNICEF 1997: 6).
3. Agrarian land reforms have been tried with varying degrees of success. Oddly enough, this is one instance where revolutionary regimes, such as those in Libya and Iran, have achieved some measure of success as compared with old established regimes, as in Brazil.
4. See Postel (1992) for detailed discussion of this topic.
5. As reported by the Middle East Desalination Research Centre (MEDRC) and *Jordan Times*, March 2001.
6. Marshall (1997).

NINE

CONFLICT AND INCAPABILITY

Malnutrition, disease and illiteracy compromise people's capability, but aggression and conflict are just as effective in reducing or eliminating interactions between people that would have supplied the energy for their communities to make steady progress. Highly uneven distribution of strife that gives the developing countries more than their fair share of conflict is a significant factor in inhibiting development in that part of the world. However, my main aim in this chapter is to show that local and foreign interests, and particularly egoistic individuals, combine to keep conflict, preparation for conflict and spending on weapons at consistently high levels in areas that urgently require progress towards human development.

THE COSTLY INCLINATION FOR PEOPLE TO FIGHT

St John's Revelations allocated two Horsemen to conflict, possibly in recognition of its devastating power, and the history of humankind more than justifies the accuracy of that prophecy. The twentieth century was particularly brutal in that respect. Although the two world wars have monopolised the attention of historians, the wider picture is infinitely worse. Plainly, the collapse of the Soviet Union and the supremacy of the USA helped to diminish global conflict, but only to a modest extent; there were still some twenty-seven ongoing major wars in 1996 (SIPRI 1997: 21). In a world badly in need of adequate nutrition, safe water and sanitation, basic healthcare and primary education, the armed forces of the world directly employ over 20 million people, over 13 million of whom are in the developing countries, whose defence expenditure consumes 2.4 per cent of their collective GDP.

Hardships before, during and after conflict

There is a heavy price to pay for conflict at all stages. Preparations for conflict require obvious trade-offs between funds for military purposes and for basic needs. War, when it comes, causes damaging dislocations and hardships. And when peace finally dawns, ordinary people have to foot the bill for decades to come in foreign debts, care for the maimed and orphaned, further violence made possible by the ready availability of weapons, and clearance of the lethal debris left behind.

The peppering of the countryside with landmines is a chilling example. Popular because of their low price, at less than $10 apiece, the mines once laid cost $300 to $1,000 each to clear. They kill or maim over two thousand people every month, mainly women and children. Despite the global hand-wringing, about '2.5 million new mines are laid each year', with the not unexpected result that 'de-mining lags far behind that of new mines still being placed'. There are now over 110 million of these deadly devices strewn over past battle-fields, almost exclusively in the developing countries, and their removal would cost over $33 billion (UNICEF 1997: 57). Angola alone has some 2 million, a painful reminder of wars that dragged on for twenty years.

Disruption to normal living conditions due to warfare and its after-effects is on a scale that is not generally understood. As a result of the Gulf War and the sanctions against Iraq, for example, infant mortality rates doubled and there was a fivefold increase in under-5 child mortality. In the five years after August 1990, when Iraq invaded Kuwait, 567,000 children died as a direct outcome of that episode and the ensuing sanctions (*Lancet*, 2 December 1995). The legacy of radiation poisoning from shells reinforced with 'spent' uranium will take longer to materialise (IAC 1997). Nevertheless, the USA and Iraq continue to blame each other for the mayhem.

Productive people into refugees

Inevitably, armed clashes turn civilians into refugees. UNHCR put the number of refugees in 1993 at 17 million. Two years later they had increased to 23 million. Significantly, UNHCR estimated that over half the refugees were children. The Hutu massacre of a million Tutsis in 1994 forced another 2 million to flee Rwanda, mostly to Zaïre. Additionally, there are well over a million Afghanis sheltering in neighbouring countries. As expected, refugee problems take a long time to resolve; hundreds of thousands of Palestinians are still living in camps, half a century after the end of events that led to the creation of Israel.

The refugee problem has two dimensions. For a start, refugees are, by definition, unable to contribute to the well-being of the communities they leave behind. Perforce, their survival from day to day takes precedence over their nutrition, healthcare and learning needs. In effect, human development for those affected is arrested or reversed. On the other hand, host countries are hardly ever in a position to spare the resources needed by the new arrivals. Tragically, it often happens that neighbouring countries suffer a reciprocal influx of refugees across their borders simultaneously. That certainly was the case in Somalia and Ethiopia.

Diversion of resources is not merely a local affair. Funds earmarked for aid have to be channelled instead into humanitarian assistance, 'most of it due to war rather than natural disasters'. Allocations for this purpose increased from about $2 billion in 1985 to nearly $10 billion in 1994, 'reflecting the upsurge in conflicts that have had a devastating impact on civilians, especially children'. During that period financing for humanitarian aid went up from 5 per cent of total development assistance to 16 per cent (UNICEF 1997: 57).

I would like to comment briefly on the financial figures given in the last few paragraphs to illustrate a more general point. As mentioned previously, an additional $40 billion a year would resolve most of the shortcomings associated with basic needs in the most needy countries. Clearing all the landmines would cost around $30 billion, and humanitarian aid, mainly to deal with the aftereffects of conflict, amounts to $10 billion annually. These, and other, facts help to explain the assertion I make in Chapter 10 that the funds needed to put the most affected nations on the path to human development are already embedded in the system. Finance is not the problem.

All-consuming civil wars

Civil wars are particularly damaging, as events in Afghanistan demonstrate all too well. In 1973, Daoud, prime minister and the king's cousin, installed himself as ruler; an egoistic individual thus set in motion a process that was to leave countless victims but no victors. He was killed in April 1978 and other leaders – Amin, Kamal, Najibullah and Hekmatyar – came and went, mostly meeting a violent end. The all-out war of late 2001 is only the latest episode in what seems like an endless saga of conflict, confusion and shifting alliances. On the one side there were Bin Laden and the Taliban, America's past protégés; on the other were the Northern Alliance, Russia's protégés, and the USA and its Western allies.

Foreign egoistic individuals have been involved, such as the Shah of Iran and Pakistani politicians and army officers; they perceived enticing possibilities for gain. It is not clear, however, why Russia intervened in 1979, but after mounting losses troops withdrew ten years later. Needless to say, the USA was embroiled in the conflict at all stages. Interestingly, on 20 July 1998 America bombed 'terrorist bases' in Afghanistan that were built and funded previously by the CIA when they assisted Muslim 'freedom fighters' in their war against the then ruling faction. This is a recurring feature in the history of conflict in the developing world whenever a leading power is involved. The local leaders start a fight, become rich, and then leave or get killed; the local populations suffer horrendous hardships; and foreign powers intervene and then end up as losers.

The Lebanese civil war from 1975 to 1992 displayed all the above features but also demonstrated the motives that lurk behind such events. As Friedman (1990: 137) recounted, 'this was not a battle over dogma or sacred texts. It was about whose militia would control the illegal ports and patronage and insurance rackets.' Friedman's words are highly significant as they apply to many conflict situations. All too frequently war emanates from the selfish interests of one or a few egoistic individuals in search of power, financial profit, prestige or glamour.

Again, the Lebanon, where foreign players were much in evidence, illustrates the futility and cost of foreign intervention. Israeli forces invaded the Lebanon in June 1982. They withdrew southwards to a zone controlled on their behalf by the South Lebanon Army, but continued to suffer heavy losses until they withdrew finally in 2000. Not to be outdone, America sent in the Marines and France dispatched troops to help the 'Lebanese authorities' to restore order. Almost inevitably, suicide bombers killed 241 Marines and 50 French soldiers in October 1983; both countries pulled out shortly thereafter. Israel and

America lost a great deal and gained nothing as a result of their involvement, but their actions were a decisive factor in the emergence of Shiite groups such as Amal and Hezbollah that became a thorn in the flesh for both countries.

Naturally, the Lebanese paid the heftiest price. No one now talks of the permanent loss incurred in the form of social capital; those able to do so – people with money, higher qualifications and talents – took their assets and left the country for good. Other losses are easier to identify: over 150,000 persons were killed, and basic services and the infrastructure were decimated. As usual in these cases, a few leaders of the warring factions still live in luxury but most were killed, some butchered with their families and pets. As in all civil wars there were very few winners and numerous losers.

A loss of complexity and human development

The most decisive impact of conflict is its effect in slowing down, and frequently reversing, the process of human development. Complexity is lost to a greater or lesser extent depending on the severity and duration of hostilities, as day-to-day interactions that supply the energy required for society to achieve stability and progress are suspended while events take their course. The second law of thermodynamics gains the upper hand and the nation drifts away from self-organised Complexity into chaos. Sadly, return to normality is not instantaneous; there are no shortcuts to evolution.

To compound the damage, conflict necessitates the reallocation of resources away from long-term spending on pressing social needs. That impedes capability – human development, if you will – even further. Defence expenditure exacts heavy penalties, even without a shot being fired, and the process is self-generating; when one state arms itself its neighbours decide to do likewise. Weapons are only the beginning, of course. A standing army has to be maintained in a state of reasonable readiness, representing a constant drain on scarce human and financial resources.

But that is hardly the end of the story. The threat of conflict, real, imagined or invented, brings undoubted benefits to repressive regimes. They have what appear to be legitimate reasons for buying weapons, maintaining a large and well-paid army, and, most damagingly, enforcing harsh military rule 'until the emergency is over'. The emergency never goes, of course; those in power make certain the status quo is retained for the longest possible time. Few, if any, decision-makers find it to their advantage not to have a major national crisis on their hands. In consequence, many regimes hostile to the USA have remained long in power on the back of sanctions imposed by the USA 'to teach them a lesson'. Cuba and Iraq might be in that category.

VESTED INTERESTS

Conflict in general and buying weapons in particular are ready means for accumulating personal wealth quickly. Those involved at the selling end are equally uninterested in reducing the threat of war. Even the peacemakers have a vested interest. When hardships caused by war become evident, groups comprising other 'selfish' individuals spring into action to offer help. And then when a country shows signs of economic distress, yet another set of individuals come forward to give advice and assistance. Though they might be working for the same government, these individuals apparently do not cross paths, otherwise the whole edifice would crumble, and that would deprive them of their livelihoods or their missions in life.

The above comments are not made lightly. A holistic approach cannot be tolerated, and that is official. Clare Short, British secretary of state at the Department for International Development (DFID) suggested in a speech to the One World International Media Conference on 3 June 1998 that 'money was not the problem' in Sudan. She considered that 'the problem was one of access, not resources'. Both sides 'should agree a ceasefire so that [existing] food could be moved in.' She was roundly criticised for her comments by aid organisations and the media. In addition, members of the International Development Select Committee of the Houses of Parliament declared themselves 'baffled' by her views at a meeting in August 1998.

Pawns in a lethal game

Domestic and foreign interests routinely use genuine local grievances to initiate strife. The Kurds in Turkey, Iraq, Iran and Syria illustrate this feature well. They have legitimate historic claims that were exploited in that way for most of the twentieth century. Whenever necessary their leaders are prevailed upon to start uprisings to order.

This happened immediately after the Gulf War when the allies encouraged the Kurds to revolt in northern Iraq. As expected, government forces subdued the rebellion easily. For strategic regional reasons, independence for the Kurds is not on the cards. On the contrary, Turkey attacks them on an almost daily basis with tacit approval from the USA. Ultimately, human development has bypassed the Kurds. They are mere pawns.

The Kurds are not an isolated case. Two factions have fought an inconclusive civil war in Kashmir for more than half a century. Someone somewhere thinks it is worthwhile to fund that conflict, and the locals consider it their duty to help in that endeavour. Two factions, but this time of a different religious orientation, continue their search for a formula that would allow them to live in peace after many decades of war in Northern Ireland. However, as past warlords turn to legitimate politics new ones rush in to take their place. Basically, the attractions are too enticing. The Basques in Spain and France are another case in point. In many instances of war the top people lead a safe and luxurious life. The same cannot be said for the foot soldiers, but then they might have their turn later. This might seem to be a cynical way to look at ethnic, religious and historic grievances, and many fall genuinely in these categories. However, a glance at the history of Africa and Latin America, say, justifies cynicism.

ARMS SALES IN THE NAME OF PEACE

Conflict is impossible without weapons, but weapons are useless without conflict: the two are self-fulfilling. The marketing of weapons and conflict is, therefore, a joint venture, and the business is considerable. Exports of weapons by the top thirty supplying countries were valued at about $22 billion in the mid 1990s (SIPRI 1997: 268). Significantly, the five permanent members of the UN Security Council, with supposedly a keen interest in peacekeeping, are also the main suppliers of arms, accounting for more than four-fifths of weapons sold.

USA: the ultimate arms dealer

Limiting the transfer of military hardware and technology is a popular stance, as evidenced by declarations at the Hague Conference in 1899, the League of Nations, and at the UN up to the present. Such sentiments are rarely translated into action. Recent shrinkage in global sales reflects, in the main, reductions in procurements by the leading powers due to the changed political climate in Europe. Competition is intensifying, as a result, to sell arms to the developing countries (Wulf 1993: 4, 6, 67). There is no conspiracy to harm these nations. Basically, certain egoistic individuals, in trying to do the best for themselves, and hence their employers, seek to sell arms to potential buyers.

The USA has unwaveringly supplied weapons to the developing world on a prodigious scale. At the same time, it has been vociferous in its condemnation of state oppression and international aggression. Nevertheless, linkage of arms sales to foreign policy, at the heart of the Kissinger doctrine, remains unchallenged. Significantly, US arms exports to the Persian Gulf rocketed by 2,500 per cent from 1970 to 1976: the outflow of money from industrialised countries for the purchase of oil following the oil price shock did not take long to become a flood in the opposite direction.[1] In 1992, largely as an outcome of the Gulf War, the USA contracted to meet half the Middle East's need for weapons. That area is a lucrative market, as 'seven of the top weapons buyers in the world are in that region, including the single largest buyer, Saudi Arabia' (Kapstein 1994: 16). It has the perfect mix of attributes: abundant oil money, leaders willing to start a fight at the least provocation, and a long history rich with grievances.

Being the biggest source of weaponry underlines the dominance of America and its focus on its own interests. To drill these points home, Powell, the then chairman of the Joint Chiefs of Staff, advised the Foreign Relations Committee of Congress in March 1990 that 'America cannot choose between military security and economic security. The two are inextricably entwined.' Additionally, according to Powell, reducing domestic sales means that 'virtually all the major contractors are paying more attention to the possibility of increased foreign sales' (Wulf 1993: 56). Wulf commented: 'it seems unlikely that the United States will voluntarily reduce the level of its arms exports' (Wulf 1993: 83). It is more probable, he added, that 'it would seek the maximum benefits from this aspect of foreign policy'.

The USA is not alone in selling arms

The USSR in its heyday was an equally enthusiastic purveyor of arms and promoter of conflict. However, the rivalry between the USA and

USSR worked best when it became a game in the course of which they equipped hostile neighbours, as happened in Somalia and Ethiopia. Nowadays Russia and other members of the CIS are in a quandary. They plan to convert some military factories to peaceful production, but conversion is costly and slow, and in the meantime the economy is in tatters. Pressure on managers to search for overseas markets for their military products is intense, and they face competition from other countries that are dumping surplus weapons fast.

The same factors influence the policies of other major exporting nations, as in the case of Britain and France; and Sweden and Israel are not far behind. Significantly, New Labour's promise to follow an ethical policy with regard to sales of British weapons abroad was forgotten soon after it won the election in 1997 (*Sunday Times*, 14 March 1999). In effect, the developing countries are expected to remain a major target for weapons sales by all the leading producers, irrespective of protestations to the contrary, and despite the obvious negative effects on global peace and prosperity.

THE GLOBAL DISTRIBUTION OF CONFLICT

Certain regions have become natural hunting grounds for the 'Horsemen' of war. Of twenty-seven major conflicts recorded throughout the world in 1996, over half were in Asia and Africa. Significantly, of 170 major clashes in the forty years after World War II, 160 were in the developing countries; two-thirds involved foreign powers (Ohlson 1988: 18). Moreover, disputes in this part of the world are long lasting. As SIPRI (1997: 22) reported, 'the longer a war or the more intense a war, the more difficult is its peace process (for example, the Israeli–Palestinian and Sri Lankan conflicts).'

The arc of crises

In short, conflict is a chronic condition within the developing countries. But the hot spots are even more focused than that. Brzezinski, President Carter's national security advisor, called the swathe that includes Afghanistan, Pakistan, Iran, Iraq, Israel, Palestine, Jordan, the Gulf States, Somalia, Ethiopia, Kenya and Yemen 'the Arc of Crises'. It is difficult to distinguish cause from effect here, but it is sufficient to say that the powers of the day went out of their way to arm everyone in that region. Between 1975 and 1982, the USSR supplied more than 7,000 tanks and self-propelled guns, 2,330 supersonic combat aircraft, and some 15,000 surface-to-air missiles to its clients in the 'Arc'. The USA equipped its own clients with 4,933 tanks and self-propelled guns, 785 aircraft, and 6,311 surface-to-air missiles (Johnston and Taylor 1986: 248).

Predictably, the 'Arc' has endured over the decades many wars and famines. Despite plentiful resources, it is also home to some of the world's most deprived and backward nations. Incapability caused by war and strife does indeed have a direct effect on human development. The pattern continues unabated, as evidenced by events in Iraq, Iran, Ethiopia, Eritrea, Zaïre, Kashmir and Afghanistan, to name but a few examples.

Again, it is difficult to separate cause from effect, but the 'Arc' has also attracted over the decades a motley collection of dictators, clandestine groups, arms dealers, foreign service operatives, and mischief-makers from all around the world. Oil, diamonds and other resources are an irresistible lure. Specialist firms were sometimes used in lieu of official forces, as happened when force was required quickly but discreetly to restore one faction to power in Sierra Leone following a coup in 1998. Reportedly, rich diamond-mining concerns were involved in that conflict (*Sunday Times*, 10 May 1998). It is not readily clear what British national interests were served by that action, but that is par for the course.

WHY DO THEY BUY AND SELL WEAPONS?

The purchase of potentially deadly weapons diverts badly needed funds away from social and economic programmes. Moreover, the indiscriminate transfer of powerful weapons to all nations is a major component in the growth of terrorism and drug trafficking, activities that harm the interests of exporting countries more than most.

The stock answer

Arms manufacturers promote exports to generate greater profits. They lobby hard to exert political influence at the top of the hierarchies in the industrialised countries and they back that effort with generous financial contributions to political parties and election campaigns. All that is perfectly understandable. Similarly, despotic regimes buy weapons to oppress civilian populations, threaten neighbouring nations, wage war, or just make money. That is also perfectly understandable. But why do supposedly civilised nations sell, and sometimes give, weapons so eagerly? The stock answer goes something like this: conflict is inevitable, weapons are as likely to deter as to encourage conflict, and countries seeking arms will always find eager suppliers. In short, the scenario goes, it would not make much difference if one or two responsible states were to withdraw from this business.

The above powerful case would be more convincing had it not been for the fact that top producing countries market their wares most assiduously and offer in addition loans, credit guarantees and deferred payments to help ease the burden on purchasers. Britain spends about $600 million of taxpayers' money annually to subsidise foreign buyers (*Guardian*, 6 January 1996). As always, the US government goes even further in subsidising the weapons' export business. It devotes over $6 billion annually to market and finance sales and spends more on research and development. This seems to be a rational defence policy, but the effort is directed at exports in the first instance. For instance, foreign customers had to pay a fee in the past to refund American taxpayers for some of the research and development costs, but the 'recoupment fee' was abolished in 1996 to encourage exports. Moreover, although there are many sources of arms, a handful of suppliers, led by the USA, are trying hard to monopolise weapons exports (Kapstein 1994: 13). Again, why do they do it?

Is the trade vital to the economy?

Weapons manufacturers often depict the trade as a critical component of the economy. That is a dubious standpoint. As highlighted by Wulf (1993: 73), a 1992 study by the US Congressional Budget Office concluded that limits on the arms industry 'would not significantly affect the vast majority of exporting industries'. Essentially, the market is relatively insignificant when viewed in the context of total exports from the leading industrial nations. For instance, although the Middle East is now the largest importer of weapons in the world and the USA is the leading supplier of arms, the region does not feature as a major export destination for the USA. In 1999, North American merchandise trade with the rest of the world amounted to $564 billion, of which only $22 billion, less than 4 per cent, involved the Middle East (WTO 2000b: Table III.3). Clearly, only a modest fraction of that sum involved arms sales. It is also claimed that the industry is a vital generator of jobs. However, in 1999 there were only 8.3 million people employed in arms production worldwide.[2] Clearly, employment does not seem to be a major factor either.

National economic considerations might not be critical, but finance is important at a tactical level. It is useful, for example, to cascade surplus or obsolete arms to 'friendly' nations, and if that results in some revenue then so much the better. Recently, NATO and Warsaw Pact countries released onto the world market gigantic amounts of arms that had become surplus to requirements. Additionally, reductions in defence spending by the industrialised countries exert pressure on states to sell abroad to safeguard their military industrial base. Having said all that, it is obvious that sales are not strategically significant to the economies of the industrialised countries. So why do they do it?

Attractive fringe benefits

For vendor states, foreign policy gains are the main attraction in selling, and giving, arms. Kapstein (1994: 18) points out that America's arms monopoly 'will provide the possibility of exercising leverage in other issue areas through diplomatic linkage'. Long-term reliance of importing nations on the goodwill of exporting countries, for the purpose of maintenance and renewal, say, is of paramount importance. In accord with Game Theory, clients have to cooperate, while the vendors retain the option to compete and acquire higher rewards. Events in the Gulf since 1990 support this viewpoint; nothing happens in that region nowadays without America's say-so.

Above all else, the opportunity for a few egoistic individuals to amass large fortunes quickly is one of the most decisive factors that make the arms trade an ever-popular activity. The trade is an efficient conduit for making profits and for siphoning monies from public purses into private pockets, legally or otherwise. The inherent secrecy provides the perfect cover for this process. 'Big hitters', middlemen who persuade governments to place large orders, can earn up to 10 per cent in fees. The commission paid to one group involved in the Al Yamamah project, by which Britain undertook to supply jet fighters, naval mine-hunters and ammunition to Saudi Arabia, at a cost of about $31 billion, was said to be $380 million (*Sunday Times*, 9 October 1994).

The full circle

The Stockholm International Peace Research Institute (SIPRI) regularly draws attention to the potential opportunities available in the arms trade for corruption on a grand scale (SIPRI 1997: 184).[3] Modern dictators and despotic ruling dynasties are especially eager to participate in this system of wealth creation.[4] But to purchase weapons repressive regimes must have the funds to do so in the first instance, and that is where loans from abroad come into the picture. We have now traced the full circle: foreign governments and bankers provide the money as a loan, a dictator places an order for weapons with the same country, his rake-off is added to the price, middlemen (who might have handled both the loan and the order) share their commission with those who were useful on both sides of the fence, and the money finally goes back to where it came from.

I left one group of people out of that neat circle: the ordinary people in the weapons-producing nations whose taxes were used to subsidise the whole operation, and the millions in the purchaser countries who then proceed to pay back the odious debts over many decades, having been denied the basic services that could have been provided had the money been spent more wisely. There is nothing new in all this; the process is well understood by the global development hierarchy.

WEAPONS DO NOT REDUCE CONFLICT

The developing countries allocated about $125 billion annually for military purposes in the early 1990s. Despite that heavy commitment to arms it is now clear that large standing armies and advanced weapons have not promoted peace; quite the contrary, as the developing world is still the stage on which local, regional and global battles are fought. On the other hand, 4 per cent of that sum would have been enough to achieve universal primary education, cut adult illiteracy by 50 per cent, and educate women to the level of men. And 12 per cent would have provided in addition healthcare and safe water for all

(UNDP 1994). One-third of the money would have been enough to meet all basic social needs to an adequate level, but I will come back to this in Chapter 10.

Equally, the suspicion that high spending on weapons does not equate with power or security surfaced during the Gulf crisis. Kuwait's weakness in the face of the advancing Iraqi forces was laid bare; the country was overrun in three hours. Crushing defeat at the hands of the Allies also shattered the image of Iraq's invincible military power. Both countries were and are heavy military spenders. Peace was not kept, and when the chips were down there was no power either.

MORE EFFORT TO MARKET ARMS AND CONFLICT

In the meantime, the costs of sophisticated weapons are escalating rapidly. Kapstein (1994: 14), in addressing this aspect, remarked that 'American firms sold 3,500 military aircraft for $4 billion in 1970. In 1975, 1,700 planes were shipped with a value of $4 billion. In 1980, 1,000 aircraft cost $6 billion. And in 1985 the number sold dropped to 919, but the value had trebled to $18 billion.' Clearly, several factors are coming together to make it more difficult for arms producers to entice leaders of impoverished nations to maintain past spending patterns.

Commentators, including SIPRI, expect that efforts will intensify to prop up sales and promote conflicts, particularly in trouble spots such as the 'Arc of Crises'. Understandably, therefore, marketing in this field is revving up to fever pitch. The Gulf War, referred to by Kapstein as 'the greatest arms sale show on earth', is of course the ultimate example. During the one hundred hours of one-sided bombing, the USA with the help of CNN exhibited its advanced weapons superiority over all. The USA and its allies were able to replenish their stocks, and the Gulf States were cajoled into buying even more weapons than before. On the other hand, about 50,000 Iraqi soldiers and some 22,000 civilians had lost their lives by the end of hostilities in February 1991.[5]

The Iran–Iraq war was an even more impressive illustration. It started in 1980 and ended in 1988 when Khomeini drank what he called 'the poison cup' of defeat. Over 400,000 people died, 210,000 were taken prisoner, and $390 billion was spent in the course of that conflict. There were no discernible gains for either side. Once the conflict had started every effort was made to keep it going. As Heikal (1992: 65) reported, 'whenever one side seemed in sight of victory Washington would begin secretly helping its opponent.' Ultimately, no fewer than fifty countries participated in meeting the demand for weapons; twenty-eight, led by the permanent members of the UN Security Council, supplied both sides (Adams 1990: 128).

Marketing effort does not have to be blatant. In November 1994 the High Court in London delivered its judgement against the British government over the Pergau Dam affair. Court action was initiated by the World Development Movement, which had maintained that there was evidence of a link between aid given to Malaysia to build the dam and British arms sales to that country (Pilger 1999: 121). That example of aid-for-arms diplomacy was not an isolated incident. In April 1993, when the British foreign secretary was on a visit to Indonesia, he announced a $100 million concessional loan for a new power station at Samarinda. It was by far the largest single aid donation to Indonesia for twenty years. It coincided with intense negotiations for an arms deal worth about $3.2 billion.

A perplexing business

Marketing conflict and weapons is a chaotic activity. In many cases the outcome is unexpected, but in most instances the secret services and the ubiquitous egoistic individual are much in evidence. Events hardly ever proceed in a predictable and orderly manner. Nonlinear contradictions and ambiguities are revealed only when the facts become known years later. Two examples, out of many that could be given, will illustrate these observations.

For years Israel retransferred sensitive American technology and re-exported American weapons to other nations, some of them hostile to the USA, sometimes with the knowledge of officials in Washington. For example, cluster bombs of American origin were sold to Ethiopia's Marxist government and US technology was transferred to China to enable it to modify its ballistic missiles to avoid interception by American Patriot surface-to-air missiles (Clarke 1995: 89). On several occasions the arms produced as a result of that joint work were exported by China to Iraq and Syria, supposedly deadly enemies of Israel and the USA.

Another perplexing phenomenon relates to the arbitrary yardsticks deployed by leading powers to designate a state as being one that helps terrorism. The USA placed Iraq on the list of countries that supported terrorism when it nationalised its oil industry in 1972. That lasted up to the start of the war with Iran in 1980, but then the USA became closer to the Iraqi regime, and eventually removed Iraq from the list in 1982 (Clark 1998: 4). That was followed by resumption of full diplomatic relations two years later. Evidently, the opportunities presented by the Iraq–Iran war were simply too appealing to be clouded by inconvenient side issues.

The above illustrations underline the point that conflict and the arms trade are governed by a multiplicity of factors that go well beyond simple national interests. The web of objectives, often contradictory and hardly ever clear, renders any attempt at comprehension futile. The examples demonstrate beyond doubt the nonlinear nature of the process: numerous elements interact and as a result unpredictable but stable patterns emerge in which causes and effects are difficult to match.

A MOST EFFICIENT HORSEMAN

My principal aim in devoting Chapter 8 to malnutrition, disease and illiteracy was to underscore the role played by these factors in reducing the capability of ordinary people to help their community make progress towards human development. My intention in the present chapter, on conflict and arms trading, was the same, but I wished to demonstrate in addition that the Horseman of War is sufficiently powerful to halt, and in many cases reverse, past progress made by whole nations.

This book is not about any particular country, but the impact of conflict on the Iraqi nation gives a useful summary of the salient points advanced earlier. It also provides an excellent illustration of a Complex Adaptive System under severe operating conditions. Turmoil in Iraq in recent decades was crowned by two bruising wars. The latest, the Gulf War, commenced with an air attack early on 17 January 1991 and went on for forty-three days. In the process, the Allies dropped some 88,000 tons of bombs. There were two thousand air strikes in the first twenty-four hours alone and most bridges and public utilities in the capital were destroyed almost instantaneously.

As Clark (1998: 10) reported, 'more than 90 per cent of Iraq's electrical capacity was bombed out of service in the first few hours.' In days, and as promised by the then US secretary of state, Iraq was reduced to a level of deprivation that is unusual even for a developing country. Layers of 'depth' laboriously accumulated over many decades were torn off in a total of one hundred hours of bombing.

Ten years after the war, sanctions against Iraq were still in operation and the people there were suffering appalling hardships, now caused by malnutrition, polluted water and shortage of medicines. Infants and children, the next generation, are particularly badly affected. Qualified younger persons, the present productive generation, have left the country in droves, and the middle classes have all but disappeared. Halliday, head of the UN humanitarian programme in Iraq until he resigned in autumn 1998, wrote that the sanctions are 'producing 5000–6000 Iraqi deaths per month' (*Guardian*, 27 January 1999).

The Gulf War demonstrated the futility of conflict as a means of resolving problems or achieving set aims. There were and are no winners, with the possible exception of arms producers and those who profited from the war and the sanctions. However, above all else, that example underlines most clearly the price paid by weaker nations when they compete against an overwhelmingly stronger opponent. Game Theory shows beyond doubt that the distribution of penalties and rewards is never in doubt in these circumstances. Basically, weapons, wars and intransigence do not lend themselves to the flexibility and pragmatism required by nations, as Complex Adaptive Systems, to achieve stable patterns that permit leisurely evolution to proceed optimally. Equally, preparation for conflict, such as excessive purchases of arms, is just as effective in diverting resources from measures that would increase national capability.

NOTES

1. For discussion of American sales in that period, see Ohlson (1988).
2. These figures were given to the author by SIPRI and were based on the latest *Annual Conversion Survey* (2001) produced by the Bonn International Center for Conversion, BICC.
3. Corruption in the arms trade, it seems, is another frozen accident inherited from the distant past. When Sultan Baibars attacked Acre, in the thirteenth century, the Venetians sold him military supplies, 'under

licence from the High Court at Acre'. See Jones and Ereira (1994).
4. See Pilger (1999), particularly the chapter on 'Arming the World', page 115 onwards.
5. Details of weapons used, casualties, and 'costs and benefits' are given in Heikal (1992).

TEN

AGENDA FOR A
NEW PARADIGM

I identified a dual paradox in Chapter 1: development bypassed many nations after half a century of focused efforts, and costs running to billions of dollars, and those involved in the project seemed unwilling or unable to find more effective policies and actions. In the chapters that followed, I was able to show that these difficulties arose from a view of development that was fatally flawed. I am not alone in expressing such an opinion. Caufield (1996: 333), for example, suggested that past efforts failed because of the false assumption that 'there was a condition called underdevelopment and that virtually every country in Asia, Africa and Latin America suffered from it'.

In taking that contention forward, I argued that the prevailing framework within which development is studied and practised is based on questionable linear assumptions. Evidence was then presented to advocate a shift to a vision of development founded in Complex Systems theory. In that way, I concluded, a rational explanation can be advanced for the above paradox. The adoption of linear prescriptions to deal with a nonlinear phenomenon was bound to end in failure, and while the experts were locked into a mind-set that predetermined their actions they were unable to explore other, radically different, means to achieve better results. The initial incentive to write this book was essentially to consider, and hopefully substantiate, this hypothesis.

In a sense, achieving that aim was the main objective. Nevertheless, the story is incomplete without discussion of the practical consequences that flow from a shift to a Complexity framework for development. The concluding remarks presented in this chapter are intended to provide that finishing touch. For reasons that will be made clear in the next few sections, the suggestions I advance later in the chapter take the form of an agenda comprising strategic and policy items, rather than the set of precise recommendations, with costs and implementation programmes, traditionally associated with studies conducted within a linear view on life.

PARADIGMS IN DEVELOPMENT

Experts, especially those dealing with local issues from afar, can, and often do, get things seriously wrong. They have a tendency to misdiagnose problems, they regularly misinterpret what those affected actually want, and, most importantly, they frequently jump to the wrong conclusion as to what needs to be done to rectify the situation. Upbringing, education, and social and geographical distance impose their own penalties. Most critically, however, experts unwittingly bring with them a powerful paradigm, the dictates of which they have been trained to obey as unassailable scientific laws. Those working in development are not immune from this constraint.

Consideration of the role played by paradigms in development is a new departure that is gathering momentum. Schuurman (2000: 8), for instance, wrote, 'The character of the debates within development studies seem[s] to have shifted from theory to paradigm.' He identified three key components to the paradigm that existed from the end of World War II to the mid-1980s: treating the 'Third World and its inhabitants as homogenous entities', 'unconditional belief in the concept of progress', and 'confidence in the role of the state to realise progress'. Schuurman's words might be different from those I used in earlier chapters, but the characteristics he listed are typical of a linear viewpoint based on assumptions of order, determinism and the efficacy of command-and-control from the top.

The development industry's assembly line

That vision carries with it the implication that development has a clear beginning and end, matched causes and effects, and universal laws that developed countries discovered some time ago. The task as seen by the specialists is obvious: the developing countries should be guided or pushed into treading the same path to success. According to that conception, developing nations move on an assembly line while the mechanics apply predefined adjustments to bring them up to scratch. That view of development has failed, hence the turmoil that has gripped the industry. Clearly, a radical change is unavoidable, and I advocate in this book a paradigm shift that would treat nations and their evolution as Complex Adaptive Systems. The proposed paradigm would not simply replace one viewpoint with another: it would change the *what*, *who*, *how* and *when* of development at all levels.

A RADICALLY DIFFERENT STYLE OF AGENDA

In consequence, the agenda associated with the new paradigm assumes an unfamiliar look that requires a few words of explanation. Recommendations drawn up within a linear framework would include a set of detailed proposals, complete with costs and timescale for implementation. Moreover, the schedule would identify the countries to which the various ideas apply. That form of presentation would be inappropriate within the concept of development advocated here in which overall patterns are the only stable and reasonably predictable feature.

In essence, the agenda items address matters of policy, and attitudes, that affect the process of development as a whole; the details are unpredictable, and to large extent irrelevant in the realm of Complexity. The proposals, therefore, focus exclusively on strategic options that would allow nations, as Complex Adaptive Systems, to assume stable, but evolving, global patterns. In other words, the agenda does not apply to any particular nation and does not include a list of specific actions. To this end, it is helpful to present a summary of the principal conclusions reached in the previous chapters to focus attention on the far-reaching nature of the changes implied by the transition from a linear to a Complexity view of development. As mentioned above, the new paradigm addresses the what, who, how and when of development and that format will be adhered to in what follows.

WHAT IS DEVELOPMENT?

Previous discussion revealed that the vision of development that has dictated the nature of past actions is seriously flawed. As described below, on the way to that conclusion a number of key questions were answered.

Nations behave as complex adaptive systems

At present, nations are seen as orderly entities whose behaviour is tolerably predictable. They are also assumed to be reasonably homogenous, and their progress is deterministically inevitable; they function in clockwork fashion and their movement forward follows a predetermined path. As such, there are few hidden surprises here; the whole is simply the sum of the parts.

However, looked at within a paradigm founded on Complexity, the way nations behave changes nature almost beyond recognition. In this case, change is driven by numerous local interactions that take place between individuals, working singly and in groups. Under suitable conditions of connectivity and regulation, the local chaos provides the energy that allows a nation to acquire self-organised, stable but evolving, patterns. As a result, progress comes mainly in the form of modest local improvements that accumulate over long periods of time. Nations' affairs, therefore, are full of surprises; *emergent properties* ensure that the whole is more than the sum of the parts.

Development is an evolutionary process

At base, development is what nations do as Complex Adaptive Systems, and what they do can be described as uncertain evolution that has no beginning or end, no shortcuts, and few signposts on the way. Nations do not follow the same path; the particular route traversed in each case is defined in part by frozen accidents inherited from the past, such as history, religion and traditions. However, prospects for the future are conditioned by two factors that are difficult to predict and guard against in advance: local opportunities and constraints, and the activities of other coevolving nations.

Under these conditions, rigid plans and policies are inappropriate. As discussed in Chapter 4, the only evolutionarily stable strategy (ESS) open to a nation is to exercise flexibility and pragmatism in order to survive, learn and adapt over and over again in accordance with its ever-changing fitness landscape. Critically, there is no evolution or progress without interactions; members of the population have to be free and able to interact (or in more traditional language to 'participate') for anything to happen.

Evolution does not promise equality

By its very nature, the evolutionary change of Complex Adaptive Systems leads to inequality and the emergence of elites and hierarchies. Average Complexity increases over time, but those with the highest Complexity stand to make the greatest gain; railing against the system and the unfairness of life does not help. The best policy in this case would be for a nation to optimise its performance within its own opportunities and constraints without being diverted by how others are doing. The rich will get richer, and the gap between rich and poor might well grow, but a nation can, and must, make substantial progress under its own steam and on its own terms.

International comparisons might be useful to a degree, some more than others, but ultimately review of the performance of a nation from year to year is the only pertinent factor. Monitoring is important, as management of a Complex Adaptive System is essentially a *reiterative process* that involves continual assessment leading to frequent but minor adjustments to encourage local interactions to proceed optimally. Again, intricate and rigid long-term plans are contraindicated in this instance.

Britain is a developing country

I chose this intentionally provocative subheading to underline a critical point arising from the above: *development is a continuous process*. Under suitable conditions, chaotic local interactions can result in stable but evolving patterns, but under other conditions the build up of Complexity could be halted or reversed. Hence, the numerous *states* currently produced by millions of diverse local interactions lead to a familiar pattern, or *attractor*, that equates with the concept of Britain, say, in the twenty-first century. Britain has changed over the centuries but mostly in slow and modest steps. Layers of 'depth' or Complexity, call it what you may, accumulated over very long periods in a sustained process of development. The cycle of survival, adaptation and learning has not come to a stop simply because Britain was placed on a list titled 'developed countries'. In that sense Britain is a developing country, and, barring unforeseen catastrophe, it will continue to be one.

Afghanistan is not a developing country

This subheading is inevitable, but is also of paramount importance. Afghanistan, along with a host of other countries, is not a developing country. The nature and scale of local interactions between members of its population are at a level that cannot provide sufficient energy for the system we know as Afghanistan to assume stable global patterns. In this case, local chaos cannot be translated into global self-organisation. In the absence of stability, the cycle of survival, adaptation and learning is fatally broken. The country swings between bouts of utter chaos and deathly order, such as that imposed until recently by the madcap rules of the Taliban. The main challenge, as I see it, is not concerned with changing developing countries into developed countries, but to enable non-developing nations to become developing nations.

WHO DRIVES THE DEVELOPMENT PROCESS?

As described in Chapter 4, egoistic individuals are the fundamental units when nations are considered as Complex Adaptive Systems. Numerous commissions have advocated greater involvement by people in projects that affect their lives. However, the basic balance of power remains unaltered; local people are allowed to come into the process at some stage of the work but remote experts and decision-makers remain in control. Top-down management of the development process is untouched in that revision of style rather than substance. A shift to the new paradigm recommended here would reverse that format. Complexity decrees that healthy change in social, political and economic life takes place at the local level and is driven by local actors: men, women and children. The state is vitally important, nonetheless, but as a facilitating institution rather than an oppressive presence.

People come first

Command-and-control from the top is not only inappropriate; it is also ineffective when dealing with nonlinear situations. Misunderstanding of this fundamental point is not restricted to efforts made by the development industry alone. For example, the WHO and UNICEF organised in 1978 an International Conference on Primary Health Care, attended by 134 member states, at which they launched a campaign to achieve 'Health for All by the Year 2000'. Recently, the WHO (2000: 14) provided a candid assessment of why the outcomes from that conference were 'at least partial failures'. Significantly, Evans et al. (1981: 1117) described in some detail 'the difficulties of putting this [the conference] objective into practice' shortly after the event took place.

The comments made on the 1978 event are highly pertinent to the themes presented here. I will concentrate, for brevity's sake, on one of the WHO's main concerns. The WHO criticised the conference 'for giving too little attention to people's *demand* for health care, which is greatly influenced by perceived quality and responsiveness, and instead concentrating almost exclusively on their *needs*'. There are many reasons why needs, as defined by experts one degree removed from ordinary people, and what these people actually want, differ; 'simply providing medical facilities and offering services may do nothing' to resolve that mismatch. There are, in truth, two different perspectives in most circumstances: life as experienced by people at large, and life as envisioned by the experts.

As demonstrated by the above example, it is necessary to put the clients – in other words, the people affected by the decisions taken – firmly in the driving seat in order to avoid going up blind alleys. That is not an easy pill for the experts to swallow, but Complexity provides scientific reasons why swallow it they must if progress is to be made. Complexity is founded on the principle that meaningful action takes place primarily at the level of the fundamental unit, the egoistic individual. The means have to be found to enable ordinary people to determine which problems they wish to address, how the problems should be tackled, and by whom. I have to labour this point because it determines to a great extent the content of the agenda presented below.

HOW TO BECOME A 'DEVELOPING NATION'

Having determined the 'what' and 'who' of development, it is appropriate to turn next to how nations could extricate themselves from the wretchedness of non-development to become truly 'developing nations'. That is the most fundamental task for the majority of nations on Earth, especially those in sub-Saharan Africa and parts of South Asia. It is also the most far-reaching outcome from a paradigm shift to a Complexity framework for development. The most important distinction is whether a nation is developing or otherwise; where it is in the hierarchy is a secondary issue.

Chapters 7, 8 and 9 defined in detail the parameters that would allow a nation to cross that Rubicon. They explored factors that encourage or inhibit the ability of individuals to take part in local interactions that provide the energy needed for their nations, as Complex Adaptive Systems, to acquire self-organised evolving patterns. Two strategic requirements were identified for optimal performance: individuals must be *free* to interact and *capable* of doing so in accordance with sensible rules that receive willing compliance from most people. Ultimately, discussion focused on basic human rights, coupled with protection for personal and property rights, nutrition, health, learning, and finally peace and security.

Human development leads the way

The first *Human Development Report*, published by UNDP in 1990, opened with a challenging thought: 'The real wealth of a nation is its people. And the purpose of development is to create an enabling environment for people to enjoy long, healthy and creative lives. This simple but powerful truth is too often forgotten in the pursuit of material and financial wealth' (UNDP 1990). A paradigm founded on Complexity provides scientific backing for this statement of principle. Fundamentally, human development must be accorded first priority above all else, including economic development.

UNDP (1999: v) is now in favour 'of the power of globalisation to bring economic and social benefits to societies', but beyond these politic words it, unknowingly, ascribes to a Complex Systems view of development: people are the prime actors, development is about giving them a better life, and a better life and wealth might not be one and the same. The evidence presented in previous chapters leads to the same conclusions. With respect to the 'how' of development: Malnourished, diseased, illiterate, oppressed and insecure people living in countries that lack properly functioning institutions cannot begin to develop, no matter how that activity is defined and tackled. Radical changes in attitudes, policies and practices are more effective in confronting these ills than the search for economic growth.

WHEN WOULD DEVELOPMENT HAPPEN?

I expect the final question, the 'when' of development, to cause considerable difficulty in the course of advocating a move to the proposed paradigm. Brought up on a linear view of life, most people would wish to know how long the process of conversion, and the associated actions, would take. The World Bank and the IMF, for instance, confidently stated that structural adjustment of target nations was expected to take between three and five years. Rostow (1960), on the other hand, expected takeoff into development to happen within ten to fifteen years. That was wonderfully precise and reassuring. It did not work out that way, but that is usual in most cases where a nonlinear phenomenon is treated as an orderly and predictable activity. The traditional response is to give some excuse and then amend the timescale repeatedly until events finally coincide with expectations. If that does not happen one forgets the whole idea and starts again. This procedure is followed in business as well as in political circles.

However, if progress is to be made in helping needy nations to enter the development process it is necessary to be brutally honest and open about what the new paradigm entails. Detailed prediction is impossible and, therefore, timescales are irrelevant to a considerable extent. What do I mean by that? Let us look at what is involved. First, the development industry, including individual nations, leading powers and international regimes, has to convert to a different paradigm at its own pace. Experience in the natural sciences suggests that paradigm shifts can be lengthy and convoluted; advocacy is not a precise art. Second, radical revisions to policies and practices, and associated institutional changes, will have to be implemented by a wide range of organisations, local and global. And finally, a period of time must elapse to allow the new actions to take effect. In short, it is impractical to give a timescale.

Then the next hurdle comes into view. I concentrated above on the point at which a non-developing nation turns into a developing nation, but when will it improve its standards of living? When will ordinary people in Zaïre acquire their own homes, complete with gardens and two cars per household? The answer is a long time, perhaps never. Basically I do not know, and no one else does either. The only rational response is that if a nation wants to start developing then it will have to change its ways and rely on itself. How aggressively and diligently it is willing to pursue that goal is affected by too many factors for anyone to express sensible views about the future. There is one aspect that is totally predictable, though: a non-developing nation can never move forward without the radical transformations described here. The reader does not have to take my word for it; the failure of the development industry since the end of World War II is more eloquent testimony than I could ever give. As mentioned in Chapter 1, $1 trillion (in 1985 dollars) given in aid by Western countries to the developing world between 1950 and 1995 did not have much of an impact (Easterly 2001: 33).

IMPEDIMENTS TO ENTRY INTO THE DEVELOPMENT PROCESS

Clearly, it is not possible to speak sensibly about timescales. On the other hand, I was able to demonstrate in previous chapters that there are powerful impediments to nations entering the process of development and then going on to optimise their performance as Complex Adaptive Systems. These restraints can, and often do, retard the timing of potential progress. To help give perspective to the agenda proposals described later, I summarise below the main barriers to achievement.

Bogus ideologies and theories

Development has been pursued traditionally within specific ideological guidelines. Contrasting approaches based on capitalism or socialism were the norm until recently, but the capitalist camp has emerged as the victor and development prescriptions now follow the dictates of that philosophy. Working within the new spirit of the age and under the watchful eye of the leading powers, agencies such as the World Bank have set out to impose on the so-called developing countries an idealised version of the capitalist system that is almost unrecognisable elsewhere. Little, if any, flexibility or variety is tolerated, and any attempt to veer from that straitjacket is perceived, and often punished, as a threat to 'world order'.[1] In effect, they are told that big government and public spending are bad, that subsidies distort the market, and that income support and social provision at public expense are unacceptable.

Conversely, I argued in Chapters 2 and 3 that the core ideologies are sets of flexible and changing beliefs that share an extensive common ground. I maintained, moreover, that the leading powers have consistently kept an open mind when it came to ideologies and political economic theories. They accept large governments and budgets, subsidies, and public services as self-evident necessities. In practice, as opposed to rhetoric, successful nations adopt policies derived from a blend of ideologies that varies to suit changing circumstances. In short, the developing nations are being prevented from following what has proved to be the only evolutionarily stable strategy open to nations as Complex Adaptive Systems.

The harmful focus on globalisation

Obsessive pursuit of globalisation is the most damaging consequence of the accent placed on the above intolerant ideological orthodoxy. Adam Smith and David Ricardo might have explained the virtues of the market, trade and comparative advantage, but they did not invent them. With or without these explanations, humankind energetically manufactured goods, offered services, bought, sold, bartered and traded across borders for thousands of years before the WTO came on the scene. Nonetheless, the WTO, the World Bank and the IMF behave as the worst kind of 'market fundamentalists'.

Preaching the gospel of free trade and globalisation with missionary zeal is not only unnecessary but poses a serious threat to the ability of struggling nations to evolve optimally. I relied on evidential presentation of facts and figures in previous chapters to argue that point, but a veritable mountain of anecdotal evidence is also at hand, and not necessarily from the 'disruptive elements' that organise protests at WTO meetings. For instance, one could not find a more middle-of-the-road organisation than the Arab–British Chamber of Commerce, but its *Journal* repeatedly draws attention to the dangers of overenthusiastic promotion of globalisation by the leading powers. The *Journal*, for example, has criticised the virtual exclusion of agriculture from the liberalisation of trade (April 1996), the primacy of the interests of a few leading powers over all other concerns (December 1999), and the WTO giving the impression of being a 'two-tier organisation, with first and second class membership' (April 2000). Significantly, the *Journal* led in October 2000 with a revealing question: 'Globalisation is here to stay, but will it benefit developing countries?'

Similarly, George Soros, whose capitalist credentials are beyond reproach, joined the ranks of those who questioned the wisdom of ruthlessly pursuing a vision of globalisation that is clearly biased against the development of deprived nations. Speaking in January 2001 on the occasion of the World Economic Forum in Davos, he said globalisation 'creates a very uneven playing field'. Interestingly, there are historic parallels from the period when today's leading economies were feeling their way forward. As mentioned in Chapter 2, for example, List (1789–1846), argued that protection was desirable in some cases to enable nations, meaning Germany at that time, to catch up with the leaders, although he had no objection to free trade in principle. Reflecting the same sentiments, Alexander Hamilton (1755–1804) presented a report to the US Congress in 1791 in which he expressed opinions that sit very comfortably with reservations voiced by present-day weaker economies.

Notwithstanding the practical and moral objections to obsessive globalisation, the destructive nature of the project is plain to see in technical terms. Essentially, globalisation demands uniformity; it bleaches all variety out of the world system. Ostensibly, globalisation presumes that one universal fitness landscape exists, or could be engineered, to suit all nations. That is fiction. In practice, the leading powers, using the formidable resources available to them and their global agencies, have set out to force all nations to compete on one fitness landscape on which these powers thrive. Viewing interstate cooperation and competition from the perspective of Game Theory leaves no doubt about the reasons for adopting such a policy or its inevitable outcome.

Excuses based on cost

Lack of progress is often blamed, cynically or otherwise, on the presumed high costs of remedial measures. In consequence, the 'market fundamentalists' are able to spread the myth that the nations concerned should exercise patience: economic development, and hence globalisation, must come first and that will inevitably be followed, through trickle-down, by progress in tackling urgent social needs. Well, evidence suggests that nations might have to wait an eternity for that to happen. During a phenomenally successful period that advanced the global economy by leaps and bounds, the poor in the developing world have become poorer both within and between nations. And the prospects are not promising. The World Bank's poverty projections suggest that up to one billion people might still be living on less than $1 per day by 2015 (World Bank 2001).

Contrary to the above assertion, effective remedial measures could be implemented at surprisingly low cost. Certain countries, as in the case of Cuba and China, were forced by shortage of funds to seek locally meaningful remedies at minimal levels of expenditure, and in that way achieved standards of health, nutrition and literacy that compare well with those in the most prosperous countries. Chapters 6 and 8 cited various examples to substantiate this viewpoint, but ample supportive evidence is also available from other sources, including all the main agencies of the United Nations. On the whole, cost and economic development are not deciding factors.

Excuses based on affordability

But can poorer nations afford remedial actions even at low cost? Confronting this element in the folklore of the development industry is, I believe, of critical importance. The story goes something like this: remedies are expensive, poorer nations have very limited financial resources, so what is the point of changing course to seek progress in human development? This is another piece of fiction. The poorest nations in sub-Saharan Africa are relatively poor but they are not penniless. As mentioned in Chapter 1, de Soto (2000) demonstrated that the developing countries have vast amounts of capital that is tied up in uses and institutional red tape that prevent its utilisation as an active tool towards development. Similarly, the facts presented previously reveal that, against all expectations, shortage of funds is not a critical issue in tackling the core problems of disease, malnutrition and illiteracy. Concerns about affordability are caused by biased spending regimes that do not allocate sufficient finance to basic programmes. Additionally, substantial sums are squandered through rampant waste and corruption.

In the early 1990s, governments of the developing countries spent about $440 billion annually, of which only about $50 billion was earmarked for nutrition, healthcare, primary education, family planning, clean water and sanitation (UNDP 1994). It is possible to cite specific instances of this warped view of the top priorities. Ethiopia, say, allocated 22 per cent of its GNP to military expenditure in 1992, and maintained that level of spending to the late 1990s. In sum, health and poverty, good nutrition and poverty, and literacy and poverty are not mutually exclusive. On the one hand, improvements can be made at low cost, and on the other hand the necessary funds are already available, though they might not be visible.

There are, of course, factors that limit governments' room for manoeuvre in reallocating funds within the existing budgets. Repayments for past foreign debts are an obvious instance. UNICEF (2001: 55) reported that for some of the world's most impoverished countries these repayments often absorb between 25 and 50 per cent of the budget. Similarly, the costs of looking after refugees and clearing landmines impose severe pressures on budgets in some cases. Nonetheless, the developing countries find the money somehow to allocate well over $100 billion annually for military purposes.

Foreign aid is a potential source of funding, although its levels have decreased in recent decades. Yet again, this element is not immune to the eccentric allocation policies that bedevil the budgets of needy countries. UNDP (1997: 113) estimated that only 10 per cent of aid goes to the most pressing social needs of recipient nations. In addition, and as mentioned in Chapters 5 and 8, one-third of aid is lost in administration and straightforward corruption, and as much as one-half of the money goes into payments to consulting firms from the donor countries. Humanitarian aid, mainly to deal with the effects of conflict, currently running at $10 billion annually, reduces the effectiveness of the available aid resources even further. Aid, therefore, displays the same paradox: money is available but spending has little to do with the most pressing needs. In any case, the efficacy of aid in assisting development is not clear-cut.[2]

Futile efforts to import development

The long way is also the quickest way for a nation to achieve sustained progress, and the route to success – basically survival and adaptation – is largely self-evident once it is recognised that nations behave as Complex Adaptive Systems. That is not an easy message for the leaders of developing countries to accept. On the whole, and having made due allowances for egoism, corruption, and all the other usual ills that afflict leaders, it is undeniable that most states would wish to take their nations forward. Understandably, they also want to do so in a hurry, without radical changes to policies, and at least cost and effort to themselves and their local elites. They pin their hopes, therefore, on the importation of the supposed experience and resources of 'more advanced' nations, a curious notion but one that seems reasonable when viewed in traditional linear terms.

I suggested in Chapter 6 that the popular story of how today's leading nations came to occupy the top branches of the global hierarchy is a myth. Their progress, evidence shows, followed centuries of slow evolution during which they added numerous layers of 'depth' across many issue areas that went well beyond simple economics. Each nation ploughed its own furrow, and progression was achieved through the accumulation of modest improvements over long periods. Moreover, their development was not preplanned; it relied on actions by most of the population, working alone or in groups, to pursue their diverse interests. Regardless, leaders of the developing countries, aided and abetted by their experts and those working for the WTO, the World Bank and the IMF, assume that there are universal laws known to the leading nations that will help them to compress the process into a few years. That is when the wheels come off the cart.

Intervention by leading powers

Nations must enter the development process under their own steam. That is the brutal message that has to be understood for any nation to take the next, reasonably obvious, steps on the way forward. Leading powers cannot give other nations the secrets of, or the resources for, success. Additionally, they cannot prevent them from making progress if they are determined to do so. However, under certain conditions foreign intervention can reduce the speed with which progress is made. That does not imply ill will; it merely indicates that the interests of the leading powers come first and if they conflict with local progress then sadly that must be sacrificed. Nonetheless, the degree of success achieved by the foreign powers, working overtly or covertly, can be controlled to some extent by the target nations, as explained later.

THE AGENDA: ENCOURAGING SIGNS

A paradigm shift in development along the lines described above is the most fundamental item on the agenda; a new dawn for development can only come about if, and when, that feat has been successfully accomplished. I have stressed all along that paradigm shifts are a long time coming, but equally once the need for the transition gains acceptance the leap to a new formulation happens quite rapidly. Advocacy is evidently the main tool in pursuing this aim. In this context, it is appropriate to highlight two hopeful signs: there is widespread dissatisfaction with the performance of the development industry to date, and the search is on for alternatives. Chambers (1997: 188) wrote, 'In an evolving paradigm of development there is a new high ground, a paradigm of people as people.' Interestingly, in surveying alternative ideas, Chambers (1997: 194) made specific reference to 'chaos and complexity theory'.

Soul-searching at the World Bank is also a pointer to the future. I underlined in Chapter 5 the critical self-appraisal that took place at the Bank when Wolfsensohn took over as president in 1995. Judging by the output of reports from that organisation the reassessment has continued; comparison of back issues of the Bank's *Policy and Research Bulletin* with more recent issues supports that impression. The April–June 1999 issue is particularly indicative as it dealt robustly, and in some respects critically, with fundamental topics relating to development policy.

The proceedings of the tenth Annual World Bank Conference on Development Economics held in Washington DC in April 1998 gives even clearer hints of the transformation slowly gathering momentum within that organisation. Stiglitz, the Bank's chief economist at the time, emphasised in his opening remarks the need for new models and instruments to pursue a broader agenda. He added that many cherished doctrines must be reassessed, including prescriptions based on the 'neoliberal model' of development. Other participants conveyed the same message, especially the care needed 'not to confuse ideology with economic science', the pressing requirement for empirically grounded analysis, and the desirability of directing attention to institutional improvements.[3] In a similar vein, the World Bank underlined the need to balance regulation against flexibility, as 'excessive restraint can lead to paralysis'. That conclusion was arrived at intuitively, but it has specific significance within a Complex Systems framework.

In short, a widening constituency is seeking reform from the bottom up. Admittedly, there is a long way to go. For example, action by the World Bank does not seem to have caught up yet with the new ideas advocated in its most recent research output. Moreover, there is so far little unanimity about the nature of the future paradigm, although I hope this book is a positive step in that direction. Nonetheless, the omens are encouraging, in spite of the difficulty of predicting the ultimate form and the speed of the forthcoming transition.

THE AGENDA FOR NATIONS SEEKING DEVELOPMENT

The decision to deal first with the nations seeking development was deliberate. Development, as defined here, is a local affair. Local actors drive the process forward and the countries concerned can do much to improve their chances of success despite the self-evident fact that their room for manoeuvre is influenced by other coevolving nations as well as by leading world powers and their global organisations. The policy changes suggested are in many respects obvious. They are those required to give ordinary people freedom and capability to interact as much or as little as they see fit. Other policy options are also included, however, to allow such nations to improve their performance at regional and international encounters.

Enhancement of basic liberties

The most significant step forward relates to the provision of basic liberties to allow individuals to interact freely but within rules that command willing general support. The benefits to the nation as a Complex Adaptive System were described in Chapter 7, but leaders intent on staying in power through imposed control often ignore three beneficial by-products. First, repression is highly inefficient due to its failure to elicit voluntary compliance by the population. Elites elsewhere discovered by experience that a measure of freedom is more effective in safeguarding their privileged status. Second, as Horowitz (1998: 38) pointed out, liberal structures provide a 'frame within which ethnic conflict is played out'. In that context Collier (1998: 18) wrote, 'Democratisation is worth around half a century of income growth in terms of its contribution to peace.' And third, the most efficient way to reduce the potential for intervention in the internal affairs of a nation by an external power is through human rights reforms and the creation of a democratic image. These measures eliminate the most popular excuse given by one country to interfere in the affairs of another.

The call here is not for parliamentary democracy along British, or any other, lines, and it does not stem from a moral standpoint. The need for reforms arises from the paramount necessity of enabling individuals to interact, innovate, take risks, and generally be different within sensible limits. The filigree of practices that have been adopted over the centuries at different locations might not be appropriate or practicable elsewhere. However, there is an absolute minimum that has to be in place for a nation to enter the development process. Regular elections, local and national, independent press and media, and separation of powers between the executive, legislative and judicial branches of government are desirable, but the degree to which they can be achieved is open to consideration.

An obvious question springs to mind: how can one make progress when the local agencies that would implement the change are themselves repressive? Admittedly, the dice are loaded against success, but the task is not impossible. The Instituto Libertad y Democracia (ILD) in Lima, Peru, provides some possible answers. The ILD was set up in 1982 with the purpose of helping the poor in Peru play a more active role in society. It has received plaudits from many quarters; in 1992 *The Economist* called it the second most important think-tank in the world. It has since extended its work to other countries in Latin America, the Middle East and Asia. From the start, the ILD argued that the best way forward is through incremental steps. Despite the name, the ILD seems to have avoided the trap of calling for outright democracy. As discussed in Chapter 7, that itself is a nebulous concept that can cause more trouble than it is worth.

The ILD approach, based on gradual changes that focus on reforming decision-making procedures, restructuring institutions, improving access to public information, and the way the law works in certain areas, seems to have succeeded because it avoided confrontation with the elite. In addition the work of the ILD relied heavily on promotion – even self-promotion – and proactive work with a wide range of already existing organisations. Possibly one of the most imaginative innovations championed by the ILD was the creation of a national ombudsman to represent the interests of ordinary citizens. Obviously, it is futile to endeavour to convince people to interact, invest and innovate in the absence of arrangements for them to seek redress when necessary.

I dwell on the ILD not for the purpose of suggesting that its work should be copied everywhere else, although there are distinct lessons to be learnt, but to make the point that with imagination and persistence progress can be made even under the most trying conditions. The one noticeable feature in the ILD approach is that it started from the existing situation and then moved forward in small steps to propose changes that made local sense individually. Some institutions charged with responsibilities in the field of human rights are already in existence in most regions within the developing world. Chapter 7, for example, referred to the African Human Rights Commission, set up in 1987, and to the African Human Rights Court, created in 1998. Performance might be disappointing, but these institutions are there and they merely require the spark that will change them into fully functioning entities.

Why have I devoted so much space to the topic of basic liberties? Essentially, it is a critical prerequisite for setting local interactions on their way, but that is not the only element at stake. I will give two examples to illustrate this point and to underline the primacy of this part of the agenda. Inequitable, and damaging, allocation of spending between rural and urban communities is attributed by most authorities to the lack of 'voice' on the part of rural people. Unless that is altered, and institutional reforms and independent media are of obvious benefit in that context, there is little likelihood of striking a better balance. Similarly, corruption is common in all parts of the world, but it is especially harmful in the so-called developing countries. It is out of control, but it is also a topic that cannot be discussed, let alone criticised, openly. Again, without liberalising reforms that nefarious activity will continue unchecked. These examples, and many others like them, demonstrate that achievement of progress on other items on the agenda will be heavily compromised unless action is taken to put human rights on a proper footing.

Prevention and resolution of conflict

In every respect, conflict is damaging to the efficient functioning of a nation as a Complex Adaptive System. Nations crippled by actual and potential conflicts have to consider three strategies. First, they must strive to implement human rights reforms, as outlined above. The power of mischief-makers, domestic and foreign, is drastically reduced in an open society. Second, they can explore effective regional conflict prevention and resolution arrangements, possibly with UN backing. And third, they should unfailingly examine the possibility of reducing military spending substantially. World expenditure in this sector was about 2.4 per cent of GDP in 1996. It is reasonable to suggest that anything above that figure at the national level must be considered extravagant; a great deal less would be even better.

As argued by al-Wardi (1996: 73), poorer countries are slow in agreeing mechanisms for the peaceful resolution of disputes. This is particularly the case in the 'Arc of Crises', principally the Middle East and Africa. SIPRI was moved to warn that 'in the absence of strong regional mechanisms African states will increasingly resort to private security forces, such as those offered by South African-based Executive Outcomes'. A proposal was made by the USA in the early 1990s to set up an African Crisis Response Force but, understandably, fears of increased American involvement led to abandonment of that idea (SIPRI 1997: 57). Nevertheless, there are signs that the situation might be changing. Mazrui (1995: 38), for example, put forward an idea 'for five pivotal powers [in Africa] to create a kind of African Security Council'. Similar suggestions have been made for the Arab countries in the Middle East to enter into peacekeeping arrangements. That would not be a totally new departure; in 1961 the Arab League positioned a military force between Kuwait and Iraq to prevent a state of tension escalating into war.

It is necessary to underline again the close affinity between heavy military spending, corruption, conflict, repression and meddling by foreign powers. All these factors are self-reinforcing. Put another way, action on any would help to reduce the ferocity of the others. And action on all fronts would produce surprisingly good returns. Admittedly, however, progress will be difficult. As outlined in Chapter 9, vast fortunes are made through arms sales, legally or otherwise, and army officers are not likely to agree a change that would rob them of their privileges. On the other hand, little progress can be made without an agreement by the military to vacate government offices in favour of the barracks. That voluntary migration is difficult to effect, but it has been done before.

Reallocation of financial resources

Human rights, institutional reforms and reduction of conflict would enhance the freedom of individuals to interact. Redistribution of existing financial resources to give priority to basic social programmes would energise the internal dynamics of the nation even further by boosting the capability of individuals to interact locally. As argued in Chapter 8, a shift in that direction would also help to make civil strife less attractive, and of course less necessary. Funds devoted to social needs, including income redistribution, and special programmes to target children, women, ethnic minorities and rural areas, should be substantially increased to fall within the range of 50 to 75 per cent of total spending. That would simply bring practice in the developing countries, where the needs are infinitely more pressing, closer to the spending norms in the industrialised economies (see Chapter 6). A large reduction in military spending would be a step in the right direction, as suggested earlier. However, human rights reforms, an independent judiciary, and reasonably free media to provide uncontrolled sources of information and facilities for public comment are indispensable tools to that end.

Improvements in efficiency

The worst act a state can commit is to seek finance from abroad, but there are different levels of risk attached to that act. By far the most harmful folly is to accept a bilateral loan from another government or bank, including the World Bank. Multilateral loans are only marginally less risky. Interest-free credits or low-interest loans from the International Development Association (IDA) are a much better proposition, but they are only given to qualifying countries. As discussed earlier, even aid carries its own risks. As Caufield (1996: 338) remarked, 'development funds, including the World Bank's, are ... largely a matter of poor people in rich countries giving money to rich people in poor countries.' Debts, and aid, are routinely seen as helpful tools in the search for development, but they often lead instead to dependency and loss of sovereignty. More to the point, they also correlate with repression and corruption.

Strategically, a state should minimise, or preferably eliminate, the need for loans and aid from external sources. To that end, it has to optimise the financial resources already available locally. Although reallocation of funds between budget heads and between rural and urban areas was advocated above, it is undeniable that that course of action has its own difficulties and constraints. Clearly, therefore, the first line of attack in the search for additional funds must involve

improvements in efficiency. Better corporate governance is an essential part of that task, but efficiency also relates to the selection of
projects and actions that are appropriate to local problems and circumstances. This aspect of decision-making was highlighted at several
stages of the discussion, particularly in Chapter 8.

Careful selection of problems and the appropriate technology to
tackle them is of fundamental importance in achieving optimal success
at minimal cost. At the end of the day, indigenous knowledge and
inherited coping strategies must form an integral part of decision-
making at all levels. Local actions offering low-cost flexible solutions
to problems of water supply and sanitation, for example, are often
eschewed in favour of major projects that impose severe commitments
in initial costs and in future maintenance and renewal. There are
powerful inducements for experts and states to follow that course of
inappropriate action, as discussed previously. However, rigid plans
allow little flexibility to alter course in line with changing circumstances. Essentially, they are the very opposite of what is required
under the highly unpredictable conditions faced by a nation taking its
first steps in development.

Equally, lack of even the most elementary aspects of governance
and public accountability are major drains on potential resources. They
are ever-present causes of waste that inhibit, and often prevent, progress from being made in funding basic social programmes. In that
respect, corruption is a major headache in the so-called developing
world. The World Bank (1997b) stressed that the power that rulers
have to intervene arbitrarily, coupled with access to information denied to others, creates fertile opportunities for corruption. Under these
circumstances, development 'hits a brick wall, as corruption is negatively correlated with investment and growth'.[4] Corruption, of course,
exists everywhere, but the difference lies in the absence of checks and
balances within the developing nations to keep that element of waste
within acceptable limits. Basically, audit systems are either minimal or
nonexistent. In some cases, a formal budget does not exist, and in a
few instances the ruling clique does not recognise any distinction
between personal and national revenues. An elementary step in re-
trieving the situation must include the creation of an independent
national audit office with wide-ranging powers. But that should be
seen as only the start in a wider project of scrutiny.

Effectiveness in international encounters

This is a relatively neglected strategic policy issue, and one that requires urgent attention. On top of all the other challenges they face, weaker countries endure many disadvantages in their relations with more powerful actors on the world stage. All too often they accept the situation as an inevitable outcome of their relative place within the global hierarchy. As a result, they do not take steps to improve their performance on that front. Furthermore, they frequently adopt a quiescent and obsequious stance in their dealings with others, and that makes matters infinitely worse for them.

However, it is possible for a country to consider policies that would improve its position in encounters with others. The task is in three parts. First, weaker nations have to create the right conditions for spontaneous cooperation to emerge. Second, they have to minimise the damage caused through inevitable encounters with more powerful players without giving them sufficient reason to become aggressive overtly or covertly. And third, they have to gain a better understanding of the critical role played by communication and a positive image locally and internationally.

For spontaneous cooperation to emerge, Game Theory provides convincing evidence that nations should intensify links with those at a similar level in the global hierarchy (Axelrod 1984: 145). A number of arrangements are already in existence designed to enhance regional cooperation, such as the European Union; Mercosur, involving Argentina, Brazil, Paraguay and Uruguay; the North American Free Trade Agreement (NAFTA); and the Asia Pacific Economic Cooperation forum (APEC). On a smaller scale, the Gulf Cooperation Council (GCC) was founded in 1981 to promote cooperation between Bahrain, Kuwait, Oman, Qatar, Saudi Arabia and the United Arab Emirates. The UAE itself brought together, in 1971, the seven sheikdoms of Abu Dhabi, Dubai, Ajman, Umm Al Quwain, Ras Al Khaimah and Fujairah. In short, the model is familiar.

The Group of 77 (G77) is possibly the most prominent in the context of the so-called developing countries. It was formed in 1964 by a declaration issued by seventy-seven countries at the end of the first session of the United Nations Conference on Trade and Development (UNCTAD) in Geneva. The G77, now involving 133 members, works with other world organizations through 'Chapters', such as those in Rome (FAO), Vienna (UNIDO), Paris (UNESCO), Nairobi (UNEP) and the Group of 24 in Washington DC (IMF and World Bank). Some would say, with good reason, that the group is too large and diffuse to be effective. However, it is in place, and represents, therefore, a potential tool that can be amended to increase its power.

Inequitable contacts with more powerful states are unavoidable, and quite necessary, but even here the odds could be enhanced through proper appreciation of the processes involved. The weaker side should aim, for instance, to increase the frequency of interactions without increasing their value by breaking each potential encounter down into smaller segments. Furthermore, nations should club together to create more effective negotiating blocs. Again, this feature is becoming obvious to weaker countries. For example, a new grouping, the G16, involving Egypt, Algeria, Argentina, Brazil, Chile, India, Indonesia, Jamaica, Kenya, Malaysia, Mexico, Nigeria, Peru, Senegal, Venezuela and Zimbabwe met in Cairo in May 1998 to improve mutual co-operation. They also agreed to present a united front at the next round of WTO trade negotiations.

Promotion and image building are often seen by poorer nations as optional extras. Reputations and labels are identified by Game Theory as powerful tools in gaining an advantage in all encounters. Leading powers have understood this requirement perfectly. Wars, in trade as well as involving weapons, are now fought in accordance with a strict public relations format, as was seen, for instance, in the Gulf War and the trade war over bananas between the USA and Europe. Repressive regimes lose in two ways: they alienate their citizens and then they proceed to give themselves a highly negative image abroad. And their efforts at public relations are often crude in the extreme, as anyone who listens to their broadcasts would readily confirm. Clearly, a change in substance as well as style is in order.

Africa is a special case

The developing world is not a homogenous mass of nations and people. Some have already taken steps to join the development process, while others are lagging far behind. Africa, in this respect, merits special attention. Obviously, it is a continent that shows clear signs of stress, including rapid increases in population, famines, AIDS at near-epidemic proportions, and conflict, to name but a few negative factors.

On the other hand, it is a region that is full of potential, which includes a vast reservoir of human and natural resources.

There is a critical reason for identifying Africa at this point. Stallings (1995: 361) cited clear indications that the previous bipolar system of military opponents is being replaced by 'a tripolar system of economic competitors': a triad comprising the USA, Europe and Japan. Although the details are far from clear – Southeast Asia rather than Japan, for instance, might be a more accurate description of the third member of the triad – it seems that the triad concept might join the free market as a stable feature of the global system for the foreseeable future. In that scenario, each of the three regional powers would endeavour to act as a focal point for nations within its sphere of influence. Global networks of trade, production, ideology and finance would continue to bind the three members of the triad at the top, but links between each 'regional hegemon' and its group of nations would also be maintained and strengthened (Stallings 1995: 352). Hence, globalisation would exhibit a significant measure of regionalism. However, Stallings (1995: 355) warned that sub-Saharan Africa in particular is 'being marginalised in the process'. Hoogvelt (2001: 173–96) argued this point similarly.

Evidence suggests that the global system has been shifting towards a tripolar structure for quite some time. Internal trade and investment activity by each triad member is on a colossal scale. In 1999, just under 70 per cent of Western Europe's merchandise trade was internal (WTO 2000b). The same is evident in the trade picture within the American region and in Asia; internal trade is predominant and that with the other triad members comes next in importance. Contrast with the marginalised regions is highly significant: Africa's share of intra- and inter-regional trade flows is a mere 2 per cent of total world merchandise exports.

The development of the triad, whatever shape it might take in future, has positive elements for nations in search of development. For a start, the grip of the USA in world affairs would be weakened, with consequential effects on globalisation and the power of world bodies such as the World Bank and the IMF. Conversely, the impact on Africa, and on parts of the Middle East, could be negative. To that end, Africa, and within that sub-Saharan Africa, needs to rise to that challenge. There is no shortage in ideas. For instance, Mazrui (1995: 36) advanced a well-argued case to implement far-reaching changes in

Africa in stages to effect an improvement in the position of women, population policies, human rights, and the avoidance and resolution of conflicts. In the latter instance, for example, he proposed the creation of an African Security Council comprising South Africa, Egypt, Ethiopia, Nigeria and Zaïre. The New African Initiative approved by the Organisation for African Unity (OAU) summit on 11 July 2001 is another notable instance. Again, the details are unimportant. My aim in giving these examples is merely to underline three aspects: the need for focus on Africa, the radical nature of the change required, and the availability of local people and ideas that would help in achieving success in that difficult task.

THE AGENDA FOR LEADING POWERS AND WORLD BODIES

The agenda for nations seeking development was presented first and was given more space. I believe that reflects the rational order of priority when development is considered within a paradigm based on Complexity. Basically, it is up to the nations concerned whether they enter the development process or not. Others might help or hinder them a little but ultimately they are in the driving seat. You have to be cruel to be kind in some instances, and development is a case in point. For as long they are fed on empty promises and ineffectual prescriptions from outside, these nations and their governments will continue to loiter at the starting gate.

There is another reason for giving everyone else second place in the order of priority. It is largely pointless to appeal to their better nature in an effort to help less fortunate people and nations. Sad to say, the world does not recognise that mode of operation. I was at pains to highlight this point at various stages of the discussion. Above everything else, nations – all nations – seek to promote their interests, and rich and powerful nations are able to go further on that road than others. There is nothing sinister or underhanded in this form of behaviour. In many ways, today's hegemonic power is relatively more broadminded and reasonable than its predecessors. In short, asking leading powers, and the international regimes they set up and fund, to behave differently is futile.

The above remarks might sound harsh or excessively sombre, but they are supported by historic evidence. Certainly, the primacy of nations in managing their own affairs is beyond dispute. For instance, a major meeting of experts convened by the World Bank concluded that end results of adjustment lending depended almost exclusively on the client nation itself; 'ownership' of programmes was highlighted as a basic condition for success (Thomas et al. 1991: 523). However, notwithstanding this key proviso, there are a number of policy issue areas in which leading powers and international regimes could be more of a help and less of a hindrance.

Recognition of development as a localised activity

The most constructive action that leading nations and global institutions can pursue is to accept development for what it really is, an evolutionary process driven by local actors. Possibly through good intentions, they decided in the past that 'underdevelopment' could reasonably quickly be turned into 'development' by rigid implementation of predetermined recipes of universal applicability. As efforts failed, they were replaced by equally ineffectual remedies. Continual experimentation based on the false premiss of linearity, as described in Chapter 5 in the case of the World Bank for example, has been misleading, diverting and damaging.

In particular, and as underlined repeatedly, diversity and flexibility are essential elements to success when nations are treated as Complex Adaptive Systems and when development is viewed as an ongoing evolutionary process. The leading powers, and their global organisations, could help by taking a more relaxed view of the practices adopted by nations in the initial stages of development. Every departure from the norms set by these powers is not necessarily a challenge to their authority or to 'world order and stability'. The powers could also contribute to the success of needy nations by limiting their involvement in the affairs of these nations. The principle advocated in this context is that involvement by others should be the exception rather than the rule.

Emphasis on integrative systemic measures

Nevertheless, a degree of intervention is inevitable. Egoistic individuals and organisations are unlikely to accept a diminution in their role. Furthermore, the developing countries themselves seek help from others, often with alacrity that verges on rashness. The ever-present lure of financial assistance makes the process irresistible. But inter-vention could be directed into more productive channels. For a start, poorer nations should be weaned off the idea that foreign money will solve their problems. Loans, it was asserted in previous chapters, can be counterproductive, and needy nations are hardly in a position to shoulder further burdens in this respect. Aid has already declined by one-third in real terms in the 1990s, and the World Bank (1998) identified a feeling on the part of donors 'that aid does not work very well'. In some ways these are hopeful signs. Loans should be seen as measures of last resort and aid should be focused, as now advocated by the Bank, on integrated efforts to tackle basic needs, poverty reduction, and systemic and institutional improvements such as those proposed above for nations in search of development.

Appropriate knowledge and experience

That imported remedies might not be appropriate at all times and places is even more difficult for foreign organisations to accept than deviations from ideological orthodoxy. Naturally, part of the purpose of intervention by the industrialised economies is to sell their prod-ucts and services. Many would assert that that is the main reason for any involvement abroad. It is, therefore, difficult for development agencies to subscribe too readily to indigenous remedies and local coping strategies. In addition, those involved in development on both sides of the divide have been educated and trained in systems that predominantly reflect Western conventions. It is abundantly clear, however, that a fresh start in this issue area is sorely needed.

Restructuring of global organisations

The above does not imply blanket rejection of all foreign methods. The aim should be to select the most appropriate solutions to problems, and that demands flexibility and familiarity with the full range of possible options. This requirement is generally well understood. Efforts have been made to encourage those working in the World Bank, for instance, to spend more time in client countries. What is needed, however, is awareness and knowledge that can only be gained through long exposure to local conditions, and sustained first-hand contact with those directly affected by the remedial actions. Restructuring of the development agencies is the only sensible policy option to satisfy such preconditions. Basically, a limited number of core staff, mainly administrative, might be retained at the headquarters, and a few more could be located at main regional centres, Africa for instance, but the bulk of manpower would comprise field officers working locally on-site on long-term assignments. A glance at the pay and conditions for those working at the UN, the World Bank and the IMF would readily identify the near impossibility of implementing such a change from within. The alternative scenario is just as unattractive, however: these global bodies could slowly drift into irrelevance. The UN has already ceased to be of major significance so far as development is concerned, and the World Bank could easily follow suit.

Reversing the commercialisation of weapons

The majority of 'fledgling states throughout Africa and Asia inherited or created by their new, independent existence national security problems and concerns'. That, according to Allen and Thomas (1995: 235), was one factor in the increasing transfer of weapons to the developing world after World War II that ultimately led to the 'commercialisation of the arms trade at the end of the 1960s'. Militarism, as I argued in Chapter 9, is highly damaging, especially because it brings repression of civilian populations and rampant corruption in its wake. Costs are imposed on arms exporting nations as well. Sadly, the interests of local rulers often coincide with the legitimate, and occasionally dubious, interests of weapons producers and their middlemen. Instability, disputes and regional suspicions are encouraged and then used as tools in marketing weapons, and that might involve covert activities by security services. These latter organisations offer exciting and lucrative employment opportunities; understandably, therefore, the individuals concerned do not view the prospect of total peace with much enthusiasm.

Leading powers could help weaker nations in need of progress by curbing overzealous activities by their weapons' producers and secret services. Both are notoriously difficult to monitor and control, but they cause serious harm to all development efforts. Furthermore, past evidence suggests that they quite frequently work to their own agendas. The bombing of a Sudanese pharmaceutical plant in August 1998 is a case in point. The American government decided in the end not to contest the court case brought against it by the owner of the factory (*The Economist*, 8 May 1999). Essentially, the proposed reversal of the commercialisation of the weapons business and a limitation on the covert activities of secret services would yield positive results to impoverished and prosperous nations alike. Admittedly, that is a tall order indeed.

A reversal of policies in this field would be of benefit to the armsexporting countries themselves. Afghanistan, again, provides a good illustration. Months before the Russian forces invaded Afghanistan in 1979 (Blum 2001: 4), the US government decided that the regime in that country should be destabilised by a jihad. Reasonably, the US secret services felt that Saudi Arabia was a natural first port of call. To start with, the project was funded by oil money through the socalled Safari Club to avoid scrutiny by Congress (Heikal 1992: 45, 66). Pretence became unnecessary when Russia moved in. Congress voted $250 million to recruit and arm warlords and 'freedom fighters', including presumably Osama bin Laden (Ranelagh 1992: 225). Tragically for everyone concerned, the 'freedom fighters' of the 1970s and 1980s – recruited, funded, armed and trained by the USA and its cohorts – turned into the 'terrorists' of 11 September 2001. It is difficult to see how this sorry episode was of benefit to the American people, let alone the hapless, and shoeless, Afghan in the street. It is daft to speak about development under these circumstances. Meddling by foreign powers, then and now, does not allow the process ever to begin.

FINAL WORDS

I have sought to show in this book that nations behave as Complex Adaptive Systems and that development is a continuous evolutionary process that follows an uncertain path with no shortcuts or guarantees. I identified in the present chapter an agenda that could help nondeveloping nations to become developing nations. That, as I see it, is the heart and soul of the development project. The biggest hurdle, however, is to convince those involved in the development industry to adopt a new paradigm based on Complexity.

In putting forward policy suggestions, my aim was to concentrate on inputs rather than outputs. Hence, I did not mention two old favourites: the population explosion and the drift to the cities. Both activities are of critical importance, but they are shaped by the prevailing social, political and economic conditions. Progress in addressing the items included on the agenda will affect these issues more positively than instruction in birth control and calls for people to stop their migration to the cities.

I fully understand that adoption of a paradigm founded on Complexity would entail major dislocations in the theory as well as in the practice of development. However, there are strong indications that scholars and practitioners have been drifting intuitively towards the concepts I have presented here. For instance, Thomas and Potter (Allen and Thomas 1995: 122) argued that development means 'restoring and enhancing basic human capabilities and freedoms'. Similarly, UNDP (2000: Glossary) defined human development as 'the process of enlarging people's choices'; the aim being to give them capability 'to lead a long and healthy life, to be knowledgeable and to have access to the resources needed for a decent standard of living'. The choices valued by people, UNDP added, also include participation, security and human rights. More tellingly, perhaps, development is recognised by UNDP as 'a process as well as an end'.

Equally, the changes in policy implied by my proposals are not as startling as they might appear on first inspection. For instance, the World Bank (1993) recommended that 'governments in developing countries should spend far less – on average about 50 per cent less – than they now do on less cost-effective interventions and instead double or triple spending on basic public health programmes.' In short, there are distinct indications that the Bank is progressively moving to a Complexity view of development without, as yet, recognising that fact explicitly.

Possibly the most encouraging sign on the horizon is the rising power of the European Union, on the one hand, and China, on the other. The tripolar global system, if it were to coalesce as predicted by some commentators, would help the development prospects of many nations. The principal benefit relates to the return of variety and pragmatism to the world stage. Approaching the same point but from a different perspective, Krugman (1995: 257) commented that under present conditions 'each of many agents considers itself too small to influence market outcomes'. In a regional distribution of power, triad members might have a better chance to influence outcomes and hence intervention might be more effective. More specifically, these trends might have a beneficial effect in reducing the rush to globalisation to manageable proportions. On the downside, and there is a downside, the distribution of rewards, with most going to the elite and their regional partners, could leave large areas of the developing world – Africa and the Middle East in particular – in limbo.

I believe that the key contribution made by this book lies in its definition of a synthesis for the diverse ideas now emerging haphazardly throughout the development industry. Complexity, I maintain, offers a sound basis for the identification of problems and selection of solutions. Critically, the book puts the spotlight where it belongs, on the factors, and actors, that really count. Ultimately, nations – as people, governments and institutions – are the masters of their own destinies.

NOTES

1. Leaders have always been fond of talking about their 'New Order'; America did not initiate that fashion. For example, Sultan Selim III introduced *nizam jaded* (New Order) throughout the Ottoman Empire in the 1790s, and Muhammad Ali imposed his New Order on Egypt in the first three decades of the nineteenth century (Vatikiotis 1991: 49).
2. See, for instance, Cassen (1994) and Thérien and Lloyd (2000).
3. World Bank, *Policy and Research Bulletin*, July–September 1997 and April–June 1998.
4. See World Bank, *Policy and Research Bulletin*, July–September 1997.

REFERENCES

Adams, J. (1990) *Trading in Death*, London: Hutchinson.

Adams, P. (1991) *Odious Debts*, London: Earthscan.

Al-Ghazali, M. (1994) *Woman's Affairs: Between Stagnant and Imported Traditions* (Arabic), Cairo: Dar Al-Shuruk.

Allen, T. and A. Thomas (eds) (1995) *Poverty and Development in the 1990s*, Oxford: Oxford University Press.

Al-Tikriti, S.T. (translator and commentator) (1986), *Ancient Iraq*, Anthology of papers, written by Soviet archaeologists from the 1930s to the 1960s (Arabic), Baghdad: Ministry of Culture and Information.

Al-Wardi, A. (1995) *The Sultan's Preachers* (Arabic), London: Dar Kufaan Publishing.

Al-Wardi, A. (1996) *On Human Nature* (Arabic), Amman: Al-Ahlia Publishing.

Amin, S. (1990) *Maldevelopment*, London: Zed Books.

Arthur, W.B. (1990) 'Positive Feedback in the Economy', *Scientific American*, February, 80–85.

Arthur, W.B. (1994) *Increasing Returns and Path Dependence in the Economy*, Ann Arbor: University of Michigan Press.

Axelrod, R.M. (1984) *The Evolution of Cooperation*, New York: Basic Books.

Baumol, W.J. (1989) *Productivity and American Leadership*, Cambridge MA: MIT Press.

Bell, D. (1965) *The End of Ideology*, New York: The Free Press.

Blum, W. (2001) *Rogue State*, London: Zed Books.

Bottero, J., et al. (2000) *Ancestor of the West*, Chicago: Chicago University Press.

Bottomore, T.B. (1993) *Elites and Society*, London: Routledge.

Brown, L.R. (1996) *Tough Choices: Facing the Challenge of Food Scarcity*, New York: W.W. Norton.

Brown, L.R., et al. (1997) *State of the World 1997*, London: Earthscan.

Buchanan J.M.and G. Tullock (1962) *The Calculus of Consent*, Ann Arbor: University of Michigan Press.

Buckley, P., et al. (1999) *The Cambridge Illustrated History of China*, Cambridge: Cambridge University Press.

Byrne, D. (1998) *Complexity Theory and the Social Sciences*, London: Routledge.

Cassen, R. (1994) *Does Aid Work?*, Oxford: Oxford University Press.

Caufield, C. (1996) *Masters of Illusion*, London: Macmillan.

Chambers, R. (1997) *Whose Reality Counts?*, London: ITDG Publishing.

Chandler, A.D. (1977) *The Visible Hand*, Cambridge MA: Harvard University Press.

Chandler, A.D., et al. (1997) *Big Business and the Wealth of Nations*, Cambridge: Cambridge University Press.

Chase-Dunn, C. (1981) 'Interstate System and Capitalist World-Economy: One Logic or Two?', *International Studies Quarterly*, vol. 25, no. 1.

Clark, R. (1998) *Challenge to Genocide: Let Iraq Live*, New York: International Action Centre.

Clarke, D. (1995) 'Israel's Unauthorised Arms Transfers', *Foreign Policy* 99, Summer.

Cline, W.R. (1995) *International Debt Reexamined*, Washington DC: Institute for International Economics.

Cohen, B.J. (1977) *Organising the World's Money*, London: Basic Books.

Collier, P. (1998) *The Political Economy of Ethnicity*, Annual World Bank Conference on Development Economics, 20–21 April 1998.

Collier, P. and A. Hoeffler (2000) *On the Incidence of Civil War in Africa*, draft research paper, Washington DC: World Bank.

Corbridge, S. (1993) *Debt and Development*, Oxford: Blackwell.

Coveney, P. and R. Highfield (1991) *The Arrow of Time*, London: W.H. Allen.

Coveney, P. and R. Highfield (1996) *Frontiers of Complexity*, London: Faber & Faber.

Crane, G.T. and A. Amawi (eds) (1991) *The Theoretical Evolution of International Political Economy*, New York: Oxford University Press.

Crosland, C.A.R. (1956) *The Future of Socialism*, London: Cape.

Davies, P. (1987) *Superforce: The Search for a Grand Unified Theory of Everything*, London: Unwin Hyman.

Dawkins, R. (1989) *The Selfish Gene*, Oxford: Oxford University Press.

Dawkins, R. (1991) *The Blind Watchmaker: Why the Evidence of Evolution Reveals a Universe Without Design*, Harmondsworth: Penguin.

Day, R.H. (1994) *Complex Economic Dynamics: An Introduction to Dynamical Systems and Market Mechanisms*, Cambridge MA: MIT Press.

De Soto, H. (2000) *The Mystery of Capital*, London: Bantam Press.

Downs, A. (1957) *An Economic Theory of Democracy*, New York: Harper.

Easterly, W. (2001) *The Elusive Quest for Growth*, Cambridge, MA: MIT Press.

Ehrenberg, V. (1973) *From Solon to Socrates*, London: Routledge.

Elliot, E. and L.D. Kiel (eds) (1997) *Chaos Theory in the Social Sciences*, Ann Arbor: University of Michigan Press.

Elliott, J. A. (1996) *An Introduction to Sustainable Development*, London: Routledge.

Evans, J.R., K.L. Hall, and J. Watford (1981) 'Health Care in the Developing World', *New England Journal of Medicine*, vol. 305, no. 19, November.

Fakhri, M. (1958) *Aristotle: The First Teacher* (Arabic), Beirut: Catholic Press.

Faraj, L.J. (1987) *King Ghazi* (Arabic), Baghdad: Yaqtha Publications.

Farrukh, U. (1970) *The Arabs and Greek Philosophy* (Arabic), Beirut: Commercial Office.

Fawzi, A. (1988) *Abd al-Karim Qassem: His Last Few Hours* (Arabic), Baghdad: Dar Al-Hurriyah Press.

Ferguson, M. (1983) *The Aquarian Conspiracy*, London: Paladin.

Ferguson, N. (ed.) (1998) *Virtual History*, London: Macmillan.

Filmer, D. and L. Pritchett (1999) 'The Impact of Public Spending: Does Money Matter?', *Social Science and Medicine*, vol. 49, no. 10.

Frey, B.S. (1984) 'The Public Choice View of International Political Economy', *International Organization* 38.

Friedman, T. (1990) *From Beirut to Jerusalem*, London: HarperCollins.

Frieden, J.A. and D.A. Lake (eds) (1995) *International Political Economy: Perspectives on Global Power and Wealth*, New York: St. Martin's Press.

Fukuyama, F. (1992) *The End of History and the Last Man*, Harmondsworth: Penguin.

Gell-Mann, M. (1994) *The Quark and the Jaguar: Adventures in the Simple and Complex*, Boston, MA: Little, Brown.

Giddens, A. (1994) *Beyond Left and Right*, Cambridge: Polity Press.

Giddens, A. (1998) *The Third Way*, Cambridge: Polity Press.

Gilpin, R. (1992) *The Political Economy of International Relations*, Princeton: Princeton University Press.

Gleick, J. (1988) *Chaos: Making a New Science*, London: Heinemann.

Gleick, J. (2000) *Genius*, London: Abacus.

Green, P. (1979) *A Concise History of Ancient Greece*, London: Thames & Hudson.

Haggard, S. and C. Moon (1983) 'The South Korean State in the International Economy: Liberal, Dependent, or Mercantile?', in J.G. Ruggie, *The Antinomies of Interdependence: National Welfare and International Division of Labour*, New York: Columbia University Press; reproduced in J.A. Frieden and D.A. Lake (eds), *International Political Economy: Perspectives on Global Power and Wealth*, New York: St. Martin's Press, 1995, pp. 47–60.

Hanlon, J. (1998) 'Dictators and debt', www.jubilee2000uk.org/news/dictators, November.

Hawking, S.W. (1988) *A Brief History of Time*, London: Bantam.

Heath, E. (1998) *The Course of My Life*, London: Hodder & Stoughton.

Heikal, M. (1975) *The Road to Ramadan*, London: Collins.

Heikal, M. (1992) *Illusions of Triumph*, London: HarperCollins.

Herman, E.S. and N. Chomsky (1994) *Manufacturing Consent*, London: Vintage.

Hoogvelt, A. (2001) *Globalization and the Postcolonial World*, Basingstoke: Palgrave.

Horowitz, D.L. (1998) *Structure and Strategy in Ethnic Conflict*, Annual World Bank Conference on Development Economics, 20–21 April 1998.

Hourani, A. (1991) *A History of the Arab People*, London: Faber & Faber.

IAC (1997) *Metal of Dishonor*, New York: International Action Center.

Ibn Khaldun (n.d.), *Muqaddima* (Arabic), Beirut: Dar Al-Jeel Publishing.

Ibn Battuta (1984) *Travels in Asia and Africa 1325–1354*, London: Routledge & Kegan Paul.

Jervis, R. (1999) *Systems Effects: Complexity in Political and Social Life*, Princeton: Princeton University Press.

Johnston, R.J. and P.J. Taylor (eds) (1986) *A World in Crisis?*, Oxford: Blackwell.

Jones, T. and A. Ereira (1994) *Crusades*, London: BBC Books.

Kapstein, E.B. (1994) 'America's Arms-trade Monopoly', *Foreign Affairs*, vol. 73, no. 3, May–June 1994.

Kauffman, S. (1993) *The Origins of Order*, Oxford: Oxford University Press.

Kauffman, S. (1996) *At Home in the Universe: The Search for Laws of Complexity*, Oxford: Oxford University Press.

Keil, L.D. and E. Elliott (eds) (1997) *Chaos Theory and the Social Sciences*, Ann Arbor: University of Michigan Press.

Kennedy, P. (1989) *The Rise and Fall of Great Powers*, London: Vintage.

Keohane, R.O. and J.S. Nye (1977) 'Power and Interdependence', reproduced in G.T. Crane and A. Amawi (eds), *The Theoretical Evolution of International Political Economy*, New York: Oxford University Press, 1991, pp. 122–39.

Keohane, R.O. (ed.) (1986) *Neorealism and its Critics*, New York: Columbia University Press.

Kindleberger, C.P. (1973) *The World in Depression, 1929–1939*, London: Lane.

Krasner, S.D. (1976) 'State Power and the Structure of International Trade', *World Politics*, vol. 28, no. 3.

Krasner, S.D. (1981) 'Transforming International Regimes: What the Third World Wants and Why?', *International Studies Quarterly*, vol. 25, no. 1.

Kravtsov, Y.A. and J.B. Kadtke (eds) (1996) *Predictability of Complex Dynamical Systems*, Berlin: Springer Verlag.

Krugman, P.R. (ed.) (1995) *Strategic Trade Policy and the New International Economics*, Cambridge, MA: MIT Press.

Kuhn, T.S. (1996) *The Structure of Scientific Revolutions*, Chicago and London: University of Chicago Press.

Lafeber, W. (1983) *Inevitable Revolutions: The United States in Central America*, New York: W.W. Norton.

Lerner, R., A.K. Nagai and S. Rothman (1996) *American Elites*, New Haven, CT: Yale University Press.

Lewin, R. (1997) *Complexity: Life at the Edge of Chaos*, London: Phoenix.

List, F. (1977) *The National System of Political Economy*, New York: Augustus M. Kelley.

Machiavelli, N. (1981) *The Prince*, trans. G. Bull, Harmondsworth: Penguin.

Malcolm, N. (1995) 'The Case Against Europe', *Foreign Affairs*, vol. 74, no. 2, March–April 1995.

Marger, M.N. (1981) *Elites and Masses: An Introduction to Political Sociology*, New York: Van Nostrand.

Marshall, S.P. (1997) 'Does Education and Training Get in the Way of Learning?', *RSA Journal*, vol. 145, no. 5477, March, pp. 36–9; lecture given on 15 January 1997.

Marx, K. and F. Engels (1998) *The Communist Manifesto*, London: Verso.
Mazrui, A.A. (1995) 'Understanding Africa at the Turn of the Millennium', *RSA Journal*, vol. 143, no. 5458, April.
McLellan, D. (Ed.) (1995) *Capital: An Abridged Edition*, Oxford: Oxford University Press.
McLean, I. (1996) *Oxford Concise Dictionary of Politics*, Oxford: Oxford University Press.
Meisler, S. (1995) 'Dateline UN: A New Hammarskjöld?', *Foreign Policy* 98, Spring.
Musawi, M. (1978) *Shiism and Reformism* (Arabic), Los Angeles: privately published.
Nicolis, G. and I. Prigogine (1989) *Exploring Complexity: An Introduction*, New York: Freeman.
OECD (2001) *Development Co-operation 2000 Report*, Paris: OECD.
Ohlson, T. (ed.) (1988) *Arms Transfer Limitations and Third World Security*, Oxford: Oxford University Press.
Ormerod, P. (1994) *The Death of Economics*, London: Faber and Faber.
Ormerod, P. (1998) *Butterfly Economics*, London: Faber & Faber.
Payer, C. (1991) *Lent and Lost*, London: Zed Books.
Peat, F. D. (1991) *Superstrings and the Search for a Theory of Everything*, London: Sphere Books.
Pilger, J. (1999) *Hidden Agendas*, London: Vintage.
Pollock, S. (1999) *Ancient Mesopotamia*, Cambridge: Cambridge University Press.
Pomeroy, S.B., et al. (1998) *Ancient Greece: A Political, Social, and Cultural History*, Oxford: Oxford University Press.
Postel, S. (1992) *Last Oasis: Facing Water Scarcity*, New York: W.W. Norton.
Qasha, S. (1998) *The Influence of Babylonian Writings on the Contents of the Torah* (Arabic), Beirut: Baysan Publishing.
Ranelagh, J. (1992) *CIA: A History*, London: BBC Books.
Ray, E.J. (1988) 'Changing Patterns of Protectionism: The Fall of Tariffs and Rise in Non-tariff Barriers', *Northwestern Journal of International Law and Business* 285; reproduced in J.A. Frieden and D.A. Lake (eds), *International Political Economy: Perspectives on Global Power and Wealth*, New York: St. Martin's Press, 1995, pp. 353–67.
Reed, M. and D.L. Harvey (1992) 'The New Science and the Old: Complexity and Realism in the Social Sciences', *Journal for the Theory of Social Behaviour* 22.
Ricardo, D. (1971) *On the Principles of Political Economy and Taxation*, Harmondsworth: Penguin.
Rich, B. (1994) *Mortgaging the Earth*, Boston: Beacon Press.
Rostow, W. (1960): *The Stages of Economic Growth*, Cambridge: Cambridge University Press.
Saad, F. (1990) *Legacy of Political Thought Before and After the 'Prince'* (Arabic), Beirut: Dar Al-Afaq Al-Jadida.
Sampson, A. (ed.) (1980), *North–South: A Programme for Survival*, London: Pan.

Samuelson, P.A. and W.D. Nordhaus (1995) *Economics*, 15th edn, New York: McGraw-Hill.

Santos, T.D. (1970) 'The Structure of Dependence', *American Economic Review* 16; reproduced in G.T. Crane and A. Amawi (eds), *The Theoretical Evolution of International Political Economy*, New York: Oxford University Press, 1991, pp. 144–52.

Schneider, W. (1963) *Babylon is Everywhere*, London: Hodder & Stoughton.

Schumpeter, J.A. (1950) *Capitalism, Socialism, and Democracy*, New York: HarperCollins.

Schuurman, F.J. (2000) 'Paradigms Lost, Paradigms Regained?', *Third World Quarterly*, vol. 21, no. 1, February.

Singer, H.W. (1989) 'Lessons of Post-war Development Experience: 1945–1988', *Institute of Development Studies*, Discussion Paper 260, April.

SIPRI (1997), *Yearbook 1997*, Oxford: Oxford University Press.

SIPRI (1999), *Yearbook 1999*, Oxford: Oxford University Press.

Smith, A. (1970) *The Wealth of Nations*, Harmondsworth: Penguin.

Soros, G. (1998) *The Crisis of Global Capitalism*, Boston: Little, Brown.

Stallings, B. (1995) *Global Change, Regional Response: The New International Context of Development*, Cambridge: Cambridge University Press.

Stephens, C. (1995) 'The Indigenous Earth', *RSA Journal*, vol. 148, no. 5460, June.

Stiglitz, J. (2000) 'The Insider', *The New Republic Online*, www.tnr.com.

Summers, L.H. (1999) 'Summers Questions Development Policy Research', *Policy and Research Bulletin*, April–June, Washington DC: World Bank.

Thérien J. and C. Lloyd (2000) 'Development Assistance on the Brink', *Third World Development*, vol. 21, no. 1, February.

Thomas, V., A. Chibber, M. Dailami and J. de Melo (eds) (1991) *Restructuring Economies in Distress*, New York: Oxford University Press.

Tickell, C. (1993) 'The Earth Summit', *RSA Journal*, vol. 142, no. 5445, December.

Timberlake, L. (1991) *Africa in Crisis*, London: Earthscan.

Toye, J. (1987) *Dilemmas of Development*, Oxford: Blackwell.

UNDP (1990) *Human Development Report 1990*, New York: Oxford University Press.

UNDP (1994) *Human Development Report 1994*, New York: Oxford University Press.

UNDP (1999) *Human Development Report 1999*, New York: Oxford University Press.

UNDP (2000) *UNDP Poverty Report 2000*, New York: UNDP

UNICEF (1995a) *The Progress of Nations 1995*, New York: Oxford University Press.

UNICEF (1995b) *The State of the World's Children 1995*, New York: Oxford University Press.

UNICEF (1997) *The Progress of Nations 1997*, New York: Oxford University Press.

UNICEF (1998) *The State of the World's Children*, New York: Oxford University Press.

UNICEF (1999) *The Progress of Nations 1999*, New York: UNICEF.

UNICEF (2000) *The Progress of Nations 2000*, New York: UNICEF.

UNICEF (2001), *The State of the World's Children 2001*, New York: UNICEF.

Vatikiotis, P.J. (1991) *The History of Modern Egypt*, London: Weidenfeld & Nicolson.

Waldrop, M.M. (1994) *Complexity*, Harmondsworth: Penguin Books.

Wallerstein, I. (1983) 'Three Instances of Hegemony in the History of the Capitalist World Economy', *International Journal of Comparative Sociology*, vol. 24, nos 1–2.

Waltz, K.N. (1979), *Theory of International Politics*, New York: McGraw Hill.

Ward, G. (1997) 'India: Fifty Years of Independence', *National Geographic*, May.

Watson, B. (ed.) (1967) *Basic Writings of Mo-Tzu and Han Fei Tzu*, New York: Columbia University Press.

WCED (1987) *Our Common Future*, Oxford: Oxford University Press.

WHO (2000) *The World Health Report 2000*, Geneva: World Health Organisation.

Woodward, B. (2000) *Maestro*, New York: Simon & Schuster.

World Bank (1993) *World Development Report 1993*, Washington DC: World Bank.

World Bank (1994) *World Development Report 1994*, Washington DC: World Bank.

World Bank (1995a) *Policy Research Bulletin*, vol. 6, no. 1, January–February.

World Bank (1995b) *Policy Research Bulletin*, vol. 6, no. 5, November–December.

World Bank (1996) *Annual Report 1996*, Washington DC: World Bank.

World Bank (1997a) *Policy Research Bulletin*, vol. 8, no. 4, October–December.

World Bank (1997b) *World Development Report 1997*, Washington DC: World Bank

World Bank (1998) *Assessing Aid: What Works, What Doesn't, and Why*, New York: Oxford University Press.

World Bank (2001) *Policy and Research Bulletin*, vol. 9, no. 4, April–June.

WTO (2000a) *Trade, Income Disparity and Poverty*, Geneva: World Trade Organisation.

WTO (2000b) *International Trade Statistics 2000*, Geneva: World Trade Organisation.

Wulf, H. (ed.) (1993) *Arms Industry Limited*, Oxford: Oxford University Press.

Zhengyuan Fu (ed.) (1996) *China's Legalists*, New York: M.E. Sharpe.

INDEX

DEVELOPMENT STUDIES TITLES
FROM ZED BOOKS

Zed Books has a reputation as the leading publisher of critical, intellectually innovative and important books in the field of Development. Amongst the many titles in this field that we have published in recent years are:

Nassau Adams, *Worlds Apart: The North–South Divide and the International System*

Aderanti Adepoju, ed., *Family, Population and Development in Africa*

Yilmaz Akyuz, ed., *Reforming the Global Financial Architecture: Issues and Proposals*

Brian C. Aldrich and Ravinder S. Sandhu, eds, *Housing the Urban Poor: A Guide to Policy and Practice in the South*

Kojo Sebastian Amanor, *The New Frontier: Farmers' Responses to Land Degradation: A West African Study*

Samir Amin, *Capitalism in the Age of Globalization: The Management of Contemporary Society*

Frédérique Apffel-Marglin with PRATEC, ed., *The Spirit of Regeneration: Andean Culture Confronting Western Notions of Development*

Akhtar Badshah, *Our Urban Future: New Paradigms for Equity and Sustainability*

Isabella Bakker, ed., *The Strategic Silence: Gender and Economic Policy*

Asoka Bandarage, *Women, Population and Global Crisis: A Political-Economic Analysis*

Tariq Banuri and Frédérique Apffel-Marglin, eds, *Who Will Save the Forests? Knowledge, Power and Environmental Destruction*

Jo Beall, ed., *A City for All: Valuing Difference and Working with Diversity*

Walden Bello, Shea Cunningham and Li Kheng Poh, *A Siamese Tragedy: Development and Disintegration in Modern Thailand*

Walden Bello, Nicola Bullard and Kamal Malhotra, eds, *Global Finance: New Thinking on Regulating Speculative Capital Markets*

Sara Bennett, Barbara McPake and Anne Mills, eds, *Private Health Providers in Developing Countries: Serving the Public Interest?*

Kum-Kum Bhavnani, John Foran and Priya Kurian, eds, *Feminist Futures: Re-imagining Women, Culture and Development*

Robert Biel, *The New Imperialism: Crisis and Contradictions in North–South Relations*

Rosi Braidotti, Ewa Charkiewicz, Sabine Häusler and Saskia Wieringa, *Women, the Environment and Sustainable Development*

Rod Burgess, Marisa Carmona and Theo Kolstee, eds, *The Challenge of Sustainable Cities: Neoliberalism and Urban Strategies in Developing Countries*

Steve Burkey, *People First: A Guide to Self-Reliant Participatory Rural Development*

Ray Bush, ed., *Counter-Revolution in Egypt's Countryside: Land and Farmers in the Era of Economic Reform*

Raff Carmen, *Autonomous Development: An Excursion into Radical Thinking and Practice*

Raff Carmen and Miguel Sobrado, eds, *A Future for the Excluded: Job Creation and Income Generation by the Poor – Clodomir Santos de Morais and the Organization Workshop*

Ricardo Carrere and Larry Lohmann, *Pulping the South: Industrial Tree Plantations and the World Paper Economy*

Fantu Cheru, *The Silent Revolution in Africa: Debt, Democracy and Development*

Fantu Cheru, *African Renaissance: Roadmaps to the Challenge of Globalization*

Andrew Chetley, *A Healthy Business? World Health and the Pharmaceutical Business*

Jacques M. Chevalier and Daniel Buckles, *A Land without Gods: Process Theory, Maldevelopment and the Mexican Nahuas*

Marcus Colchester and Larry Lohmann, eds, *The Struggle for Land and the Fate of the Forests*

Christian Comeliau, *The Impasse of Modernity: Debating the Future of the Global Market Economy*

Bill Cooke and Uma Kothari, eds, *Participation: The New Tyranny?*

Carlos M. Correa, *Intellectual Property Rights, the WTO and Developing Countries: The TRIPS Agreement and Policy Options*

Emma Crewe and Buzz Harrison, *Whose Development? An Ethnography of Aid*

Peter Custers, *Capital Accumulation and Women's Labour in Asian Economies*

Mariarosa and Giovanni F. Dalla Costa, eds, *Paying the Price: Women and the Politics of International Economic Strategy*

Bhagirath Lal Das, *An Introduction to the WTO Agreements*

Bhagirath Lal Das, *The WTO Agreements: Deficiencies, Imbalances and Required Changes*

Bhagirath Lal Das, *The World Trade Organization: A Guide to the New Framework for International Trade*

Diplab Dasgupta, *Structural Adjustment, Global Trade and the New Political Economy of Development*

Eugenia Date-Bah, ed., *Promoting Gender Equality at Work: Turning Vision into Reality for the 21st Century*

Korrie De Koning and Marion Martin, eds, *Participatory Research in Health*

Oswaldo de Rivero, *The Myth of Development: An Emergency Agenda for the Survival of Nations*

Wim Dierckxsens, *The Limits of Capitalism: An Approach to Globalization Without Neoliberalism*

Boru Douthwaite, *Enabling Innovation: A Practical Guide to Understanding and Fostering Technological Change*

Siddharth Dube, *In the Land of Poverty: Memoirs of an Indian Family, 1947–97*

Mark Duffield, *Global Governance and the New Wars: The Merging of Development and Security*

Graham Dunkley, *The Free Trade Adventure: The WTO, GATT and Globalism – A Critique*

Gustavo Esteva and Madhu Suri Prakash, *Grassroots Post-modernism: Remaking the Soil of Cultures*

Saskia Everts, *Gender and Technology: Empowering Women, Engendering Development*

Edesio Fernandes and Ann Varley, eds, *Illegal Cities: Law and Urban Change in Developing Countries*

Priyanthi Fernando and Gina Porter, eds, *Balancing the Load: Women, Gender and Transport*

Jacques B. Gelinas, *Freedom from Debt: The Reappropriation of Development through Financial Self-reliance*

Anne Marie Goetz, ed., *Getting Institutions Right for Women in Development*

David Gordon and Paul Spicker, eds, *The International Glossary on Poverty*

Denis Goulet, *Development Ethics: A Guide to Theory and Practice*

Wendy Harcourt, ed., *Feminist Perspectives on Sustainable Development*

Betsy Hartmann and Jim Boyce, *A Quiet Violence: View from a Bangladesh Village*

Bertus Haverkort and Wim Hiemstra, eds, *Food for Thought: Ancient Visions and New Experiments of Rural People*

Christine Heward and Sheila Bunwaree, eds, *Gender, Education and Development: Beyond Access to Empowerment*

Susan Holcombe, *Managing to Empower: The Grameen Bank's Experience of Poverty Alleviation*

Terence Hopkins and Immanuel Wallerstein *et al.*, *The Age of Transition: Trajectory of the World-System, 1945–2025*

Rounaq Jahan, *The Elusive Agenda: Mainstreaming Women in Development*

Jomo K.S., ed., *Tigers in Trouble: Financial Governance, Liberalisation and the Economic Crises in East Asia*

Karin Kapadia, *The Violence of Development: The Political Economy of Gender*

Michael Kaufman with Harold Dilla Alfonso, eds, *Community Power and Grassroots Democracy: The Transformation of Social Life*

Shahrukh Rafi Khan, ed., *Trade and Environment: Difficult Policy Choices at the Interface*

Martin Khor, *Rethinking Globalization: Critical Issues and Policy Choices*

Nabil Khoury and Valentine Moghadam, eds, *Gender and Development in the Arab World: Women's Economic Participation*

Meri Koivusalo and Eeva Ollila, *Making a Healthy World: Agencies, Actors and Policies in International Health*

Rajni Kothari, *Poverty: Human Consciousness and the Amnesia of Development*

Serge Latouche, *In the Wake of the Affluent Society: An Exploration of Post-development*

Arthur MacEwan, *Neo-liberalism or Democracy: Economic Strategy, Markets and Alternatives for the 21st Century*

Joanna Macrae, *Aiding Recovery? The Crisis of Aid in Chronic Political Emergencies*

John Madeley, *Big Business, Poor Peoples: The Impact of Transnational Corporations on the World's Poor*

John Madeley, *Food for All: The Need for a New Agriculture*

John Madeley, *Hungry for Trade: How the Poor Pay for Free Trade*

Hans-Peter Martin and Harald Schumann, *The Global Trap: Globalization and the Assault on Prosperity and Democracy*

John Martinussen, *Society, State and Market: A Guide to Competing Theories of Development*

Manfred Max-Neef, *From the Outside Looking In: Experiences in 'Barefoot Economics'*

Manfred Max-Neef, *Human-scale Development: Conception, Application and Further Reflections*

John May, ed., *Poverty and Inequality in South Africa: Meeting the Challenge*

Patrick McCully, *Silenced Rivers: The Ecology and Politics of Large Dams* (New Updated Edition)

Zakes Mda, *When People Play People: Development Communication through Theatre*

Kidane Mengisteab and Ikubolajeh B. Logan, eds, *Beyond Economic Liberalization: Structural Adjustment and the Alternatives*

John Mihevc, *The Market Tells Them So: The World Bank and Economic Fundamentalism in Africa*

Ronaldo Munck and Denis O'Hearn, eds, *Critical Development Theory: Contributions to a New Paradigm*

Axel I. Mundigo and Cynthia Indriso, eds, *Abortion in the Developing World*

Klaus Nurnberger, *Prosperity, Poverty and Pollution: Managing the Approaching Crisis*

Klaus Nurnberger, *Beyond Marx and Market: Outcomes of a Century of Economic Experimentation*

Leif Ohlsson, ed., *Hydropolitics: Conflicts over Water as a Development Constraint*

John Overton and Regina Scheyvens, eds, *Strategies for Sustainable Development: Experiences from the Pacific*

Helen Pankhurst, *Gender, Development and Identity: An Ethiopian Study*

Govindan Parayil, ed., *Kerala: The Development Experience. Reflections on Sustainability and Replicability*

Susan Perry and Celeste Schenck, eds, *Eye to Eye: Women Practising Development across Cultures*

James Petras and Henry Veltmeyer, *Globalization: The New Face of Imperialism*

Riccardo Petrella, *The Water Manifesto: Arguments for a World Water Contract*

Claire Pirotte, Bernard Husson and Francois Grunewald, *Responding to Emergencies and Fostering Development*

Majid Rahnema with Victoria Bawtree, eds, *The Post-development Reader*

Gilbert Rist, *A History of Development: From Western Origins to Global Faith* (New Updated Edition)

Kalima Rose, *Where Women Are Leaders: The SEWA Movement in India*

Eric Ross, *The Malthus Factor: Poverty, Politics and Population in Capitalist Development*

Wolfgang Sachs, ed., *The Development Dictionary: A Guide to Knowledge as Power*

Wolfgang Sachs, *Planet Dialectics: Explorations in Environment and Development*

Saral Sarkar, *Eco-Socialism or Eco-Capitalism? A Critical Analysis of Humanity's Fundamental Choices*

Frans Schuurman, ed., *Beyond the Impasse: New Directions in Development Theory*

Ian Scoones *et al.*, *Hazards and Opportunities: Farming Livelihoods in Dryland Africa*

Vandana Shiva, *The Violence of the Green Revolution: Third World Agriculture, Ecology and Politics*

Vandana Shiva, *Staying Alive: Women, Ecology and Development*

Paul Wolvekamp, ed., *Forests for the Future: Local Strategies for Forest Protection, Economic Welfare and Social Justice*

David Woodward, *The Next Crisis? Foreign Direct and Equity Investment in Developing Countries*

Mathew Zachariah and R. Sooryamoorthy, *Science in Participatory Development: Achievements and Dilemmas of a Development Movement — The Case of Kerala*

For full details of this list and Zed's other subject and general catalogues, please write to:

The Marketing Department, Zed Books,
7 Cynthia Street, London N1 9JF, UK
or email Sales@zedbooks.demon.co.uk

Visit our website at: http://www.zedbooks.demon.co.uk